ISBN 978-1-331-17656-5
PIBN 10154365

This book is a reproduction of an important historical work. Forgotten Books uses state-of-the-art technology to digitally reconstruct the work, preserving the original format whilst repairing imperfections present in the aged copy. In rare cases, an imperfection in the original, such as a blemish or missing page, may be replicated in our edition. We do, however, repair the vast majority of imperfections successfully; any imperfections that remain are intentionally left to preserve the state of such historical works.

1 MONTH OF
FREE
READING

at
www.ForgottenBooks.com

By purchasing this book you are eligible for one month membership to ForgottenBooks.com, giving you unlimited access to our entire collection of over 1,000,000 titles via our web site and mobile apps.

To claim your free month visit: www.forgottenbooks.com/free154365

English
Français
Deutsche
Italiano
Español
Português

www.forgottenbooks.com

Mythology Photography **Fiction**
Fishing Christianity **Art** Cooking
Essays Buddhism Freemasonry
Medicine **Biology** Music **Ancient
Egypt** Evolution Carpentry Physics
Dance Geology **Mathematics** Fitness
Shakespeare **Folklore** Yoga Marketing
Confidence Immortality Biographies
Poetry **Psychology** Witchcraft
Electronics Chemistry History **Law**
Accounting **Philosophy** Anthropology
Alchemy Drama Quantum Mechanics
Atheism Sexual Health **Ancient History**
Entrepreneurship Languages Sport
Paleontology Needlework Islam
Metaphysics Investment Archaeology
Parenting Statistics Criminology
Motivational

MOIRS

OF

ND BARÈRE

a

EDITIONS.

The ordinary Small Paper Edition is printed on specially-made fine laid printing paper.

5 copies of the Small Paper Edition are printed on Japanese vellum.

50 Large Paper Copies are printed on Arnold's unbleached hand-made paper, royal 8vo, with proofs before letters of the Portraits.

5 copies of the Large Paper Edition are printed on Japanese vellum, with proofs before letters of the Portraits in two states, namely, one impression on Japanese vellum and one on India paper.

BERTRAND BARERE

OF

TRAND BARER

CHAIRMAN OF THE COMMITTEE OF PUBLIC
SAFETY DURING THE REVOLUTION

NOW FIRST TRANSLATED BY

DE V. PAYEN-PAYNE

IN FOUR VOLUMES—VOLUME I

LONDON

S. NICHOLS

SOHO SQUARE AND 62A PICCADILLY W.

MDCCCXCVI

MEMOIRS

OF

*CHAIRMAN OF THE COMMITTEE OF PUBLIC
SAFETY DURING THE REVOLUTION*

NOW FIRST TRANSLATED BY

DE V. PAYEN-PAYNE

IN FOUR VOLUMES—VOLUME I

LONDON

3 SOHO SQUARE AND 62A PICCADILLY W.

MDCCCXCVI

REGISTERED

TRADE *MARK.*

ENTERED AT STATIONERS' HALL

1896

H. S. NICHOLS, PRINTER, 3 SOHO SQUARE, LONDON, W.

TRANSLATOR'S PREFACE

THIS work was first published in Paris in 1843, two years after Barère's death, under the editorship of M. Hippolyte Carnot—the son of his colleague on the Committee of Public Safety, "the organiser of victory," and the father of the martyred President of the Third Republic—and of M. David, the friend, but no kinsman, of the famous painter. Hitherto it has not been translated into English, although from his well-known hatred of England, we should have thought that Englishmen would have been interested in hearing what his views were.

Macaulay wrote a lengthy review of this work, which appeared in the "Edinburgh Review" of April, 1844. Although he starts with an expression of open-mindedness, the article is a diatribe against Barère from beginning to end; there is scarcely a page that does not bristle with derogatory epithets. He sums up his extreme verdict thus:

"Our opinion, then, is this: that Barère approached nearer than any person mentioned in history or fiction, whether man or devil, to the idea of consummate and universal depravity. In almost every particular sort of wickedness, he has had rivals. His sensuality was immoderate; but that was a failing common to him with many great and amiable men. There have been many men as cowardly as he, some as cruel, a few as mean, a few as impudent. There may also have been as great liars, though we have never met with them or read of them. But when we put everything together—sensuality, poltroonery, baseness, effrontery, mendacity, barbarity, the result is something which, in a novel, we should condemn as caricature, and to which, we venture to say, no parallel can be found in history."

Now Macaulay never knew Barère, while Carnot did; and this is his opinion. He expected to meet a furious demagogue, a bloodthirsty tribune, and he found a man of polished wit, of literary expression, with all the elegant manners of the old school. The publication of these Memoirs he considers a duty to history and a service to one of the founders of French liberty, on whom calumny had been poured with no uncertain hand. Without trying to excuse his mistakes, he is shown to be a man of undoubted courage, rigid incorruptibility, and unselfish devotion to the great ideas of the French Revolution. Some of the phrases which have been attributed to him are proved to be inventions or to have been twisted from their original meaning; and we must recollect that his southern nature expressed more than it meant. His grand appeal of the 23rd of August, 1793, for a Levy in Mass, likening the Republic to one vast besieged city, should excuse worse utterances than his. It runs : "Two hundred and fifty forges shall in these days be set up round Paris to make gun-barrels, in the sight of Earth and Heaven. From every hamlet to their departmental town, from every departmental town to the appointed seat of war, the Sons of Freedom shall march; their banner is to bear ' The French People risen against Tyrants.' The young men shall go to the battle—it is their task to conquer : the married men shall forge arms, transport baggage and artillery, provide sub- sistence; the women shall work at soldiers' clothes, make tents, serve in the hospitals; the children shall scrape old linen into surgeon's lint; the aged men shall have themselves carried into public places, and there, by their words, excite the courage of the young, preach hatred to kings and unity to the Republic."

In one of his famous reports to the Convention he invented, or, at any rate, gave publicity to that masterpiece of invention, the suicidal sinking of the *Vengeur*, going down on the 1st of June with two hundred men shouting " Long live the Republic ! " whereas they were in reality rescued by British boats. Carlyle was at first deceived by this account, and calls Barère, with Burke, " the Anacreon of the Guillotine "; but he acknowledges that he was in- genious, even genial, supple and graceful—an indis- pensable man, able to produce an orderly report

from the wildest confusion, working all night through,
and often uttering Tyrtaean words to the fourteen
armies on the frontiers.

We leave the reader to judge between these
diverse opinions, but we can have no doubt that
he will read this elaborate *apologia* with interest,
depicting as it does the inner working of that great
Committee of Public Safety which caused one nation
to resist successfully the whole of Europe in arms.

CONTENTS OF VOL. I

CONTENTS

CONTENTS

CONTENTS

EXTRACTS FROM A MANUSCRIPT ENTITLED "THE LAST
DAYS OF PARIS UNDER THE OLD RÉGIME" *continued*:

HISTORICAL NOTICE

ON

BARÈRE

THE Republicans of France gave a noble example in 1815. In face of the dangers of their country, they forgot that the man who had been charged to direct its defence against the invader, had but lately destroyed the edifice which had been so painfully raised upon foundations reddened with their blood. They agreed to identify their country's cause with that of this man, to rally to him loyally, and to silence, as long as the national welfare required it, their most ardent political vows.

Napoleon, on his side, felt how necessary the adhesion of these citizens, whose services France had not forgotten, of whose devotion she was aware, and whom she knew incapable of neglecting the true interests of her liberty, how necessary the adhesion of these citizens was to obtain the adhesion of the nation, and to calm the just suspicions which the past could not fail to inspire. He called one of them—the one who had personally opposed his despotism most frankly and directly—to a seat at the councils of the Government, whose policy included most distinctly the guarantees demanded by the country. And Carnot soon saw rally round him a large number of the old dauntless champions of liberty, joining their self-sacrifice and patriotism to his. They included men who had long marched at his side, and others who in cruel strife had sometimes proved his persecutors.

Among the latter was Bertrand Barère. These two former members of the Committee of Public Safety had never set eyes on each other since the period when they had worked together for the defence of their country, without ever experiencing any sympathy one for the other. When the characters of these two men are compared, it is easy to explain their aversion. After more than twenty years a new national danger reunited them. As long as France did not need their services they had remained strangers to one another.

Then I saw Barère for the first time. I was too much of a child for my father to have dreamt of seriously teaching me contemporary history. The traditional calumnies taught then, as now, in schools, had warned me to expect a furious demagogue, a bitter and bloodthirsty tribune. How can I recognise him in this man with his playful wit, his literary diction, his elegant manners of the old school? Afterwards I saw him at Brussels in his exile; at Paris the day after the popular triumph which had recalled him to France; at Tarbes, his native town, with one leg already in the grave: everywhere the same. I always heard him express himself as to the Revolution with the freedom of speech of a man who had placed his own biography in the scales of historical justice, and who had seen upright intentions and services rendered to his country triumph over errors, and even faults.

In the course of our conversations, Barère often spoke to me of his Memoirs, and expressed a wish to entrust their posthumous publication to me. His entreaties became more pressing when I went to visit him amidst his mountains in 1836. He thanked me for having accomplished the same pious duty with regard to another patriarch of our great political assemblies (Grégoire). How could I refuse to accept this touching proof of confidence, shared with a friend—the famous artist who has devoted his brush to perpetuate the figures of so many veterans of liberty? Fearing lest his Memoirs should experience the fate of many important political documents, hidden from posterity by hands that shun the day, Barère had been careful, in concert with M. David and myself, to place them beforehand in safety, and they were only brought out when the death of their author struck the hour of their publication.

The editing of these Memoirs occupied the last years especially of Barère's life; but the collecting of the materials was the result of patient and continual care. He was the more anxious to explain the deeds of the Revolution, because, not only had he been one of the principal authors of them, but also one of those who had suffered the most from hasty and passionate judgments; the more fitted to tell of the Revolution because he had gone through all its phases; the better situated to accomplish this task because, endowed with an immense mental activity and suddenly finding himself driven from public life, Barère set to work directly the political soil had ceased to tremble under his feet. From the first days of the Empire, he spent his time in jotting down the recollections with which his splendid memory was so richly stored, in arranging the documents he thought necessary to support them in portfolios, and in examining the opinions of contemporary historians in order to rightly judge them.

The result of this persevering labour was a truly colossal accumulation of materials, but these were somewhat in confusion, and had been chosen with no critical acumen. They have served as a basis for the Memoirs, whose first pages were written during the Empire, while the last were traced by a hand on which death was soon to lay its icy grip, but which had never trembled under the weight of old age.

Autobiographical memoirs should be seen ; the eye loves to compare sheets written in a running hand, in which ideas flow rapidly, with those laboured passages in which numerous erasures occasionally display the author's embarrassment. It likes to play the geologist with the additions, in studying the change of times in these different strata of thought. Printing unhappily destroys all these shades. We must tell our readers how we have endeavoured to preserve the chief part for them, and, firstly, in what condition Barère's manuscript was left.

The Memoirs are composed of :

1. A series of manuscript books, of 800 pages in all, written fairly closely. Nearly every page has in the margin either an explanatory note or some new passage, with a sign to show where it should go.

2. A great number of detached sheets to be inserted.

3. Finally, six large bundles of notes to be inserted in the text, and documents to accompany it — all in perfect order.

The work of revision has consisted in comparing all the notes, and when it has been necessary to choose between several various readings the most complete has always been preferred. As for the documents, those which it has been possible to include in the text, without interrupting or delaying the narrative, have been admitted either word for word or in substance, the rest have been placed at the end of the volumes. Lastly, some fragments that were of real interest have been borrowed from other manuscripts of Barère. These loans have been chiefly made from a very voluminous collection of biographical notices, to which the author had given the title of "The Men of my Time," but which remained in outline among his papers. Among them there are sketches of Mirabeau, Talleyrand, Sieyès and La Fayette. We need not add that, in accordance with a wish formally expressed by the author himself,[1] we have scrupulously respected, not only Barère's thought, but his style, with its new expressions, its frequent negligences, and its old-fashioned phrases, with its peculiar qualities, particularly its southern stamp.

We said just now that, added to the manuscript of the Memoirs were a certain number of passages composed at a later date, sometimes under the influence of new opinions. As it appears essential to us to place the reader in the best position to judge the work and the writer, we have marked the passages as often as possible. When a man leaves *all his papers* after his death, he exposes himself to the revelation of many contradictions in the eyes of his testamentary executors. We have found many in Barère's writings; they did not surprise us and have not changed our respect for his character.

For, we hasten to declare, these variations never touch the fundamental points of opinion: the legality of the Revolution and of its acts never was doubted for an instant by Barère. The energy of these convictions,

---

[1] Letter from Barère to M. Carnot, dated Tarbes, 23rd of September, 1837.

increasing with years, in the midst of mental worry and bodily suffering, of persecutions, privations and isolation, is a fact that we state with pride; it is shared with nearly every man of the great revolutionary epoch, even with those whose life is least free from reproach.

Barère's Memoirs will certainly rank among the most important documents for the knowledge of this period. They will shed desired light over facts that have remained in darkness in spite of the efforts, sometimes by the efforts, of historians.

In introducing them to the public, we do not pretend to guarantee any fact or any judgment; but while truth, in our opinion, will gain by their publication, we believed, and we do not hesitate to declare it, we were rendering a service to the memory of an old artificer of our liberties. All the men who devotedly toiled together in this great work—and there is not a doubt that Barère did so—all, whatever their faults, deserve a share of national gratitude.

These Memoirs will not exculpate the author from all the reproaches that have been showered upon him; but they will efface many unfavourable prejudices. His character has been one of the most ill-treated by history. Every party chief has found his apologists: one system has been made to exalt the Girondins, another to justify Danton, another to canonise Robespierre; but as for Barère, he has remained with no one to defend him against slander, which has been poured out freely, since proscription closed the mouth of its victim.

This slander, which attacked him so cruelly, he speaks of on every occasion in his private journal, and in one place he defines it thus bitterly:

"It is a power amongst corrupt nations. Ingratitude and envy are at its orders. It has an iron hand which holds an envenomed pen. It has a heart of mud and a head of bronze. It ever strikes at genius, virtue, talent and merit. It clings to all in power to serve their passions and to be paid for its biographies and lying anecdotes. It is deaf to all pity, purposely and spitefully deaf. It listens neither to facts nor to justifications. Its wounds leave scars that never disappear."

Elsewhere he remarks :

"I have given over to autobiographers and biography-makers, to partisan journalists, all that concerns me as a politician and representative of the people. All of it belongs to the public. But everything connected with my character—my philanthropic leanings, my literary labours, my private opinions and my feelings as a man—is my inalienable and inaccessible property. History and posterity alone can deal with them. Contemporary justice is worse than an evil passion, worse than tyranny or atrocious persecution. I do not acknowledge the jurisdiction of this exceptional, usurping tribunal."

After reading an article published by the *Revue Encyclopédique*, in 1826, in which a biographer's errors were exposed, he writes: "This is the first act of public justice I have obtained since 1789."

We must acknowledge, however, that Barère, by his doubtful conduct, has laid himself open to the severe judgment of which he so indignantly complains. He has exposed himself to be mistaken for one of those political knaves, always leaning to extreme opinions, who know how to profit by the triumph, and avoid the reverses, of each party. Barère also joined several parties in succession, but he only shared their misfortunes, and he always played the part of moderator in their counsels. His opposition to the deeds of the 31st of May, to the

establishment of the revolutionary tribunal, to the severe
execution of the law against suspected persons—these are
positive facts. We could quote several others. They are
also acts of courage: moderation always demands them.
Barère possessed that kind of courage which consists in
exposing one's life dauntlessly, as much as any other man
of his time; the story of his life will prove it. Besides,
did he not work continuously in the midst of daily perils
of which we can hardly form any idea? The firmness
he lacked was that which braves desertion and isolation.
He does not leave his post in the hour of danger; he
fights like the rest, often better than any; but when
defeat comes, he accepts the yoke of the conqueror with
a deplorable facility. Legendre expressed this in his
picturesque style: " Little Barère always rides on the
crupper of those who have the best horses."

Barère's versatility on these occasions has been styled
trickery and cowardice, which it was not. We must erase
these words from his life, and endeavour to speak of him
differently.

What he can be reproached with—at any rate in our
opinion—are his frequent, but sincere, hesitations and
contradictions, his thoughtlessness in choosing his political
banner, borrowed probably from his legal training, which
made him more inclined to see cases to plead than
convictions to uphold, and from his artistic feelings often
clinging more to the form than to the thing itself; and,
again, from his continual fear of provoking hostility, which
arose from his weakness, doubtless, but more from his
need of praise, and from that other want, so imperious
for a man essentially sociable and worldly, that of living
at peace with all who surrounded him. This fear became
the source of more than one error in Barère's life; but

nothing authorises us to believe that on any occasion it conquered his patriotism and attachment to liberty. His agreeable manners made him generally liked by his colleagues. I have heard some say: "Barère was a good fellow." This praise would sound strange in some ears, but it shows perfectly the opinion that these iron men must have had of him, so much out of his element among them.

Barère was not one of those powerful minds who dominate their time; he was not even one of those strong men whom circumstances cannot shake. On the contrary, we continually see him governed by them. So he could be said to be the echo and mirror of the Revolution—changeable but always striving towards the same goal. His plastic, often poetic, imagination reflects by turns its boldness, its uncertainty and its discouragement; they were reflected in his words and deeds.

Besides, he knew himself well :

"I have not made my age," says he, "an age of revolution and political storms, full of excited passions, interests, needs and thoughts, full of systematic corruption, public violence and treachery. I have not made my age, I have only had to obey it. It has commanded like a Sovereign so many peoples and kings, so many geniuses, wills, and even events, that this submission to one's age and this obedience to the spirit of the century, cannot be blamed either as a crime or as a fault. We have all been governed by those *fata victricia* to whom the ancients raised altars ! "

This passage is taken from the notes that Barère had prepared to serve as an introduction to his Memoirs, at the top of which he wrote these words of Jean Jacques Rousseau :

"Posterity will justify me, I am sure; this consoles me for the insults of my contemporaries."[1]

We are about to borrow from these very notes a more detailed reply to the accusations against his character:

" I am tired of the libels that perverse or corrupt men have showered on my political career. I take up my pen in the last years of my life to edit these Memoirs hastily after twenty-six years of revolution and disaster. I have waited all this time in order to write more coolly and impartially about events which have so agitated the minds of men and so profoundly influenced France and Europe.

"If my memory must go down to posterity because of the great events in which I have shared, I wish at any rate that it should reach posterity as it really is—that is to say, with a reputation for frankness, patriotism and disinterestedness, with the proofs of the zeal for my duty and with the respect for the rights of the nation of which I have always been fully conscious.

"I have only too well learnt—no doubt from the ignominy poured on me by my enemies and the secret agents of the Court of St. James', from the end of 1794 until this day (December, 1815)—what the justice and opinion of men are worth, and how absurdly credulous are the selfish and inattentive public of the capitals of Europe—always greedy of novelty, calumny, exaggeration and spite.

"But I have served my country; I have striven to

---

[1] Letter from Jean Jacques Rousseau to M. Dupeyron, written from Wootton, in England, 8th of January, 1767.

prevent its being divided up like Poland or ravaged by
barbarians ; I have exposed my life a hundred times to
foreign and reactionary assassins ; I have been obliged
to pass the best years of my life in the Committee of
Public Safety, which in thought I always called the *den
of lions*, because the National Convention, in appointing
it, had condemned me to live by the side of Robespierre,
Collot, St. Just and Couthon.

" For twenty-seven months I bore the result of my
labours to the tribune, encouraging the good citizens,
celebrating the brave deeds of our armies, moderating
popular passion, and illuminating with a few rays of
military glory the excesses of that terrible time. I never
celebrated anything but *defensive war*, which is the only
legitimate form—what a nation does to escape a foreign
yoke.

" This period of my life, the most laborious and the
strongest, gave to my political and moral existence the
most overwhelming blow, for it deprived me of everything
—glory, public gratitude, honour and patriotism, all were
withered by a few slanderers.

" But Providence, who alone protected me, Providence,
in whom I always trusted, in whose hands justice and
the future alone are placed, has allowed me to survive
my powerful enemies more than twenty years.

" My quiet and respected life under the Consular
and Imperial Government in Paris was a permanent
refutation of the calumny, and the silly credulity it imposed on.

" If I had succumbed in the isle of Oleron, in the
Saintes prisons, or in the deserts of Guiana, under the
burden of proscription, my death would have brought
upon me a sort of disgrace, not only in the minds of the

common herd, but perhaps in those of sensible men, who believe that everything that is printed, and not denied, is truth itself.

" One should not judge a public man on reports accredited in drawing-rooms, or on newspaper articles, but on attested facts, often unknown or overlooked by contemporaries.

" I have never under-estimated the judgment of the public ; I have done all to deserve its approbation, because I know it is unfettered and always honest ; but I despise a passionate and venal opinion. Thus, far from separating myself from the opinion of men, I have laboured to conciliate it in these Memoirs by the sincerity of my remembrances and revelations. Tired of passing my life in making continual useless apologies for the *truly national* government, which saved France in 1793 and 1794, I resolved to place facts in these pages which are not to be found either in the journals or in the public proceedings of the Convention, but which, having taken place in committees of the Government, form an essential portion of the political and legislative history of these extraordinary times.

" These Memoirs will justify me in the eyes of right-thinking men and of the true friends of France, who have not basely deserted her in her days of trouble and misfortune, and who have passed judgment on her unnatural children who took up arms against her. I dare to flatter myself that I deserve their approbation. I hope that France, taught by experience, will appreciate our labours for her defence and glory better. Then evil passions will have sunk in their foul slime, the policy of the enemies of the people will have unveiled its mysteries, and the memory of its true defenders will perhaps be honoured. Yes, I truly believe that *the future will be just.*

* * * * * * *

"Justice has been dealt out to me for my work and opinions in the Constituent Assembly; or rather, my enemies have not managed to slander this first part of my political existence.

"Calumny has dealt with my career in the midst of the National Convention. As the reward for about six hundred reports, and for twenty-seven months' continual toilsome work in the midst of storms, I was proscribed on the 12th of Germinal,[1] year III., then transported to the isle of Oleron, shut up for three months in the castle of Saintes, and for six months in the prison, and sent to die, first in the deserts of Guiana, and then on the wild shores of Madagascar.

"There is in France no other example of such revolting injustice, ingratitude and oppression, to be compared with the conduct of my enemies from 1795 to 1815.

"It will be sufficient, however, to recall the numberless persons whose lives and liberties I preserved in Paris; to ask the opinion of my department, where, through my care and influence, not one drop of blood was spilt during the whole Revolution.

"I can also call up in my favour that very severe and minute analysis of my work, reports, and speeches which appeared in the indexes of the *Moniteur*. I will only quote a few extracts:

"Page 320.—'When the shops of Paris were looted on the 28th of February, 1795, Barère cried, "As long as I am one of the people's representatives, I shall wage pitiless

---

[1] 2nd of April, 1795.

war with those who violate the rights of property, who place pillage and theft in the seat of public morality, and who cover these crimes with the mask of patriotism." '

" Page 323.—'Barère compares the foundation of the revolutionary tribunal to the vengeance of the most evil despots. He appeals for juries, and, contrary to all custom, he reads in the tribune a passage from the *Catiline* of Sallust as to the danger of such tribunals.'

"Further on.—'He demands the punishment of the authors of the September massacres, which had a parallel only in the bloodthirsty anarchy of Charles VI.'s reign.'

" Pages 312, 313.—'He demands the penalty of death for those who propose agrarian laws or the division of property.'

"In the spring of 1794 I ordered the disbanding of the revolutionary armies and the discontinuance of the public or civic meals.

"On the 31st of May I opposed the violation of national representation, and I did it *alone* at the peril of my life.

" In my military reports I celebrated the great deeds of our victorious armies; this is perhaps my greatest crime in the eyes of despotism and its hangers-on.

"As for the atrocious speeches that, with evident dishonesty, they attribute to me, I have denied them in public, either in the tribune or in my defence in the Convention. I never said that 'money was minted at the Place de la Révolution.' I defy my calumniators to find these words in any speech of mine. The *Moniteur* attributes them to a chairman of the finance committee. As for the expression, 'Only the dead do not return,' they have been turned from their original meaning. What I said of the calamities of the war, they have applied to the massacres of the Revolution.

"Can anyone believe that if I had been unfortunate enough to deliver the former of these phrases from the tribune, that the *Moniteur* and other newspapers would have not reported it? or that, if this accusation were true, that my unjust and powerful accusers would not have replied in the year III. to my challenge to produce their proofs?"

This is the explanation that Barère gives to the expression, "Only the dead do not return": General Houchard, at the battle of Hondschoote, had spared the lives of some English soldiers he could have exterminated on the Dunes; and some time after, at the capture of Valenciennes, these same soldiers made the French officers and representatives submit to the most outrageous insults. In reporting these acts of ingratitude, the orator of the Committee of Public Safety expressed his regret that these barbarians had not been treated with the utmost severity of the law of war.

One can conceive the importance that Barère must have given to the disavowal of words, of which his enemies took advantage to attribute to him the reproach of inhumanity, which people who knew him personally could not possibly believe. Even if he had uttered them, or others like them, the deduction they pretend to draw from them would not be permissible. At any time it is, to say the least, thoughtless to judge a man by his words without comparing them with his deeds; but in an age of revolution it becomes iniquitous. Who can stop himself from uttering passionate words in the midst of the tumult of passion? Who could be held responsible for all the expressions uttered in heated debate? Barère, less than any man. Barère, impressionable in the highest

degree, and so jealous of shining in oratory that a striking
expression was for him the greatest of successes. Did I
not find even in the speeches of Grégoire, the preacher,
expressions full of revolutionary passion? But are a few
expressions to weigh more in the balance than a whole
Christian life consecrated to giving them the lie direct?

Besides, historians who note so scrupulously the bar-
barities of the revolutionary vocabulary, if they dived
deeper into our political speeches so discreet and chaste,
would be surprised perhaps at fishing up a very curious
catch. For my part, I do not believe that in Barère's
most vehement outburst one could find anything to compare with the cold, cruel irony of the celebrated phrase,
"Order reigns in Warsaw." To complete the comparison,
it must be remembered that the orator's words were
spoken against the enemies of France or of the Revolution, while those of the minister alluded to the misfortunes of a people united in the bonds of the most
righteous friendship with us. And yet who would dream
of taxing the man whose mouth uttered these words
with ferocity?

I am not aware that Barère has ever been accused
of having embezzled from public funds. This crime
was not one of his age. But those who have any
doubts on this point are invited to read the passage
in which he recounts how in 1794, when he was one
of the rulers of France, at the head of three or four
public offices, he found himself obliged to borrow to
the amount of £400 from an old friend of his father,
an old priest, formerly one of the King's chaplains at
Versailles. After his return from exile in 1830, Barère
was still saving to pay back both principal and interest
of this forty-year-old debt to the family of his friend,

which he had never been able to wipe off, and which he looked upon as sacred.

But one cannot better ward off the attacks on Barère than by recounting the public proofs of esteem and confidence that were showered on him by his fellow-countrymen at all periods of his life.

In 1789 they chose him as an elector, and then as a deputy to the States-General.

In 1791 they nominated him as a member of the Supreme Court of Appeal, which was then filled by election.

In 1792 they sent him to the National Convention.

In 1795 Barère, whilst shut up in the prison at Saintes, and just about to undergo his trial before the Criminal Court on most atrocious accusations, receives a deputation of soldiers from his native county. They come to respectfully present him with the national flag, with which he had entrusted them three years previously.

In 1797, whilst in hiding to avoid the execution of the warrant of transportation against him, his department nominates him as deputy to the Council of Five Hundred.

In 1805 and 1810 he is nominated as a candidate for the Legislative Body.

In 1815 he is again nominated as their representative in the Parliament during the Hundred Days.

Finally, after another banishment of fifteen years, and forty-five years after his first election, his fellow-countrymen elect him once more for the Chamber of Deputies, and for the General Council of the Department of the Upper Pyrenees.

Such perseverance, under such circumstances, honours the electors no less than the object of their choice.

We have taken from the notes of the preface to his Memoirs the statement of the personal motives that persuaded Barère to take up the pen. It remains for us to show from these same notes that loftier motives had their share in it too. Painfully affected by seeing the events of the Revolution so little known, its intentions so badly understood and so altered by historians, Barère wished to undertake the re-establishment of the truth ; his narrative was preceded by general reflections, and by very severe judgments on contemporary accounts. By his broad, lofty manner of comprehending and explaining the duties of an historian, it can be seen that he contemplated a greater task than merely writing personal recollections ; by the colour and strength of his style one recognises with regret that he has not written them all with equal care. Besides, it is easily seen that these notes, written on odd sheets in no order, belong to different periods.

"If I have written my Memoirs, in spite of my repugnance to reappear in the political arena, where I have been so unhappy, even in type, it is not with the purpose of traducing my enemies before the bar of public opinion, but that the truth as to several crises of the Revolution may be made known, that party passion may be unveiled, and that certain mysterious or notorious men may be unmasked.

"My views in writing these Memoirs are disinterested. In the opinion of my contemporaries I have discovered no room for justice or truth. I have dedicated the period of my exile and my last years in France to the collection of my recollections of the Revolution, my observations on the chief events and most remarkable men of my time.

I was not willing to give way to the entreaties of my friends and former colleagues, who derided posthumous works and considered the attempt to gain the approbation of posterity as trickery. All these personal ideas and interests have affected me but little; only strong-minded souls and disinterested hearts support without difficulty the absence of contemporary eulogies and passing reputation in a society more desirous of novelty than of justice. The sole honest reward of the author of posthumous works, or of historical memoirs left to posterity, is the consoling thought that his labours will one day be appreciated and perhaps honoured, that ignominy or oblivion will enshroud the slanderers and enemies of liberty.

    * * * * * * *

"When one sows the principles of liberty and equality, and establishes institutions to preserve these principles, on the soil of France, five generations imbued with contrary prejudices, customs and interests must pass over this cleared ground before similar germs can be developed; political and moral roots take a century to come up.

"The minorities of these five generations are disappointed in their hopes during this long century of struggling; if they are impatient for the future, they are banished by the usurpers or heirs of power, they fall victims to their precocious love of the liberty of their country.

"But the sixth generation, unsoiled both by the abuses and excesses inseparable from revolutions, and by the vengeance and corrupt servility of reactionaries, will understand the political language of the Constituent Assembly and the National Convention better. It will be more just to the men of high thoughts and strong resolutions; the names of these democratic legislators, who with one hand fought with allied monarchs, while with the other they were formulating free constitutions, will be mentioned with gratitude.   The remembrance of the awful struggles they had to go through will recommend their labours and their courage to a just posterity.

*   *   *   *   *   *   *

" I have seen the reigns of Louis XV. and XVI., the States-General, the Revolution begun on the 14th of July, the Constituent Assembly, the Legislative Assembly, the National Convention, the fall of Louis XVI. and his solemn sentence, the counter-revolution of 1795, the Directory and its sudden fall, the Consulate and its undertakings, the Empire and its wars, its conquests and abdications, the restoration of the Bourbons by foreign armies, that halt of the returned nobles in the mire, in blood and gold, the new popular revolution of 1830, the reign of Louis Philippe, and, lastly, the pitiless quackery of the political doctrinaires.

" I have seen all these events in the course of eighty years ; I have been enabled to note them from the heights of the tribune and from the depths of exile ; I have written the recollections of my life and the biography of the men of my time.   It is a frank, true work in an age of lies and hypocrisy.

"The history of the notable period from 1789 to 1830 is only half known.   The facts and results, it is true, are known by all.   But the true history of a revolution is not made up of these elements alone, whether they be official or passionate, which contemporaries published or changed as they liked.   History ought to go back to the causes of political, military and civil events.   Chance and passion note these events without discernment or honesty, and they only form annals.   Truth and justice have to make history of them.   These inexorable guardians of bygone times do not content themselves with narrative or description—they must explain and reveal, they must go into cabinet councils and legislative committees, they must squeeze into the closets of diplomatists and be present at the head-quarters of commanders, they must attend private influential meetings as well as those in public squares, where the most opposite factions assemble. History owes to posterity the secret of first causes. But it cannot fulfil this task before time has placed men and things at the requisite distance they have to be at, in order to be rightly judged, before time has allowed the depositaries of governmental and revolutionary secrets to reveal what they had kept hid either through interest or passion ; individuals must have written their memoirs and related what has come within their ken.

✻   ✻   ✻   ✻   ✻   ✻   ✻

" It is only a politician and philosopher who can know all the changes of position, of principle and of doctrine that the regeneration and constitution of the new social state have caused in France since 1789. It is only a statesman gifted both with genius and patriotism who can discern the resemblances and differences of these positions and principles. It is only a diplomatic writer who can honestly and sagaciously appreciate the events and intrigues by which this great Revolution was surrounded, and the means employed by its powerful enemies and the different springs they set in motion among the highest and lowest, both in France and abroad.

✻   ✻   ✻   ✻   ✻   ✻   ✻

" The great days of the Revolution and the huge hopes it raised must have been witnessed to obtain a fair idea of this extraordinary, unlooked-for epoch. One must have received the deep impressions of liberty at the moment of the emancipation of a people grown old under the oppression of anti-social institutions, in order to portray faithful pictures and to write fruitful recollections of them.

*   *   *   *   *   *   *

"There exists in the desert a small and unfortunate race of Arabs; they scrape at the foot of the pyramids and thus obtain from these gigantic monuments a little mortar and a few bricks, with which to build a few huts and crouch in them to gain shelter from the sun, wind and sand—that is the profit they obtain from the pyramids. To others they leave mere sterile admiration. This is what one may say of the authors of histories, summaries and memoirs on the French Revolution.

*   *   *   *   *   *   *

"Where are the enlightened and disinterested contemporary witnesses of this great Revolution? Who are the historians who have fathomed the causes and results of this terrible political and social movement? Some have dealt with it diffusely, as Lacretelle and Thiers; others concisely, as Mignet and Roederer. Summaries and analyses of the Revolution have appeared; but not one single true, impartial, severe history, passionless, uninfluenced by party spirit and undertaken by a courageous friend of liberty and equality. Since 1789 each epoch has had its spirit, its tendency, its dominating figure; each party has had its triumph and defeat, its mistakes and its crimes; each day, each great event has had its anniversary and has been plunged into the same Lethe: few of these days have dwelt in the minds of men.

*   *   *   *   *   *   *

"One can quote as true the anecdotal works of Froissart, Philippe de Comines, Dangeau and St. Simon. But who can trace the features of each of the men of the

Revolution? Who can turn trustworthy traditions and uncontested facts to profit, so as to catch the look, bearing, idiosyncrasy, fine oratory, political blunders, short-sightedness, clumsiness or crowning mistake of each of the great actors of this memorable time? Who has the talent to individualise the chief persons honestly, picturesquely and philosophically? What pen can be truthful enough to make certain political faces stand out clearly, and manage to make men distinguished for talents or errors appear themselves and not other men. The knowledge of how to place persons and facts in relief, of how to give them that appearance of greatness that events have given them, or of how to portray those fixed human types granted by Nature to revolutions, is not given to every writer. And yet the period of the French Revolution was rich in originalities, in striking physiognomies, in extraordinary talents, in statesmen created by events and by the love of liberty, inspired too by excessive passions, by every noble sentiment and by every concentrated hatred."

Bertrand Barère was born at Tarbes on the 10th of September, 1755, of a lawyer and a farmer's daughter. His father possessed at Vieuzac, in the delicious valley of Argelès, a little fief, whose revenue consisted of feudal dues. He added, early in life, this name to his own, either to distinguish himself from other members of his family or from obedience to a custom which endeavoured to hide inequalities of rank, already offensive to public feeling. Besides, Barère renounced these feudal rights before they were abolished by decree, a fact which is attested by a resolution of the inhabitants of Vieuzac thanking him for it.

Born of a father who had defended the privileges
of his province at the risk of his liberty, brought up in
a country of professional men, and educated in the parliamentary city of Toulouse, the seat of a distinguished
bar and the home of essentially academic writers, Barère
must have felt the influence of these beginnings, and
thus we find the chief impulses of his life spring from
this collection of facts.

We shall see him flung into the midst of the whirlpool of French and European socialism, in which local
interests disappear, entering into it with all the ardour of
youth and the convictions of the new philosophy, but not
forgetting his province of Bigorre and preserving it intact
in the great geographic upheaval of 1789, and, after half
a century of triumph and defeat, of battle and exile, like
a true child of the mountains, wanting to breathe his last
breath among them, and proud of bearing the title of
municipal councillor in the chief town of the department
created by his care.

We shall see him become one of the agents of the
most powerful centralised government, of which he will
feel the necessity ; but his mental habits will ceaselessly
protest against the preponderance of great capitals, and
when he writes his Memoirs, the first words traced by
his pen will be impregnated with this thought.

We shall see him living in the most brilliant and
alluring seat of action, and the part he will reserve for
himself will be the translation of this action into words.
The former member of the Academy of Floral Games
will borrow epigrams from the Eclogues of Virgil for his
reports to the Constituent Assembly.

The first years of a life which was destined to be so
roughly tossed were spent in quiet, in the midst of a

perfectly united family that he always remembered most affectionately. A little manuscript bearing the date of 1797, in which Barère seems to have jotted down his private impressions under the title of " Melancholic Pages," will give us the chief features.

"I have devoted this pious monument," says he, "to the dear memory of my parents. Alas! I lost them when I still needed their wise counsels and the sight of their virtues and their courageous souls.

" My father was celebrated for his defence of the rights of the people in the assembly of the delegates of Bigorre, in which he was president of the Commons by virtue of his office as sheriff of Tarbes. He was exiled through the machinations of a treasurer of the Assembly, whose accounts he wished to audit so as to discover the deficit. The president of the Assembly, a bishop, helped in this act of injustice.

" My mother, descended from the noble family of the Naïs of Lavedan, inherited from them her proud spirit and lofty thoughts, which I deem an honour to inherit. She cherished me beyond all else, doubtless because of my physical and moral resemblance to herself. She was fifteen when I was born, and when I was a youth and used to walk with her at the waters of Cauterets, St. Sauveur and Bagnères, on returning from Toulouse, strangers took us for brother and sister.

" It gives me great pleasure to recollect all these little details, which draw tears from my eyes when I write them. During the long years of my exile how many times have I not congratulated myself that Nature had ordained that my dear parents should not witness the sad misfortunes of their son! They would never have survived them, I

am sure; I know their deep feeling. They both died
before the first days of that terrible Revolution, whose
despotic results were so fatal to my country.

✻   ✻   ✻   ✻   ✻   ✻   ✻

"In one of the short holidays that public affairs allow
me, I visited the gardens of Betz, near Soissons, which
had great celebrity and which I thought even superior to
their reputation. They were designed by Robert for the
Duchess of Monaco, quite in the English style.

"Returning one day from the tombs, erected at great
expense in the depths of the forest, a crowd of ideas
weighed on my heart; its wounds reopened. I sank
down under the shade of the poplars and the weeping
willows, by the side of a stream which runs through the
wide glade. I perceived that I was near a marble funereal
urn, placed on a broad stone plinth and surrounded by a
vigorous growth, contrasting with the thoughts that a
tomb ought to inspire. It was a superabundance of life
round death.

"There I felt one of the sweetest but most melancholy
of pleasures, that of thinking of my dear mother, who
had died prematurely through grief at my unhappy marriage. How, said I to myself, can Nature break such
pure delightful bonds as those that bind together a
mother and son? How can one die at forty-five in the
full vigour of one's strength and mind? A thousand
thoughts rushed through my brain, saddened by these
reflections, and my imagination carried me to the future
world, where I saw myself united to my mother in
the Elysian Fields, or in the Paradise that our religion
has adopted as the resting-place of the good and virtuous.

"Then turning my looks to the tomb near which I was
seated I could only pronounce the words, 'Across that.'

"Indeed, yes! it is across the tomb that the unfortunate would like to be, when injustice and persecution
come upon them.

"Enough attention is not paid to the preliminaries of
the great events of life. And yet they are warnings that
Providence gives us, but by which we rarely profit, either
because they pass unnoticed or because they come too
late. When I was married in 1785, there were great
family rejoicings at Vic and at Tarbes. I went to the
altar with my young bride at midnight; the church was
in dazzling brightness; we were surrounded by relations
and friends. My heart was full of sadness, and when
I uttered the solemn words, *Yes, I will*, tears flowed in-
voluntarily down my blanched cheeks. Only my mother
perceived this, and after the ceremony took my hand
and squeezed it to her breast.

"My mother, whom I loved more than life itself, remembered it with sadness; she had a presentiment that
the marriage—which had been the result of prudence
rather than of sentiment—would not be a happy one.
Nature had endowed me with a sort of aversion or
contempt for riches. Its secret warning had been
despised, and my marriage was most unhappy."

We shall not apologise for having made such a lengthy
quotation; on the contrary, we shall continue culling from
Barère's manuscripts, especially from those not intended
for publication, in which he unconsciously described himself without being preoccupied by the idea that they would
be read. Behind the display of sentimentality that romantic
novels had brought into fashion, one cannot mistake their
true feeling. Barère has been sometimes called an actor,
he ought to have been called an artist. He shows this

in the expression, in the exaggeration perhaps, of his
feelings; but with him it is so natural that his monologue
hardly differs from his public harangues. Does not this
prove that the part he plays is true to himself?

At fifteen, and by means of a special dispensation,
Barère began his legal studies at Toulouse. The parliamentary bar was then rich in justly celebrated names,
Taverne, Désirat, Monyer, Faget, Duroux, Jamme, Roucoule,
and many more, to whom succeeded a younger generation
no less celebrated, Janole, Mailhe, Veyrieu, Faure, etc.
We borrow these names from a list that one of their
equal famous successors drew up in 1840, on a solemn
occasion.[1] M. Romiguières does not forget to mention
Barère de Vieuzac, then the member of every Academy,
the man to be met in every drawing-room.

The first forensic success of the young barrister had
been the defence of a poor work-girl, accused of infanticide,
and already condemned to death by the seneschal of
Limoux; his first literary success was the Eulogy of
Louis XII., which was followed shortly afterwards by
those of his minister, Cardinal d'Amboise, of Chancellor
Séguier, Montesquieu, Rousseau, Pompignan, etc. Several
of these works gained prizes and opened to him the
portals of the principal Academies of the South. At last,
a startling case founded his oratorical reputation; it was
that of a young girl that has been seduced, abducted and
married in a foreign country, the County of Venaissin,
by a Knight of Malta, who wished to repudiate her, after
several years of married life, under the pretext of their
unequal social positions.

---

[1] Speech at the opening of the Royal Court of Toulouse, by
Romiguières, Royal proctor; born 1775, died 1847.

Barère did not stop at making a noble use of his talents, he profited by the credit these talents began to give him among his colleagues to persuade them to establish a *Charitable Debating Society*, for the purpose of defending poor prisoners. We are not aware if this institution lasted for any lengthy period, but in reading about it in Barère's Memoirs we recall with satisfaction that we ourselves helped to organise a similar institution, attached to a charitable society of the Metropolis.[1]

The Academy of the Floral Games elected the young lawyer as a member in March, 1788 ; he was already a member of the Academy of Sciences of Toulouse. He took the place of M. Férès, reader and librarian of the Count of Provence. The speech he delivered on his reception was a success, derived doubtless from the philosophical ideas which were scattered over it, since it provoked, it is said, this outburst from the President, M. de Cambon : " This young lawyer will make his way. What a pity that he has already imbibed of the impure waters of modern philosophy ! Believe me, this lawyer is a dangerous man."

About this time a family lawsuit led Barère to Paris. As he was setting out his father said to him : " You are going into a country which will soon become dangerous. The situation is too strained; there must soon be an eruption."

" I at last found myself in this famous capital," Barère says, " electrified by the rapid, inevitable and continual motion of men and things. A thousand confused contradictory ideas rushed through my brain. I cannot give an account of the first impressions produced

---

[1] The Prison Committee of the Society of Christian Morality.

by the immense population, rushing and knocking against
each other, and civilising themselves in the midst of
wealth and poverty, of knowledge and ignorance, of
power and slavery.

"The idea came into my mind to put my feelings
and observations into some order by writing every evening
what had occupied or struck me during the day. It
was a newspaper that I edited for myself alone, and to
account for my time in a country where it flies so
quickly with its long wings."

This journal still exists in manuscript. When, fifty
years after, Barère thought of publishing it, and wrote the
preliminary preface that we have just quoted, he gave
it the title of "The Last Day of the Old Monarchy
in Paris." What a curious book it might have turned
out, edited on the crater of a volcano about to erupt!
Without altogether answering for what one would expect
from such a situation, the work is of a fairly lively
interest.

The young traveller is at first more attracted by
sights so new to him than occupied with public
affairs. In fact, if we study his calling, it is certain
that the bar and the Academy would have offered him
an atmosphere more suited to his nature than the dan-
gerons toils of the Committee of Public Safety. Invincible
circumstances were necessary to make of the lawyer of
Toulouse one of the governors of revolutionary France.

The chief things that strike him on his arrival are
the monuments, the statues, the pictures, the learned
societies, the law courts and the theatres. He is present
at the speech given on his reception by the author of
"Estelle and Némorin," who took the place of the writer
of "Epoques de la Nature" in the French Academy. In

the Academy of Sciences he listens to the eulogy of
Buffon by Condorcet, better suited for the task than
M. de Florian. He frequents the Lyceum, where
Fourcroy, Champfort, Lebrun and La Harpe teach and
talk. He meets Tippoo Sahib's ambassadors at the
theatre. The palaces he visits, the plays he sees, the
music he hears, of which he is passionately fond, such
are the subjects which inspire his pen. If his picture
of Paris contained nothing but this, De Mercier would be
by far preferred by all readers. But soon a reflection of
the spirit of the times begins to appear, and his account
resembles more historical memoirs. In it one hears of
the insubordination of the Parliament applauded at the
Théâtre Français in this verse of the Cid :

" Désobéir un peu n'est pas un si grand crime ; "[1]

and the hatred of an intelligent public seize this allusion
to the King's counsellors :

" Je leur couvre de fleurs les bords du précipice."[2]

The philosophical opinions of the writer are seen in his
animated pages on the luxury of the great and the widespread misery ; the halls of Versailles and the boudoirs
of Luciennes suggest bitter reflections to him, and his
imagination compares the shrill sounds of the machine
at Marly to the cries of an unhappy people, working and
suffering for its masters. Then, suddenly, love for his
country interrupts a rural lunch with this exclamation :
"We were under green foliage not half so good as the
groves of our Bigorre country, and the butter made round
Paris will never be so good as that of the Pyrenees."

---

[1] "To disobey a little is not so great a crime."—CORNEILLE.
[2] "I cover the edge of the precipice with flowers for them."—
RACINE.

Important matters now take a more prominent place. Between the representation of a bállet and an excursion into the country, we find the account of a political event.

The struggle of the Parliaments, whose history Barère knows thoroughly, gives him an occasion to digress. He tells of the arrest of D'Esprémesnil, of the judicial court held at Versailles, and of the establishment of the plenary court. The hope that this raises in his breast proves the point at which he has arrived; he is favourable to constitutional progress, but far from any revolutionary ideas.

" A plenary court alone ought to register all the taxes and laws for the whole kingdom. It is composed of men devoted to the King from their position, and still more by their views. The members are nominated for life. They only have the right of remonstrance ; *only the will of the King makes a law.* These words need no commentary, they are those of an Eastern Prince. However, if circumstances oblige the people to give way to the plan proposed by the Court, this new court can gain energy and influence over politics, its constitution may be improved. It is a kernel that a fine fruit may surround in the future. The States will want a seat in it and the provinces will have representatives on it; the Commons will sit by the side of the Parliament; we shall one day perhaps be worthy to be free ; and we shall at last profit by our frequent trips to London without being obliged to become such cruel rebels as the proud inhabitants of that island."

The fall of Brienne, Necker's recall, the re-opening of the Paris Parliament, the second assembly of the Notables, all these events, that took place during young

Barère's stay in the capital, are the subjects of as many chapters in his account of his travels.

Finally the States-General are summoned and France is in the midst of the birth-pangs of the great assembly that is to effect her regeneration. Barère leaves Paris, where the news of his father's death has reached him, without suspecting that he will be called upon to play an important part in the destinies of his country. What should prove this is that he only arrives home in March, when the elections were beginning, having broken off his diary in the middle of a description of the antiquities of Nîmes.

Nominated in succession elector, President of the Committee of Grievances, and finally First Deputy of Bigorre in the States-General, Barère leaves in May to be present at the opening of the Assembly.

He then possessed a reputation at the bar of Toulouse that augured for him the most brilliant future. The patrimony he had just inherited was almost entirely founded on the existing state of things—that is to say, feudal dues and a judicial charge on the *sénéchaussée* of Tarbes. Yet he resisted much flattery from the privileged party, who wished to use his talents, and he did not hesitate to join the reformers' party.

Barère rapidly gained in the world the success that his looks and his brains promised him. Madame de Genlis thus describes him.:

"He was young, with a very good reputation, much wit and an insinuating manner, an agreeable exterior combined with manners both noble, gentle and reserved. He is the only man I have ever known to come from the depths of the country with a tone and manners that would not disgrace the Court and society. He was lacking in knowledge, but his conversation was always pleasant and attractive ; he displayed much good sense and a reasonable taste for arts, talent and country life. These gentle feelings, combined with a sharp wit, gave a touch of interest and true originality to his character and person." [1]

However, the ambition of the young deputy began to carry him towards a more serious goal. From the moment of his arrival he began to connect himself with Bailly and Mirabeau, who welcomed him kindly, and their encouragement emboldened him to speak in a discussion in which the most celebrated orators had spoken. The question was upon the constitution of the Assembly and the name it should adopt. Barère declared in favour of the .National Assembly that an unimportant member had just suggested, which was a much better title than the puzzling verbose definitions proposed by Sièyes and Mounier. But he originated the idea that this title should not be definitely adopted before the minorities among the nobility and clergy had abandoned their respective orders to rally to the Third Estate. This delay would leave, in his opinion, no reason for deputies to desert who were equally devoted to the liberties of their country. We can see here already a half-and-half opinion, no doubt to be accounted for in a maiden speech, but which shows the character of the politician.

On the same day, the 17th of June, when the Commons took the great resolution of calling themselves the National Assembly, Barère, who was not satisfied with only speaking, took up journalism as well. He began the issue of the *Point du Jour (The Dawn)*, for

---

[1] " Précis de la conduite de Madame de Genlis depuis la Révolution." Published at Hamburg on the 12th of March, 1796.

the purpose of reporting the debates in the dramatic style that newspapers have now generally adopted. On the 20th of June he reported the meeting in the Tennis Court on his knee, the position in which the brush of David has represented him. In the first numbers of the paper, he was bold enough to echo the general discontent at the Royal Session of the 23rd of June : "It is like a thick cloud," said he, "which hides the throne from the eyes of the citizens."

On the 13th of July, thirty-six deputies, elected by ballot, were charged to go to Paris to calm the popular clamour. Barère was one of the number. Their difficult and dangerous mission developed into a triumph, for in the interval the Bastille had been taken.

Then came the night of the 4th of August, which has been called the "Saint Bartholomew of privileges." During his stay in Paris, Barère, as counsellor of the *sénéchaussée* of Bigorre, had published a pamphlet against the venality of judicial offices, and had proposed a few means of suppressing it.[1] His electors having given him a mandate that suited his own personal opinions, he profited by the occasion to carry it out. Then, in order to make his own conduct conform with his words, he gave up the office he had acquired by birth.

Having become a member of the Committee of General Warrants *(lettres de cachet)* together with Mirabeau, Frêteau and Castellane, and having undertaken the real work together with the last named, he presided over the inspection of the entries in the calendars of all the

---

[1] *The Venality of the magistracy destroyed.* With this quotation from Montesquieu: "Venality is good in monarchies because it makes men do as a family duty what they would not undertake for virtue."— *Esprit des Lois*, lib. v., ch. 19.

State prisons.   There were thirty-two in Paris alone, situated in the most obscure districts, of which the magistrates were entirely ignorant.   Thanks to the active solicitude of the two deputies charged with this obscure painful work, a crowd of captives were set at liberty.   Two abominable abuses, established by the royal despotism especially in its own interests, or to pander to the pride, the hatred and the greed of powerful families, were unearthed and repressed.   One was the detention of people they wished to get rid of under the pretence of madness ; the other, more recent and more difficult to discover, was getting them imprisoned abroad by taking advantage of the complaisance of foreign Courts.   One Créqui, having offended his family, lay thus forgotten in the citadel of Stettin.   "He was one of that privileged caste that did not interest me," says Barère, "but he was unfortunate and persecuted.   I saw in him only a man.   I told Montmorin, then Foreign Minister, of the order of the National Assembly, to free Créqui, banished and buried alive, 200 leagues from his country and relations."[1]

We have said that, in the new plan of the division of France, Barère had preserved his province of Bigorre under the name of the department of the Hautes Pyrénées. Such was the origin of the gratitude this department never ceased to show him.   Barère, after his election to the General Council towards the end of 1833, reprinted the " Observations " which the resolution of the National Assembly had determined in 1790.[2]   One must read in his

---

[1] Defence of Barère before the National Convention.

[2] Observations presented to the National Assembly by M..Barère de Vieuzac, deputy for Bigorre, on the necessity of making a department of that country, of which Tarbes should be the chief town.— 21 Dec., 1789.

Memoirs the account of his applications to the Committee
of Division into Departments, of his struggles with the
deputies of Béarn, who wanted, because they represented
an ancient kingdom, to absorb the principality of Bigorre,
and with the deputies of the town of Saint Gaudens,
who were attempting the same thing on behalf of
Comminge. One may judge of the importance he
attached to his success by this last sentence in his
"Observations" :

"May Bigorre preserve for ever, under the title of
department, its ancient independence and continue to
tax itself and be governed by its own representatives! If,
unhappily, this petition of its deputies had not obtained
all the success it deserved, they would not be able to
resolve to return to their country to witness, and perhaps
be the victims of, the despair that the degradation and
disgrace of this fine land would cause to their constituents."

If we ourselves have given an importance that may
be thought exaggerated to this feature of Barère's life,
the reason is because it is not merely a question of local
patriotism, but of an opinion that held the principal place
in his mind. All his conduct reveals a marked tendency
to federalism, both his attachment to municipal institutions, which goes so far as to make him sometimes
advocate those of the old regime; his repugnance for
the centralisation of large capitals, which inspires in him
frequent diatribes against the influence of Paris; and his
political alliances with the Girondins, whom he defended
on the 31st of May. If severe expressions on their
doctrines and conduct are remarked in his later reports
and writings, the reason was because he recognised that
in reality the appeal to the provinces had been, as far

as they were concerned, a means of fighting the Republic, just as the accusation of federalism served as a pretence to repress anti-revolutionary efforts. With Barère, on the contrary, provincialism was doubtless a sincere deliberate opinion. We ourselves have heard him say: "The country must be fertilised; without that you will not get true freedom." Besides, his Memoirs contain, on this point, the explanation of quite a system in which he relates the foundation of the Republic.

It must not be thought that we do not find in his manuscripts and in several of his reports passages composed in an anti-federalist spirit. These contradictions are the peculiar mark of his mind, according as he looks at things from the point of view of his favourite theories or is affected by the necessity of the times.

When the Assembly was deliberating on the new judicial organisation, Barère proposed the establishment of the jury in civil as well as in criminal cases, just as in England. "But," says he, "the routine of the old magistrates and barristers, together with judicial prejudices, caused the first part of the motion to be adjourned." When Cambacérès brought it up again later in the Convention, he again supported it warmly.

As member of the Committee of Feudal Domains, Barère made a series of reports on the national forests, the domains and forests to be reserved for the king, etc., from August, 1789, to the May of the following year. Following his lead, the Assembly decreed that the property of the Crown could be alienated to provide for the needs of the State, that the King, like every other citizen, should pay land-taxes, that he should possess the right of hunting only over the properties of the Civil List and in parks surrounded by walls, etc. In the name of the same committee, Barère decreed that the Protestants, banished by the Revocation of the Edict of Nantes, should return to France, and recover their property which was unsold and which had been under the administrations of the Domains.

Among the other decrees of the Constituent Assembly of which Barère was the principal instigator, we ought to cite that which abolished the right of forfeiting to the Crown the property of an alien on his death, and the other, which granted a pension to the widow of Jean Jacques Rousseau.

When the death of Mirabeau was announced, he proposed that the whole of the Assembly should attend his funeral.

On the 13th of May, 1791, he proposed to recognise the right of negroes to active citizenship, provided they fulfilled the conditions demanded by law.

On the 6th of July he warmly supported the first penal measures against the emigrant Nobles. "They are," said he, "bad citizens, who, being enraged at losing the playthings of vanity or the pensions of despotism, will never pardon us the abolition of the peerage, or the laws with which freedom has endowed France."

Thirty years later he wrote: "What can one do with a vast country in which, after an imprudent amnesty granted to 100,000 emigrant nobles, in arms for fifteen years against their country and against liberty, a minister, worthy of that caste of political assassins, dared to say that France was, during their emigration, not in French territory, but at Coblentz, with the King?"

Age had not weakened either his anger or his energetic speech, as one may see. But we blame this vehemence with difficulty when we recollect our own indignation on hearing a minister of the King declare in a full House the same doctrines, distinguishing between one's moral country and one's national country.

On the 12th of July, 1791, after the arrest of Louis XVI. at Varennes, Barère printed in the *Point du Jour* an address to the department of the Eastern Pyrenees, in which he boldly demanded a republic. However, when he was sent by the Assembly as the thirtieth to protect the return of the Royal Family to the Tuileries, he fulfilled its command as zealously and as firmly as his colleagues. Grégoire and himself had charge of the young Dauphin, whom they carried in their arms, while other deputies conducted his parents through an exasperated and threatening crowd.

This event, while giving an opening to republican ideas and their exponents in the Assembly, at the same time united in a common interest the partisans of a constitutional monarchy, who had up till then been divided on the most important points. Barère, who had not been among the former, now joined them to oppose the revision. This attempt, organised by those who, already frightened at the progress of liberal institutions, wished to restore to royalty part of its prerogatives, only found thirty-five opponents, of whom Barère was one. It was an abortive attempt from the point of view of its supporters, but it was sufficient to decrease distinctly the popularity of the new constitution. In the discussion that took place, Barère caused the propositions of the ministers as to the taxes, which had been proposed by Beaumetz and Duport, to be rejected. He established this principle, now a recognised one in political law, that in the matter of taxes there are not two authorities, the only one is the people—that is to say, the deputies elected by it in a representative government.[1]

We have just said that Barère was not a Republican in the Constituent Assembly. In fact, there he was a moderate Parliamentarian, and his talents had shone with sufficient brilliance for the Constitutionalists of the Court to think to give him the post of Home Secretary, in spite of his youth. This last vote with Pétion, Buzot, Robespierre and Grégoire, with reference to the revision, led him into a new path; not that this vote was contradictory to his opinions up till then, but it placed him in relations with a party to which hitherto he had been a stranger.

Barère in his Memoirs charges the Constituent Assembly with having committed suicide, and he adds: "All wise men would have wished it to prorogue, whilst forming itself into a legislative assembly to carry its own constitution into execution." He forgets that he himself had spoken thus : "You have been wise and magnanimous in following the noble and generous emotion that has rendered you all ineligible for the coming Legislature. A creator is not a part of a created universe, and those who have given their country a constitution do not, so to speak, belong to the social state that they have formed ; ancient lawgivers have set you the example."[2]

This is another of the contradictions we have spoken

---

[1] " Opinion of M. Barère, Deputy of the Department of the Upper Pyrenees, spoken in the Sitting of the 27th of August, 1791, against the Initiative of the King and his Ministers concerning Public Taxes." Printed by order of the National Assembly.

[2] " Speech of M. Barère, spoken on the 19th of May, 1791, on the Unlimited Re-election of Members of Legislatures."

of.   Public opinion, which had at first applauded the
disinterestedness of the Constituent Assembly, has come
to look on it as a political mistake.   Barère allows his way
of looking at things to be so easily governed by the
dominant opinion around him, that he thinks that he
has never looked at them in any other way.

In the same speech from which we have just quoted,
according to his tactful method, he takes a half-way
position between those of Cazalès and Robespierre ; he
proposes to restrict the right of re-election to two legislatures only, after which two years must intervene before
a man can be re-elected.

There is one serious question of political history that
appears to have greatly exercised Barère's mind, and has
left numerous traces in his manuscripts.   Madame de
Staël states it very clearly in these words : " Was there
a constitution in France before the Revolution ? "[1]   It is
a question on which many writers have founded the
legality or illegality of the French Revolution.   In a
somewhat recent work, a prolific legist has gone so far
as to declare the National Assembly a usurping power,
for not having remained, according to the limits prescribed by this pretended constitution, a third order in
the States-General ; he has styled as felony the oath in
the Tennis Court, by which the deputies promised not to
separate before having given France[2] a fundamental law.
Besides, party polemics had already dealt with this point.
M. de Villèle, in 1814, had protested against the granted
Charter, saying that Louis XVIII. had not the right to
change in any way the form of ancient French govern-

---

[1] Locré : " The Civil, Commercial and Criminal Legislation of
France." (1826).

[2] "Considerations on the French Revolution," Part I., chap. ii.

ment. Such a doctrine could not displease a prince who had written : France must be given that ancient constitution which alone can make her happy and glorious,[1] and had it not been for the dangers of this retrograde enterprise, he would not have brought himself to renounce it.

However that may be, from the dawn of the Revolution, and even before the Revolution, as we shall see, the same question had occupied men's minds. Calonne answers it in the negative in a work rebutted by M. de Montyon; but before that the Duc de Choiseul, writing to a French ambassador at Vienna, and Turgot writing to Dr. Price at London, turned their attention to it.[2]

These two important letters on which Barère founds his opinion tend indeed to prove the absence of any ancient constitutional law of the State. A solemn reply of Louis XVI. to the remonstrances of the Bordeaux Parliament, as to the ownership of alluvial land (29th of July, 1786) is still more explicit. Here are a few sentences from it : " It is not within your province to weigh in the balance my rights and those of my subjects. I alone am the supreme guardian of the interests of my people, which cannot be separated from my own. Your decrees and resolutions can never give you a title to resist my authority."

In the Court of Judicature, held on the 6th of August, 1787, to register the edicts on the stamp duty and the

---

[1] Letter of Louis Stanislas Xavier, dated from Hamm, the 28th of January, 1793.

[2] Turgot finishes his letter thus : " Do not reply in detail by post, for your answer will be most certainly opened by the authorities, and I shall be considered a great deal too friendl to liberty for a minister, even for a minister in disgrace."

land tax, the Keeper of the Seals having expressed the same theories of absolute power, and having stated that the King, the sole administrator of his kingdom, alone had the right of making taxes, the senior president of the Parliament relied on the existence of primary institutions to refute him.

"The constitutional principle of French monarchy," said he, "is that the taxes should be consented to by those who have to pay them."

Besides, the last quarrels of the Parliaments with the Crown and its ministers are really nothing more than a great historical debate on this point.

Were those men wrong, who, from such a state of things in France, considered it necessary to create a fundamental political law? In that Barère found a complete justification of the Constituent Assembly and the entire Revolution. His opinion was contrary to that of M. Locré, whilst he placed himself at the same point of view, with perhaps a juster historical sense ; no doubt an important work, but the work of a legist rather than of a philosopher and statesman.

In the month of October, 1791, after the closing of the Assembly, Barère took the seat to which his department had elected him in the Supreme Court of Appeal. In the month of September, 1792, the same department nominated him a member of the National Convention. He had spent a few months' holiday in the Pyrenees, necessary after the fatigues of a session lasting uninterruptedly for two years and a half, and he only returned to Paris two days before the 10th of August. He was not concerned in the events of this day, nor in any of the political events until the beginning of the sittings of the Convention.

"This day," says he, "was the day of unmaskings. The hypocrites of the Court and Cabinet of the Tuileries, the accomplices of the Emigration, the deputies of the Legislative Assembly favourable to royalty, were shown in their true colours. The least far-seeing then understood that the Crown, possessing no stability except by relying on the constitutional principle and having itself become an ally of the foreigner, must be shattered to atoms in face of the anger of a people indignant at such treachery. Louis XVI., after having sworn a solemn oath to the Constitution, in the month of September, 1791, regretted the abdication of that old despotism on which he had been nourished. The rights of hereditary monarchy with its patrimony of the people seemed to him the only legitimate rights. Far from frankly adopting constitutional monarchy, he asked help of arms from absolute monarchs to re-establish him in his ancient sovereignty of divine right. History has collected and unveiled the authentic documents of this impious alliance and of the autograph solicitation of Louis XVI. to the Courts of Austria and Prussia for a military intervention in the affairs of France. This hypocrisy irritated the people against him: treason could no longer remain on the throne. Louis XVI. was unmasked, combatted and conquered by the people. A deposed king has no longer a right to live. With Louis XVI. perished constitutional monarchy."

The republic was enthusiastically decreed in the first sitting of the Convention. Barère seems to blame the Assembly for not having a regular debate before sanctioning this great measure ; "one fitted," as he says, "to sanction such a change by the opinion of the nation." The Assembly had a truer grasp of the situation. These great resolutions, by which a single word changes the form of a State, cannot be subject to contradictory criticism, like the articles of a constitution. They happen when everyone is impressed with their necessity, but it is important that their originators should display no hesitation, if they wish to gain for the new power all the moral strength it needs. From the 10th of August the abolition of royalty was an irretrievable step, no one could doubt it. A National Convention having replaced the provisional government of the Legislative Assembly, the republic was established; the only further point was to give it legal sanction. The new Assembly could have no doubt of its own competence. Why then should it hesitate? Why should it have submitted to the delays of a debate the expression of its mind, which was already made up? This is proved to have been the feeling of all, because only two voices, to which Barère did not join his, were raised to demand an adjournment, two who were far from protesting against republican government, they were those of Quinette and Jean Debry. But, we repeat, Barère never had a dominating leading mind; his republican opinions begin on the 21st of September, 1792.

We say his republican opinions, for we do not suppose that readers of his Memoirs will take those bitter expressions seriously in which he pours out his discouraged patriotism. Those who are opposed to these opinions will not fail to deduce from them that Barère himself did not believe in their possible application; but those whose honesty will not permit them to detach these few phrases from the whole will judge them otherwise. As we have said, Barère was an artist, subject more than other men to the intoxications of success and the faintheartedness that follows defeat, and all the contradictions expressed by such alternatives.

"The Republic," says he, "no more suits the French than English government would suit the Turks."[1] "To found a republic, take republicans, disinterested men, possessing patriotism, honesty, manners and education; but to pretend to found a republic with men who have been slaves and monarchists, intriguers, and up-starts, is a senseless scheme."[2] "The French can never get out of the small, brilliant circle that royalty has drawn round them. They will never be able to raise themselves above monarchy and social inequality."[3] "The Republic lasted for seven centuries on the banks of the Tiber; it has lasted seven years on the banks of the Seine. It suited grave patriots like the Romans; it is not at all suited to fickle cosmopolitans like the French. Rome had political customs; Paris has effeminate ways. The Capitol was both the temple of Mars and of Jupiter; the Exchange is the temple of Fortune as well as the temple of Power. The Romans loved liberty in their very nature, they possessed its principles and habits; the French have habits and governmental traditions that are opposed to the liberty and energy of a republic,"[4] and so on.

We shall not quote further, but the predilections of the author can be seen as easily as his regrets. Besides, the following is one of his last thoughts:

"The Republic is the desire of all lofty natures and free hearts; it is the Utopia of the energetic and ardent, who have been brought up in the knowledge of civilisation

---

[1] Memoirs.   [2] MSS.   [3] Idem.   [4] Idem.

and the sentiments of independence ; it is the government of good sense, of justice and economy ; it is the inevitable tendency of the human race. The position of political states, moulded by the kingly yoke, doubtless displays a distressing disproportion between the desire and the reality, between the actual state of institutions, persons and things, and the immense advance in knowledge of the present generation. But, later, the desires of enlightened free men will be accomplished ; time is the implacable, irresistible revolutionist destined to bring youth and civic virtue into the state of society." [1]

Barère has been sometimes declared to be one of the members of the Orleanist party. Since we have begun to examine his opinions, we must exhaust the subject.

The relations of Barère with the house of Orleans began, as he himself tells us, during the Constituent Assembly. Introduced into the society of Madame de Genlis, he often had occasion to meet the head of the family and his sons, whose praise he chants every time he names them. Their connections became intimate enough for them to ask Barère to accept the guardianship of a young person related very closely to the house of Orleans, which Barère did accept. [2]

---

[1] Manuscripts.

[2] This person, after having married brilliantly, fell into distress, and received help from her old guardian ; she was still living when he was recalled from exile by the Revolution of July. The following anecdote of the time was told me by an eye-witness :

One day a lady, dressed entirely in black, came to see Barère, and gave herself out to be the lady's-maid of Pamela Fitz-Gerald. "You serve a lady of whom I have always been very fond," said Barère to her ; "let me hear news of her. Is she happy?" ."Alas, no !" replied the supposed lady's-maid, and then she added that her mistress often spoke gratefully of the care bestowed on her by her guardian. "I should very much like to see her again, my good

Among Barère's manuscripts we find the following references to Joseph Egalité:

"At the Constituent Assembly he served the Commons very effectively by inducing a minority of the nobility to ally themselves with them. Political intriguers, giving themselves the names of patriots, endeavoured to exploit the influence and wealth of the Duke of Orleans by urging him to take possession of the throne, but it has always been apparent to me that he never seriously contemplated that step. . . . No one of his contemporaries could say of this Prince with any truth, 'This man had that aim.' . . . . All his actions seemed to me to be directed towards avenging himself for the affected indifference of Louis XVI. and the outrageous scorn of the Queen, who detested and persecuted him. . . . . He acted moderately and disinterestedly after the flight of the King on the 21st of June, 1791. Far from profiting by this circumstance, neither himself nor any of his party endeavoured to seize supreme power. This intention

---

Pamela," pursued Barère, looking at her scrutinisingly; "tell her that I have carefully kept her likeness, which I carried into exile with me."

"You have her likeness," cried the stranger. "Oh, sir, let me see it."

When it was shown her, she could not help exclaiming:

"My God! how pretty I was!"

"You are Pamela herself; you can no longer hide it," said Barère.

"Yes; I wished to kiss you. You no doubt think me very changed? I have suffered so much. I will tell you all about it."

Then, taking hold of the likeness very quickly: "Let me have it; I want to show it to Mademoiselle A——."

She went out, with tears in her eyes, after having clasped his hand, and Barère never saw her again.

Some time afterwards he learnt that the heroine of this anecdote had died in a boarding-house.

did not even exist in any member of the Constituent
Assembly.   On the contrary, he publicly declared he
would accept neither the regency nor any position that
would place him at the head of affairs. . . . . He
had not been willing, in July, 1789, to be the President
of the Assembly, after the union of the Three Estates.
It had been offered him by the Commons, who were in
a majority. . . . . In November and December, 1792,
the Duke of Orleans was an object of fear or jealousy
to both the parties that divided the Convention.   The
Mountain suspected Dumouriez, who, they supposed, had
aims against the Assembly.   The Girondists were
working to gain possession of the mind and military
force of the General of the Northern army to obtain
political power and influence. .   . . The latter had
proposed a decree of banishment against all the members of the house of Bourbon who were still in France. .
The Mountain pretended that this decree was merely a
ruse to disguise their royalist opinions, and two days
later they had it reported.

"I knew the plans of both parties, and as soon as I
knew the subjects of their hatred, I warned my colleague
Egalité.   I explained to him how the Mountain wished
to keep Roland out of the ministry and how the Girondists
wished to deprive the Duke of Orleans of his seat for
Paris.   One day in December we were walking on the
Terrasse des Feuillants while the Assembly was sitting.   I
endeavoured to induce Egalité to ask for a few months'
leave and go to the United States, the only place of refuge
in which he could wait until the events that appeared to
threaten France had passed by.   The Duke of Orleans,
far from disapproving of my opinion, thanked me, and
told me he must consult M. Pétion on this point, in

whom he had full confidence. He asked me to wait for
him on the terrace, and went to Pétion's house. He was
then living in a house near the Tuileries' orangery on the
side of the Rue Saint-Florentin. Pétion and his friends
were of an opposite opinion to mine; this I learnt in
another walk on the terrace the next day. . . . . M.
Roederer, in his "Esprit de la Révolution" (page 191),
alters the history of the Convention, which he could not
have known personally, as he was in hiding at Le Pecq,
near Saint-Germain, from the 10th of August. He writes:
'Thus the Girondists thought to annihilate the Mountain
by rendering the possibility of the coronation of the Duke
of Orleans impossible.' Never did such a plan or such
an idea exist, even remotely, on the benches of the
Mountain. Everybody was then for the Republic, no one
for monarchy. The Duke of Orleans sat on the benches
of the Mountain; but he saw much of Pétion, Gensonné,
Guadet and other Girondists, who met at Pétion's in the
evening. Guadet was on intimate terms with General
Valence, who was always attached, with his whole heart,
to the house of Orleans. Hence M. Roederer has only
falsified this period and slandered that half of the Convention called the Mountain. . . . . Egalité was seated
at the Convention near M. Mailly, and, seeing the
divisions of the Assembly, said to him: 'If my eldest
son were here, he would vote with the Right (the Girondists), but my younger son, Montpensier, would vote as I
shall.' [1]. . . . . Dumouriez wished, like another Monk,

---

[1] Here the MS. contains some details of the reception of the
Duke of Chartres into the Jacobin Club, and extracts from a correspondence as to the negotiations that were begun to elect him a member
of the Convention at Sarreguemines. In a paper edited by himself,
the young Duke said: "I was born under a lucky star. Opportunities
offer themselves; I have only to take advantage of them."

to dispose of the Crown and to place the Orleans branch
on the throne, which he would raise by his army of Jem-
mapes, although it had been conquered and routed at
Neerwinden. Before besieging the fortress of Lille, he
organised his armed counter-revolution and his political
expedition on Paris. He wished to realise his Utopia of
a monarchy, voted by all the cantonal Presidents, united
and assembled on the ruins of the National Convention.
Dumouriez meditated this horrible treachery with his staff,
in spite of his army in Belgium, in spite of the approval
of the frontiers, and in spite of the whole of France, now
free and indignant at such monstrous disloyalty. . . . .

"At the National Convention Joseph d'Orleans gave a
vote of *Death* against Louis XVI. This vote was heard
of at Coblentz without grief, but not without furnishing
a pretext for getting rid of the voter. The intrigues of
the banished princes at Paris were underhand but powerful. ·
They had agents in the Commune, at the Cordeliers',
the Jacobins', and even in the Convention. All the
anti-revolutionary machinery acted at once. The Duke
of Orleans was compromised in the disloyalty of
Dumouriez, and arrested on the 4th of April, 1793, at
the Palais Royal, with one of his sons, thirteen years
old, the Duke of Beaujolais. Montpensier was arrested
at Nice. His eldest son left the Army of the North on
the 5th of April, after the decree against its general had
been declared. Transferred to Marseilles with the idea
of postponing the case and saving them, Egalité and
his family were first shut up in the castle of Nôtre
Dame and then in the fort of St. Jean. There they
remained till the month of October. The Committee
of Public Safety, who had given over its powers over all
the officials to the Committee of General Surety, did no

concern itself either with prisoners or accused; it had forgotten that the Duke of Orleans was at Marseilles; that was none of its business. But the enemies of the Duke did concern themselves with him ; his ruin had been decreed at Coblentz, and their agents got him brought back from Marseilles, in order to hunt up accusations against him, and get him condemned to death. His death appears to have been the work of exaggerated republicans. In my opinion, which I expressed at the time to several deputies, they were only the blind instruments of aristocratic hatred. It was the treacherous indefatigable intrigues at Coblentz which, by the movement of the sections and by party spirit, brought about the ruin of the whole of that minority of the nobility which had joined the Commons in June, 1789, and many of whom had served the cause of liberty in the service of the Republic. Both of these were irremediable crimes in the eyes of the emigrants; and the Count of Provence was the most corrupting and treacherously clever intriguer that the Bourbon family ever produced.

"Contemporary biographers—that is to say, the class of men least worthy of credence, because they are the most impassioned and venal—have accused the Revolution of eating its own children, like Saturn of old. 'Thus perished this Prince,' say they, 'sacrificed to the implacable hatred of his enemies by those very men whose cause he had embraced, whose enemies were his own enemies—a sad, memorable example of the vicissitudes of fortune and the inconstancy of popular favour.'

"No, the French nation is not guilty of the death of the Duke of Orleans. The people were attached to him by gratitude and sympathy. Louis XVIII. must be accused of this, he who secretly intrigued at Paris to excite the people against his broth'er, Louis XVI., against Marie Antoinette and Madame Elizabeth; this is proved by letters and documents at Vienna in the Emperor's cabinet, from what Prince Charles says."

We do not know what Barère could have dissembled in the preceding notes; but it is our duty to assert that all those that we know of, while proving his fairly familiar relations with Joseph d'Orleans and his very benevolent disposition, drive away the idea of political connivance.

In 1833 Barère, having retired to Tarbes, received a letter from one of his former colleagues in which the latter, acting as intermediary for King Louis Philippe, asked for information on the circumstances that had led to the catastrophe of Joseph Egalité; especially he wanted to know if his sentence had been discussed in the Committee of Public Safety, and by how many votes it had passed. Barère replied to the appeal of his friend by a fairly detailed narrative of the events, in which he explained that the Committee of Public Safety did not exist at the time of the arrest of the Duke of Orleans, and that never came within his province, the latter's sentence being the exclusive work of the Committee of General Surety.

Shortly afterwards, Barère's colleague sent him a £40 note from the King, who had asked for these explanations; and after that time a like sum was sent regularly every year addressed to Tarbes by the head of the house of Orleans.

Such is the origin of that kind of pension of which men have spoken in such a variety of ways. A former clerk of the Committee of Public Safety, who had kept up an attachment for Barère, then managed the King's cabinet. It can easily be imagined that the request for historical information from the old member of the Convention was simply a pretence to smooth the hardships of his lot. Having been deprived of his heritage, all Barère's resources consisted of a little pension, obtained by a few friends from the Home Office, in consideration of his literary work, and from the Ministry of Justice, in consideration of the magistracy he had held.

We have had before us the minutes of the work sent by Barère to his colleague. They contain, with a little additional information, the same facts and suppositions that we have just quoted from his notes.

It seemed to be settled in advance that Barère's place in the Convention should be among the Girondists, both from his literary talents, the opinions he had upheld in the Constituent Assembly, and from his tendency to federalism, which he makes no attempt to disguise in his Memoirs. On every occasion he attacks the deputies of Paris with extreme violence; he accuses them of establishing a monopoly of power for the profit of the capital and hostile to the departments, especially those of the South. In fact Barère was intimate with the greater number of the deputies from the Gironde, and he was counted, for some time rightly, as one of them. And yet, while quite disapproving of the *coup d'état* of the 31st of May and even courageously opposing it, he did not embrace their cause or imitate their action. He felt that every obstacle to the march of the Revolution and to that of the Assembly charged with protecting the scene of action where this Revolution was being accomplished, was a crime, not only against the country, but against the liberty of the world; he felt that every opposition from within aided the plans of the conspirators and aliens. The efforts, 'the manœuvres, let us say, with Barère, while regretting the expression, the intrigues of the Girondists had the appearance of the interests of a clique, thinking little of the affairs of the nation. The appeal to the people, which was their rallying cry during the trial of Louis XVI., was an appeal to civil war. It put in question the Conventional Government, that the country had created to carry out its salvation. It offered a handle to cowardice to avoid the immense responsibility that an immense power brought with it. It was not thus that the majority of the Assembly had understood its mission; it aspired to march in the van of the revolutionary movement, and to be first in the breach in the hour of danger. "These courageous republicans," said Barère, in speaking of his colleagues; "these men who wished to deliver France from the bane of royalty, were not astonished at being banished by a fickle, changeable people; they accepted and underwent the consequences of their heroic decrees. This made Cambon say, when a reactionary deputy threatened him with the kingly wrath: 'To conquer liberty we have burnt our ships.' It is a lofty, consoling thought that, by exposing themselves to the hereditary anger of kings, these representatives did their duty, and courageously sacrificed themselves to the general welfare and the national freedom."[1]

Barère's fame in the Convention Assembly dates from the sentence on Louis XVI. The case commenced under his presidency, and he was given the delicate painful task of *giving the tone* to the serious matter. The first example is often a decisive one, and his certainly contributed to

---

[1] Manuscript.

establish that order and lofty magisterial propriety, which continued to reign during the course of the inquiry. In the dealings of the president with the prisoner, he was thoughtful and dignified, and he displayed energy and tact in repressing anything that might disturb the solemnity of the sittings. Without losing his popularity he knew how to observe a thousand little considerations, that the King and his defenders recognised; this was no easy matter in the face of a mob irritated by recent misfortunes, among which were doubtless to be found many widows and orphans of the 10th of August, a mob inclined to suspicion because it had already seen much treachery.

The motion having been proposed to refer the requests preferred by the counsel of Louis XVI. to the Committee of General Surety, Barère said: "We ought to give all the latitude that natural law establishes to the defence of the deposed monarch; we ought to encourage all those who want to exercise that most fascinating of commands, that of officious defender. The measure proposed is immoral and impolitic."[1] He tried in vain to induce Target, and encouraged Malesherbes, to accept the mission that Louis XVI. had offered to both of them.

Everyone knows what Barère's vote was;[2] and the

---

[1] Sitting of the 14th of November, 1792.

[2] The text of this vote is too impregnated with Barère's personal opinions for us to omit it here:

"If the manners of the French were civilised enough, and public education widespread enough, to receive important social institutions and humane laws, I should vote under those circumstances alone for the abolition of the death penalty, and I should express here a less barbarous opinion. But we are still far from that state of morality; I am obliged to examine with strict justice the question put before remarkable speech he uttered on the 4th of January against an appeal to the people had a great influence on the decision of the Assembly.   He contested the principal motion, cited by the partisans of this measure, as a superfluous one, that is to say, the necessity of binding the whole nation to the step the Convention was about to take.   " The nation had bound itself of its own accord to your decree," said he, "because it has created you its representatives, because it has sent you here after Louis Capet, arrested, suspended from his functions and imprisoned, had been accused of conspiracy against the State; because the nation has invested you with its unlimited powers and reposes boundless confidence in you; and, lastly, because you are the National Convention of a representative Republic. It has always seemed to me that the appeal to the country was made by the Legislative Assembly after the events of the 10th of August; and that the country

---

me. Imprisonment until the conclusion of peace does not present to my mind any solid advantage; a king deposed by a nation seems to me a false diplomatic step. Banishment appears like a call to arms to the foreign powers and another reason for interest in favour of the outlaw. I have recognised that the penalty of death was prescribed by all laws, and I must sacrifice my natural repugnance to obey them. In the tribunal of natural law, he who kills another unjustly should perish; in the tribunal of our practical law the penal code condemns to death the conspirator against his country, and him who has imperilled the internal or external safety of the State; in the tribunal of national justice, I find the supreme law of public safety. This law tells me that between tyrants and nations there can be only war to the knife. It tells me also that the punishment of Louis, which will be a lesson to kings, will also be one to rebels, anarchists, pretenders to dictatorship, or to any other power similar to royalty. The laws must be deaf and inexorable to all modern ambitious scoundrels. The tree of liberty, an ancient author has said, grows when it is watered with the blood of any kind of tyrants.

" The law says *death*, and I am here but its mouthpiece."

replied to that appeal by forming a National Convention."

But hardly had sentence been given than Barère strove to annihilate all traces of division. The proclamation to the French people that he composed on the 23rd of January, on the orders of the Convention, is a model of moderation worthy of preservation.

"This political crisis has environed us with contradictions and storms," he writes, "but yet the divergent opinions had honest motives. Feelings of humanity, political ideas more or less restricted, fears more or less thought out on the extent of the powers of the representatives, divided them for a few moments; but the cause has departed; the motives have disappeared; respect for freedom of opinion should cause these stormy scenes to be forgotten. Only the good they did has remained, by the death of the tyrant and tyranny; and this sentence each of us shares equally, together with the whole nation. The National Convention and the French nation should now have one mind, one feeling— that of civic fraternity."

Barère has often been declared to be a thorough poltroon. We have shown how much credit must be given to these assertions, but the time has come to give proofs. In fact, if Barère's conduct on certain decisive occasions is compared with the acts of the most lauded daring of our times, one may be allowed to be surprised at the reproach and to appreciate all the better the difference of the times.

From the month of October, 1792, he was one of the first to rebel against the hideous, fearful authority of Marat in the tribune, declaring that such a man ought rather to be in Bedlam than in the National Assembly. "If anything could have changed my opinion," he says in his speech against the appeal to the country, "it would be to see it shared by a man whom I cannot name, but who is known for his sanguinary opinions." Then he added, in speaking of Robespierre: "I shall declare my opinion, although it is the same as that of another man who uttered republican sentiments when we were under a monarchy, and only monarchical principles now we have a republic."

On the 5th of November, when Louvet foresightedly launched an accusation at Robespierre of aiming at the dictatorship, the order of the day was voted by the majority. Barère endeavoured to find reasons for it that Robespierre thought insulting. In fact he expressed himself in a way most likely to stir up the hatred of an ambitious man. "To accuse a man of aiming at dictatorship," he had cried, "one must suppose in him some force of character, genius, audacity and great political or military successes." Then he struck at him at the same time with the weapons of biting sarcasm and ridicule in calling him a man of a day, a little manufacturer of revolutions, and awarding him a crown formed of cypress on the 2nd of September. "I claim as our country's," he added, "this precious time we are wasting on personal quarrels. Do not let us lend importance to men that general opinion will know how to put in their place; do not let us set up pedestals for pigmies." On the evening of the same day, on the Jacobin tribune, in the spot where Robespierre gained his greatest triumphs, in his presence and amidst the clamour of his followers, Barère dared to repeat the same expressions.

The evening before he had boldly declared against the growing power of the Commune of Paris, which he repeated on several occasions: the 10th of November, the 2nd of December, 1792, the 26th of February following, etc.

On the 31st of May and the 2nd of June he took up the defence of the accused both against the Commune and against Robespierre, Danton, Hébert and Marat, and he cried in the midst of the seated Convention: "You have struck off the head of a tyrant, you ought also to strike off the head of the insolent soldier, this Henriot, who dares to violate the national representatives."

Lastly, in the very height of the Terror, in a report on the roads and bridges, he made this paraphrase of Chénier's famous hemistich, "Laws and not blood!"':

"We shall succeed in increasing the means of wealth and industry by public works whose utility sanctions their expense, by high-roads, by roads necessary for commerce, by the opening of navigable canals and by connecting them with the chief rivers of France. By multiplying such works and ways of communication does one succeed in civilising a State and in making its people prosperous, and not by a horrible profusion of penal laws and a terrible amount of tortures."

Let us add, to Barère's credit, that nearly all his courageous acts were inspired by the dominant sentiments of the passage we have just read. And he did not only protest in words in the name of humanity. He opposed the creation of a revolutionary tribunal proposed by Carrier, Danton, and Lindet, and he especially sought to demonstrate the necessity of a jury. He opposed the law relating to suspected persons, both the one of April 1st, 1792, stirred up by Saint-Just against the nobility, and that of the 10th of June, which deprived accused persons of every form of protection from justice, and was the exclusive work of Robespierre and Couthon, which

made the Convention vote their bill without ever sub-
mitting it to the Committee of Públic Safety.

At the same time, the position of the members of
the executive, and still more, that feeling of responsibility
which characterises periods of public devotedness, forbade
them to indulge in internal divisions that might stop the
forward movement. When the majority spoke, the minority
had to give way, for the safety of the State was at stake.
Once having become responsible for an act by sharing in
it, instinctively one endeavours to find just and necessary
reasons for one's action.   This is what Barère often did;
but he rarely neglected the opportunity of smoothing the
necessary severities of the politics of the time.   It was
generally by personal requisitions, under pretence of
public services, that he saved his *protégés* from the
severity of general laws, a humane method that had also
suggested itself to Grégoire.   Barère estimates that the
number of exemptions he thus obtained was over 6,000,
particularly for scholars, artists, literary men, etc.   He had
come into connection with a great number of them as
a member of the Constitution Committee, having made
an appeal in the name of that committee to all men
well versed in moral science to invite them to forward
their views on constitutional institutions.   Our impartial
duty would not be fulfilled if, after having proved the
accusation of cowardice attached to Barère's name to be
unjust, we omitted to mention the facts that reveal in him
a leaning to tack about and an absence of moral firmness.
Our duty is to show up every side of his nature.   Nevertheless, we will shorten a list that might become unduly
lengthy.

When disorder is at its height, when, according to
Barère's expression, one might think one saw in the

Convention the assassins of liberty rather than its founders, when the Jacobins yelled for the exclusion and accusation of the Girondists, and Guadet replies by proposing to abolish the municipal authorities of Paris and transfer the Assembly to Bourges, Barère manages to get a half-and-half Bill passed, the appointment of a commission of twelve members charged to inquire into the plots imperilling the Republic.

But some days after, as this Commission furnished a pretext for an armed insurrection of the sections, he himself proposes its suppression. It is true that at the same time he proposes to deprive the Commune of the armed forces of the department, in order to place it at the disposition of the Convention.

When the two parties are nearly coming to blows, and indecision as to the result makes the country intolerably anxious, Barère eagerly seizes the idea of giving the crisis an indirect issue by the voluntary ostracism of the chiefs on both sides. But immediately after his courageous demonstration of the 2nd of June, he is seen failing to back up the measure of hostages that he had proposed, and following the tide.

We have said that Barère was one of the Constitution Committee. This committee, formed in October, 1792, is the one that presented its report on the 15th of February following, Condorcet being its spokesman. It must not be mixed up with the second, of which Hérault de Séchelles and Saint-Just were the most active members, and formed the Constitution of 1793.

This constitution, that the nation expected would end all troubles and unite all parties, was welcomed by the 48,000 primary assemblies, with the exception of one. Barère was entrusted with drawing up the decree of the

27th of June on the convocation of these assemblies, while preferring the work in which he had co-operated, yet he shared the general enthusiasm. He wrote as follows :

" Here it is, this constitution so greatly looked forward to, which, like the stone tables of Moses, has come out of the holy mountain accompanied by thunder and lightning. Do not let anyone oppose it as only the work of a few days. In a few days the knowledge of every century has been collected. In one spot equality has laid down its benefits with touching simplicity; further on, civil and political liberty have concisely and severely engraved their rights. In another place property, that wealth not only of owners, but also of those that are not, because all can and ought to become owners, has laid down its limits, and dedicated this base of all political society; property, which, under the laws of a wise republic, is ever the reward of toil, economy and virtue, is solemnly recognised and assured ; philosophy has stipulated for the liberty of worship, politics for the peace of Europe, reason for education for all, the republic for popular societies, society for public works, humanity for aid to unfortunate citizens, and justice and law for the safeguard of so many rights."

Many years later he wrote again :

" This constitution has been condemned without a possibility for judgment having been given, since not one of its articles has been carried out. People have never thought, or had the time to think, of making France really republican in interests, education and legislation. So being republican only in name, Bonaparte obtained a cheap victory on the 18th of Brumaire."

The Committee of General Defence, which had been

created by the Legislative Assembly, and had rendered great services, was renewed by the Convention. Barère became a member first, and then its president. His Memoirs contain some curious particulars as to the disputes that arose in this committee between Danton and Gensonné, about Belgium. However, in the spring of 1792, the dangers of the new-born republic, at home and abroad, showed the necessity of concentrating the power into the hands of a small number of men, who would devote themselves to the whole work and danger of this collective dictatorship. The circumstances were so serious that a single thought, that of the public safety, absorbed all minds, and it was with this name that the Convention baptised the committee in which its confidence placed the destinies of the country. Barère, in a most enthusiastic speech, while recounting the immense needs of the situation, showed the whole extent of the duties imposed on the new chiefs of the government.

"Liberty," he said, "has become the creditor of every citizen. Some owe her their industry, others their fortune; these their advice, those their arms—all owe her their blood. So everyone in France, without distinction of sex or age, is called upon by his fatherland to defend his liberty. Every physical or moral faculty, every political or industrial ability, belongs to her; all the metals and elements must pay her tribute. Let everyone take his post in the national military movement that is about to take place. The young men will fight, the married will forge arms, transport the baggage and artillery, and prepare the food; the women will work at the soldiers' clothes, will make tents, and become nurses in the hospitals for the wounded; the children will make lint out of old linen; and the old men, again taking up the duties they had among the ancients, will be carried into the public squares, and will encourage the spirit of the young warriors, they will propagate hatred to kings and the unity of the Republic. The houses of the nation shall be turned into barracks, the public squares into workshops, the cellars will do to prepare saltpetre; all saddle horses will be requisitioned for the cavalry, all carriage horses for the artillery; hunting-pieces, swords and pikes will be used at home. The Republic is now nothing but a huge beleaguered town; France must now be nothing but a huge camp."

To meet such a huge mass of work, and in order that their work may not be hindered by squabbles as to their powers and jurisdiction, the twelve citizens who composed the Great Committee[1] divided amongst themselves the different parts of the government. Each exercised the most absolute authority in his ministry; but a third of them must sign an executive document to render it legal, in accordance with the decree of institution. These signatures were exchanged between the members present in a purely formal manner. Billaud-Varennes and Collot-d'Herbois managed the correspondence with the departments and the representatives who were away on any mission in the provinces. Saint-Just had asked to see to the legislation, and Couthon shared this work with him. When Robespierre entered the committee, he was charged with preparing general questions. Later, these three members established and directed a central police office. Carnot was the War Minister; Jean Bon Saint-

---

[1] This name, which has been ratified by history, was given to the second Committee of Public Safety, formed in July, 1793, to distinguish it from those which preceded and followed. Barère was a member of the first.

André directed the Admiralty, Prieur (from the Côte-d'Or) the manufacture of arms, Robert Lindet and the other Prieur (from the Marne) the Commissariat. Barère, who in the first Committee of Public Safety had shared the Foreign Office with Danton, continued at his post with Hérault de Séchelles; but this colleague, who was nearly always on special missions, and who was afterwards arrested, left all the work to him. The Admiralty was also confided to him during the absence of Jean Bon Saint-André, which lasted several months. At the same time he was in command of the Public Education Office, the charities, public monuments, theatres, etc. We shall have to speak presently of his military reports, which are over two hundred in number. In addition, he found time to attend the sittings of the Assembly, to speak frequently in the political campaigns, and to make several lengthy reports on foreign affairs, administration, legislation, the navy, the woods and forests, etc. His report " On the means of making the French language universal" is complementary to Grégoire's on the same subject. His report " On the means of abolishing beggary in the country" contains the account of the principles that the Committee of Public Safety had summed up in the axiom: "The unfortunate are the governors of the earth; they have the right to talk as masters to the governments who neglect them." The substitution of outdoor relief for hospitals and workhouses is the foundation of the system propounded in this report. He had also prepared several plans for institutions on behalf of foundlings and abandoned mothers, but the events of July stopped their being carried out.

Finally, it was owing to his report that the École de Mars was organised, where, under the direction of Prieur of the Côte-d'Or, our most celebrated savants, in a few booths on the plain of Sablons, taught many patriotic young men.   This school was the nucleus of our finest institutions for public education.[1]

Such a quantity of work did not only need that exceeding facility that no historian denies that Barère possessed, it also needed less dissipation than he is generally accredited with, or else it needed that devotion of true belief that makes a man able to silence his passions.   But, supposing he was able to direct these almost herculean toils whilst leading a life of pleasure,

---

[1] In the margin of a newspaper which accredits Robespierre with the creation of the École de Mars, Barère has written : " It was Barère who made the report and prepared the decree establishing this school. Robespierre was not even present at the Committee of Public Safety on the day that Carnot proposed the idea."

In speaking of the inner working of the Committee of Public Safety, we cannot help showing up the strange blunders of an obituary notice published by the *Times* about the time of Barère's death.   We mention them because the article contains, as well, information which must have been supplied by friends of Barère.   The writer, who subscribes himself " A Cosmopolite," says that he was introduced to Barère forty years before by Thomas Paine.   This fact seems to point out the famous Lewis Goldsmith, author of " Crimes of Cabinets," who was, in fact, introduced by Paine to his former colleague, as is proved by a letter of the former which we have in our possession.

According to the English biographer, Robespierre and Carnot were members at the same time of the Committee of Public Safety and that of General Surety (which their establishment rendered impossible).   Barère was only member of the former, which, he adds, did not concern itself with home affairs.

Next come some most romantic details on the life of Billaud-Varennes.   The author makes him become a monk, and take the name of *Padre Varenas*, in a Jacobin convent in one of the Spanish colonies. He sends him to Mexico in 1810 to stir up revolution, and at last makes him take flight and die at New York in 1817.   Such lies need no refutation.   Billaud is known to have spent twenty years at Sinnamari, and then, in 1816, to have taken refuge in the Republic of Hayti, where President Pétion welcomed him warmly.   There he died in 1819.

he must have been a colossal genius, greater even than Mirabeau.

The supple mind and indefatigable activity that distinguished Barère were highly appreciated by the Committee. Dr. Souberbielle, then a member of the revolutionary tribunal, has told us that one day Robespierre expressed this opinion of his colleague in his presence, in terms not devoid of spite: "Barère may have committed mistakes, but he is an honest man, who loves his country, and serves it better than anyone. As soon as work is to be done, he is ready to undertake it. He knows everything, he is acquainted with everybody, he is fit for everything."

In addition to the special business of each branch of the administration with which each member dealt in his office, there was a gathering every evening to talk over general affairs. Then it was especially that Barère was so useful in playing the part that the nature of his talents had marked out for him.

"When, after several hours of animated debate, which kept us till late at night, our tired intellects could only with difficulty recall the course of the discussion, and were about to lose sight of the principal point, Barère used to speak, and after a quick, clear, summing-up he placed the question squarely before us, and we only had to say a word to solve it."

It is in these words that one of Barère's colleagues (Prieur of the Côte-d'Or) explained to me one day how precious Barère's presence was in the Committee of Public Safety.

The office of reporter was a natural consequence of the summings-up of which we have just spoken. Barère was almost always given this duty, which he carried out with undeniable cleverness. But this is also, perhaps, the cause why he was the object of so much hatred. He was often compelled to express in the name of the committee opinions by no means his own, which he had no doubt opposed, and for which he was obliged to find apologies, hence he has often been held morally responsible for what was not his, and it has been possible to tax him with weakness by contrasting apparently contradictory opinions. No one but Barère was ever, perhaps, placed in such exacting circumstances : a more energetic character would have either declined the work or have been overcome by it.

And yet the part he played was a necessary one. If the committee of the Government had shown itself divided in the Assembly, it would have been deprived of all command : every day a like scene would have been witnessed, as when Barère having proposed in the name of a section of his colleagues the banishment of the political prisoners, of which the prisons were full, Collot-d'Herbois violently opposed him and styled him a supporter of the aristocrats. The task that Barère had set himself was a brilliant but difficult one ; whilst other members of the committee, who had been able to make a speciality for themselves, found a compensation for the evil they could not prevent in the knowledge of the good they did, Barère, condemned to be a party to everything, had to present it all to the nation under favourable colours.

If, in forming a juster opinion of the duties imposed on the reporter of the committee, we do not credit him with opinions not his own, we must also deprive him of some of the merit of his labours. Pen in hand, he was present at the private debates, often rich in broad views, wise opinions and energetic statements, and by help of his memory he reproduced the tenor of them ; so much so that one or other of his colleagues might have laid claim not only to his share of the omniscience of the reporter, but also to some of those picturesque chiselled expressions which are more abundant in the reports of the committee than in any other of Barère's works.

His war reports form the chief part. Carnot, Prieur and Lindet furnished him almost daily with the material of some speech on the successes of our arms. What they worked at in the silence of their offices, they left to their colleague the pleasure of publishing. The public and the Assembly were so accustomed to consider him a bearer of good news that his presence in the House excited an unimaginable enthusiasm ; his entrance was greeted with cheers and everybody cried, "Barère to the tribune !" The debate in hand was interrupted to listen to him. His reports, when read aloud in the camps, electrified the soldiers, and he himself relates with just pride how they have been heard to rush on the enemy with shouts of "Barère to the tribune !" Then it was that a decree of having deserved the thanks of the country was the best and most coveted reward.

Barère was in his right when he said in speaking of the revolutionary eloquence :

"It was the first time, either in France or Europe, either among ancient or modern nations, that the national tribune, devoted to legislative debates and politics, has exercised an important influence on the army, in rising to a new kind of eloquence. This is the first time that the representatives of a nation have spoken in the name of liberty and equality to numberless battalions, have celebrated the exploits and great deeds of the national forces, and decreed rewards to its armies, that conquered so many kings."

One may read in the Memoirs how much this Committee of Public Safety, which was obliged to fight the whole of Europe, thought, nevertheless, of the duties of peace; and one may rest convinced that, if it had enjoyed peace, many public works would not have waited until our days before being carried out. The beautifying of the Tuileries and of the Champs Elysées, the completion of the Louvre, and the housing of the National Library had seriously occupied the time of the committee. In the plan proposed by Barère, who was in charge of the public buildings, the space of the present library was to have been converted into a square ornamented with fountains in front of the Opera. Other circumstances have brought about just the contrary.

Besides, public opinion has already thought better of several errors, and even before history had begun to enlighten it, the minds of those men who are above party prejudice had formed their judgment. In a note of Barère's we find the following:

"General Subervic, a member of the Chamber of Deputies, formerly Lannes' aide-de-camp in the war in Italy, came to see me in Tarbes, where he was inspecting a regiment of cavalry. We chatted much of Bonaparte, and one thing leading to another, he told me he had heard these words from the very mouth of the General, who was talking of France with his officers, words which spoken abroad were as the judgment of posterity: 'Since the Revolution of 1789 there has been but one real energetic government in France, which was the Committee of Public Safety.'"

The note finishes thus:

"Later, during the Empire, General Subervic heard Napoleon say, 'To write the history of the French Revolution well is very difficult. I only know one man capable of doing it well, and that is Barère. But he would have to give up certain prejudices.' Napoleon was doubtless alluding to my labours on behalf of the Republic that he had overturned. He called my love for my country and my devotion to liberty, prejudices. But he did not know, or did not wish to know, that to have any influence on the government of a great nation, one must, before all else, do all for one's country and nothing for oneself; that one must be the man of the country and of the age. To act on other principles is, in truth, to have prejudices, and Napoleon was not free from them."

Barère often thought of writing the history of the period of the Revolution. He thought out the skeleton in hundreds of ways. Sometimes he called it a "Study," or "Thoughts," or "Recollections," or "Lessons of the Revolution"; sometimes it is a "Secret History," or simply a "Political Diary," some "Chapters taken from the Great Work of the Revolution," or a "Picture of Paris and the Provinces" during this astounding period; or, lastly, an account merely of the "Men," the "Periods," and the "Great Days."

He proposed to collect his military reports to the Convention. With the explanatory notes that he would have added we should have possessed an invaluable history of the wars of the Republic, written in the style of the time.

Lastly, he had the idea, of which he has left some sketches, of describing "The Mysterious Personages of the Revolution." This title was very promising. In times of political disorder there are indeed a certain number of characters dragged off so quickly by the storm that they stand out for too brief an instant before the historian to allow him to seize their features: more often than not they only show him one side of their character. Other actors in revolutions have a part so contrary to their nature imposed on them that reason refuses to judge them, and passion makes monsters of them. Yet when a corner of the veil that envelops them is raised, they are proved to be most sensitively human. It is the duty of their surviving contemporaries to fill up these historical *lacunæ*.

We have not mentioned half the plans Barère conceived and sometimes sketched out. The quantity of them is a proof of the different points of view from which he looked on facts.

But what we ought chiefly to regret, for he alone perhaps could have done it well, is the incomplete "History of the Committee of Public Safety." We may perhaps publish this work separately, in the meantime we shall not be blamed for giving a few extracts from it, which will show the author's plan and manner.

PRELIMINARY IDEA.

THE National Convention had at first, from the 22nd of September, 1792, a Committee of General Defence, composed of twenty-five members, and all the Convention might be present at its debates. The northern frontiers were threatened, the King of Prussia was already occupying the eastern fortresses, Longwy and Verdun, and was advancing into Champagne. Every day this committee was occupied with measures for defending the territory of France; but it was by no means capable of dealing with its difficult and honourable mission. Unexpected events, and the heroic courage of the volunteers, who had rushed from every department, did more than the Committee of General Defence, composed of party politicians exasperated by hate and ambition, and so divided that only unforeseen events could save the nation and its liberty.

The principal incident was the treason of General Dumouriez, who, after the disaster of Neerwinden, thought that, with the help of the remains of the army he commanded, he could march on Lille and then on Paris, and seize the power in order to establish a monarchy. This shameful betrayal, the odium of which fell equally on both parties in the Committee of General Defence, as each side was accused of sharing the profit, led to the abolition of this committee. The Convention replaced it by a Committee of Public Safety of nine members of its own choosing.

FIRST COMMITTEE OF PUBLIC SAFETY.

It was established on the 5th of April, 1793. It was at first occupied with the means of defence and the providing of armies when all the frontiers were invaded, when internal dissensions began to stir up the south, and civil war was being organised in the west. But the two parties in the National Convention spent every day in abusing and attacking each other, instead of saving their country. The ambition of the municipality of Paris, who thought itself the sole founder of the Republic by virtue of the events of the 10th of August, brought in armed forces into the midst of these stormy debates. By bringing up forty-two guns with lighted fuses the municipality exacted the violation of the national representation, by commanding the Assembly to arrest twenty-two members, whom it styled Girondists and Federalists. The Committee of Public Safety, taken thus unawares by this conspiracy of the municipality of Paris, could offer no show of resistance, nor deliver the Assembly ; so the national representation was violated by a military surprise. The Convention felt the need of forming another Committee of Public Safety composed of more energetic men, capable of using means to make the national authority respected by all the factions and parties who were already fighting for the rags of the infant Republic.

SECOND COMMITTEE OF PUBLIC SAFETY.

It was at the beginning of July, 1793, that the second Committee of Public Safety was nominated by the Convention. It was to consist of twelve members, but only nine were chosen at first; the three other places were filled up in August and October. It started on its duties at the moment when forty-three departments had been estranged by emissaries of the faction that had been beaten on the 31st of May and by deputies that had taken refuge in the west and south ; at the moment when federalism was raising its standard against the National Convention; when the English and Spaniards were buying the surrender of Toulon, and were seizing the arsenals and fleet there. This committee, far from recoiling before dangers so imminent, hastened to take up this immense responsibility, to save national unity, to preserve the integrity of France, and keep hold of the liberty it had won.

I shall always be proud of having been a member of this committee from July, 1793, till October, 1794, and to have been its mouthpiece and reporter to the Assembly, and even to have been its victim. I am writing of the labours, debates and public characters of the men who made up this second Committee of Public Safety, whose principal events and mighty recollections I am tracing. Two generations have already passed over the tombs of the members of the Convention; I am the only one left of the Committee of Public Safety. Alone have I survived long years of proscription and exile, as if I were destined to dissolve the prejudices that remain against my contemporaries and to publish to the new generation, so intelligent and so friendly to justice, the truth about the opinions, labours and services of this committee, so slandered and still more misunderstood. Now that the actors have left the stage and the conquerors and conquered rest for ever on this vast battle-field, truth and justice, who never rest but on tombs, can at least make their powerful voices heard.

I shall not say anything of all that the *Moniteur* and the newspapers reported of what was said or done in the national tribune — those are official acts, public documents; but I shall speak of what happened at debates, of the proposals brought forward by the authorities of that time, either among the members of the Convention or the members of the committee. It is the interior working of the committee which is not known. There are mysteries of extraordinary power that ought to be known, either to prepare for the future by the experience of the past, or to submit to the supreme judgment of human opinion both men and facts, either misunderstood or not known at all, or slandered by foreigners or distorted by party spirit. To relate sincerely the facts as they happened is to restore honesty to historians and truth to history. When I come to the events of the 9th of Thermidor, so like those of a battle-field, I shall only name the leaders of the reaction whose cause or pretext was this inevitable catastrophe. These revolters against the Revolution, putting on the garb of the Convention, were more allied to Coblentz or St. James' than to national liberty. The idea of a Third Committee of Public Safety arose among them, composed of the most pronounced reactionaries and the wildest deputies.

THIRD COMMITTEE OF PUBLIC SAFETY.

I shall not concern myself with this committee, which was nominated in the heat of the so-called Thermidorian reaction, in the month of October, 1794. It is enough to name Tallien, Fréron, André, Dumont, Boissy d'Anglas, etc., to see what fury and vengeance the renegades of liberty bring into their persecutions. "Get out of it so that I may get in" was the first maxim of these great statesmen, created on the 9th of Thermidor. But in order to ensure the success of this counter-revolution, the actors in which had been sent from the Cabinet of Coblentz and subsidised by that of St. James', the new committee only dealt at first with the means of getting rid of the members of the former one, either by abuse in the daily press under the direction of Tallien and Fréron, or by accusations, proceedings, proscriptions and revolutionary measures.

History, whose business it is to know all and tell all, will relate the political and financial villainies of the time. The world will be told how the last Committee of Public Safety made itself notorious by dissipating almost one hundred millions in specie that the former Committee of Public Safety and the Committee of

Finance had collected, thanks to the care of Cambon and Ramel, and had placed in the cellars and rooms of the Treasury to replace the assignats when they should be withdrawn from circulation. History will discover what deceitful treaties, contrary to the welfare of the nation, were made by this committee and the ambassadors of the Catholic army. These treaties received an unexpected check by the premature death of the son of Louis XVI., who had been imprisoned in the Temple. History will reveal by what division between the committee and Coblentz the armed sections of Paris became inimical to the Convention, in spite of the sacrifices granted by the anti-revolutionary slaughters at Tarascon, Avignon, Toulouse, Marseilles, Nimes, Lyons, Nantes, and especially Paris, in the subsidised, fomented riots of the 12th of Germinal and 1st of Prairial, 1795. This committee had to separate itself forcibly from its natural allies and hired accomplices, wishing to justify its doings after the 9th of Thermidor. It had to invoke the aid of a young general of artillery, who shot down the sections and population of Paris in the name of the reactionary Convention. This severity and these atrocities, that the committee had rendered necessary, took place on the 13th of Vendémiare.

These three committees being thus different in period, mission, aim and work, it is easier to estimate the value of each. At any rate, public opinion can judge them more justly than their contemporaries, who were ignorant of causes and their consequences, who were blinded by passion or party spirit.

    *   *   *   *   *   *   *

General Foy, in 1823, in one of his speeches, said: "The saving of the nation is not written in laws. In the

hour of danger men save their ,country as quickly and
in what manner they are able.   France made its noble,
enormous effort in 1793."

Frenchmen have needed thirty years to understand
this historic truth, although they were eye-witnesses of
it.   What abuse and libel the political writers and orators
have poured on this solemn period when France and
Liberty were saved !

*   *   *   *   *   *   *

I am undertaking the composition of Memoirs to assist
the labours of historians of this formidable committee,
which preserved the national independence and the liberty
and territory of France.   Whatever may be the excitement
of parties, the strength of prejudices, the injustice of men
and the ingratitude of reactions, it will be of no use for
historians to write in favour of this difference of opinion ;
they will not prevent the Committee of Public Safety from
occupying an important place in the annals of France, in
the history of Europe, and in the account of its social
regeneration.   Who would have had the means of suddenly
and energetically defending and saving the country at this
dangerous moment, when the fate of France still hung in
the balance and its existence as a nation was still so pro-
blematic, if there had not existed a political legislative
gathering, numerous and disinterested, devoted and huge
in its enterprises and courage, in the midst of a nation
but yet uninstructed as to its rights? The National Convention, with its Committee of Public Safety, was the only
body able to oppose the whole of Europe, and to resist
the armed alliance of all the oligarchies and monarchies
subsidised by the Tory English Government.   It was the
Committee of Public Safety that created fourteen armies,
organised them and gave them plans of campaign which,

when heroically carried out, foiled the plots of Pilnitz and baffled the bribery of St. James'. It was the Committee of Public Safety that started the factories of rifles, of gunpowder and saltpetre, of cannon and of all the necessaries for keeping and transporting a million of men. It was the committee that prepared and founded so many noble institutions, such as the École de Mars, the abolition of beggary, the organisation of public works, a vast scheme of canals, a normal school and a series of public monuments, to be re-established, preserved or started.

It preserved all the statues, columns, and other artistic remains that were to be found on the property of the emigrant nobles or of the religious orders ; it was on the side of all men of light and leading in opposing the mutilation of monuments and the destruction of bindings and books in the public libraries. It could not prevent the violent acts of popular meetings which, having no artistic feeling, only saw in these objects the symbols of slavery and despotism. The only thing that can be imputed to it was the displacement of the royal tombs at St. Denis. This was a decree of the Convention which was passed as a mark of hatred against royalty, in order to destroy the superstitious traditions still clinging to it ; but the committee itself founded a museum at the Petits Augustins, wherein to preserve these tombs as artistic monuments and pages of our monumental history.

The committee had had the idea of opening up communicating canals between all the large rivers that would have been rendered navigable by destroying all dams and other obstacles. It commanded the Minister of the Interior to get the plan examined by the Council of the Woods and Forests and by other civil and

military engineers.   All were in ,favour of this splendid
plan that would increase the means of internal communication a hundredfold.   A large map of this scheme
of canals was drawn up and handed over to the
Ministry of Public Works and Education, presided over
by M. Barère, who had been specially ordered to see
to the execution of the plan.   But at the time of the
Revolution of Thermidor some of the offices of the
committee were plundered ; the representatives who had
been sent on missions to the departments hastened to
bear off the portfolios containing their compromising
correspondence.   Documents were given over to a kind
of official plundering under the committee of 1795, and
the map disappeared.   The trace of the works ordered
for the great plan of canalisation alone remained.   The
new committee, seeking to obtain popularity by using
the plans and labours of its predecessor, wrote officially
to M. Barère, who was then confined in the Castle
of Oleron, to ask him for an account of this map
which had been deposited at his office.   He answered
that his office had been ransacked of its papers, books,
money and furniture on the 13th of Germinal, by the
order of the new Committee of General Safety ; that
everything was sealed up in his rooms at M. Savalette's,
one of the commissioners of the Public Exchequer.   This
reply caused them to break the seals in M. Barère's
rooms, and the Committee of General Safety took
possession of everything, by the old law of disinheritance
no doubt, or by the new one of "Might is right."   But
the map of the canals was not found, because it was
still at the office of the committee that had had it
drawn up.   However, it was probably not lost, for a
member of the Convention, M. Maragon of the Aude,

who had been for some time employed on the Languedoc
Canal, made a great report to the Conseil des Anciens in
1797, on the necessity and means of opening up water
communication over the whole of France. M. Barère
recognised in this the analysis of the works prepared
under the direction of the Woods and Forests, during
the time of the Committee of Public Safety.

15th of May, 1793. — The excesses of the demagogue Marat, the secret ambition of the municipality
of Paris, which took all the credit to itself of the victory
of the 10th of August, the underhand intrigues of the
leaders of this municipality, and the plans of Federalism
carried out in the southern departments, preceded the
arrival of an envoy from the English Government in
Paris. He introduced himself to the Foreign Minister,
and showed him his letters of credit, and his authority
for making proposals for a general peace. The minister
having informed the Committee of Public Safety of his
arrival, it nominated five of its members to listen to the
proposals of this envoy, although such a mission excited
much distrust at a period when France was in such straits,
both in the interior, at Paris, and on the frontiers.
The five commissioners were Treilhard, Cambon, Lindet,
Barère and Guyton-Morveau. On the next day, the 16th
of May, Mr. William Pitt's envoy came to the committee-
room, where he found the five members of the committee
and the Minister of Foreign Affairs. He affected an air
of great satisfaction and even presumption ; his language
was cautious, and at first he only expressed himself in
general terms on the necessity of peace for all the
European Powers, and for France most of all, against
whom they were all arrayed.

But Cambon, getting impatient, asked him to explain

the proposals of his Government clearly. The English envoy then declared that France should revoke certain ultra-radical reforms that the first National Assembly had voted, and should place herself again under her fundamental laws. This emphatic, assertive tone displeased them so much that Treilhard told him to state clearly the proposals of the British Government. Treilhard's tone was so decided that the envoy drew a diplomatic note from his portfolio, the reading of which shocked them even more than his preamble. The proposals he read were as follow :

1. That the old States-General were to be recognised, and that they should vote by houses.

2. That the clergy and nobility should possess their former privileges, and the Third Estate its former rank and name.

3. That the Parliaments were to be re-established.

"All that you propose is impossible; the only shred of these old institutions that exists," cried Lindet, "is the hatred the nation bears them." "The Parliaments are abolished ; they will never return," added Guyton-Morveau.

The British envoy went on reading :

4. That the form of a republican government, as yet neither constituted nor organised, should be done away with.

At this all the members of the committee insisted that the conference should cease, the English proposals being an insult to the National Convention and to the French people.

"You do not reckon on having to deal with the Republic," says Barère, "since Mr. Pitt asks for the form of government to be changed. This insolent contradiction in your proposals proves that you and your master are dissimulating. Explain your meaning."

Then the English envoy declares that it is thoroughly understood that, as the basis of peace, France should be in harmony with the form of the majority of European governments, who have formed the coalition to obtain this prime result—the unity of the monarchical principle.

Cambon immediately seizes the diplomatic note with impetuous indignation, and tells the English envoy that the commissioners will make their report to the Committee of Public Safety, and that the Foreign Minister will acquaint him with their decision. Thus finished the insolent message of Pitt's emissary.

On the next day the result of the conference and the diplomatic note were submitted to the meeting of all the members of the Committee of Public Safety. General indignation prevailed; the English envoy was regarded either as the visible sign of some plot being hatched in the provinces, or simply as a spy sent under the pretence of diplomacy to sound public opinion in Paris and the National Convention.

The Committee of Public Safety, having conferred together with the Foreign Minister, bade him expressly convey to this envoy of Mr. Pitt the intimation that he must leave France within two days. But, as at the end of this time he was still in Paris, the minister was summoned and made personally responsible that he should leave immediately; and so France rid herself of him. He had to be conducted to Calais and put on board. This diplomatic spy had only been sent to get a closer view of the state of France, the character and political significance of the National Convention, and its Committee of Public Safety.

The Question of the Secret Service Money.—The secret service money appeared to Danton a means to be employed against the Committee of Public Safety, whose severe honesty was incontestable.

Either Danton reckoned, in his customary way, on filching funds for his bribery and revolutionary ambition through the Ministry of Foreign Affairs, to which he had managed to get one of his sworn friends (M. Des-forgues) appointed, or he reckoned one day to accuse the Committee of Public Safety of extravagance, and of employing, etc., on the score of this secret service money, the funds entrusted to it in an improper manner. Danton seized the moment when no member of the committee was present in the Convention to bring forward, in his stentorian voice, an urgent motion to grant it fifty millions of secret service money, either to obtain reliable information abroad or to influence the provinces, and especially to lessen the number of the leaders and agitators in La Vendée.   Danton explained, in order to smother opposition, if any should appear, how very necessary this secret expenditure, uncontrolled, uncensured, was to the policy of the Government.

The motion was carried unanimously, so great was the confidence of the National Convention in the progress of the Committee of Public Safety, which had deserved its confidence by success and unremitting toil, although these had been won and performed without any secret funds or extraordinary occult expenditure.   An usher from the Convention brought the decree as to this secret service grant to the committee at three o'clock in the afternoon, while it was debating on the foreign and civil wars.   All the members were astonished at receiving such a message; they indignantly protested against the proposer of such an important and delicate a motion as the secret expendi-ture of national money.   Carnot made it clear that there must be some other motive in this demand for secret funds, so huge and useless, and so little in accordance with the progress and policy of the government of the National Convention. Other members observed that, on such a motion, the committee that had asked for nothing ought at least to have been heard on the need or advisability of this strange, huge vote. But, in order not to recriminate the very susceptible mover of the proposal, nor to give any opportunity of a collision in the Assembly, the committee unanimously resolved that the decree granting the fifty millions of secret service money should be placed in the pigeon-holes for official documents in the Council Hall, and should be disregarded; that not a copper of these fifty millions should be taken or used; and that after the country had been delivered from foes abroad and in La Vendée, that the decree and the money should be publicly returned intact to the National Convention by the reporter of the committee, with the declaration that they had to fight enemies, not to corrupt men.

This was done in 1794, after the great victories of the time. Barère, the reporter of the commitee, was charged with the carrying out of this restitution of the decree, and the grant of the untouched secret service money at a full meeting of the House. His speech was enthusiastically received. *Then honesty was in fashion.*

* * * * * * *

The Convention proclaimed a democratic constitution, approved by the first Assemblies. But being flung as it was in the midst of such a frightful storm, being compelled to quench civil war in the west and south with one hand, while with the other it was sustaining the brunt of a combined attack from all the armies of Europe, the

Convention was not hypocritical enough, like other governments, to talk of constitutions and laws at the very moment it was breaking them. It felt the need of having exceptional powers during war at home and abroad; it solemnly proclaimed that constitutional laws should be suspended until universal peace had been obtained by victory. It said boldly, as the consuls used to say to the Romans, " Let the safety of the people be the first law." France was warned of the political and military situation, and knew a revolutionary war was rendered necessary by circumstances.

The Convention did not usurp all its powers; it received them by the votes of the nation. It was not simply a meeting of legislators ; what good would ordinary laws have been against the invasion of the whole of Europe ? The accumulation of power was as terrible as the circumstances that produced it ; it was the despotism of liberty, a despotism that has its fury, fanaticism, excesses, mistakes and victims, like any other. But, at any rate, this despotism was not an hereditary scourge like monarchy. It was fated to strike terror into the enemies of France. The Convention, at its first meeting, unanimously proclaimed the republican form of government, and inspired kings, oligarchies and emigrant nobles with a kind of torpor that enabled it to prepare the means of defence, which had been very inadequate up till then.

The excesses of the Revolution were the work of its opponents, who placed it in the position of either conquering or being annihilated. The faults of the oppressed are really those of the oppressors, and a man is guilty of those excesses that he purposely provokes.

Originally the Convention only wished to establish

democratic liberty by means of representative institutions, to found equality by laws and customs, to uproot all ancient aristocracy, and to resist the ambitions of new aristocracy. Abroad the Convention never wished to conquer or invade other territories, except to defend itself. Foreign princes and their accomplices in France compelled the Convention to struggle against their combined attacks as a band of hunters track lions to their dens; they must attack to defend themselves, conquer in self-preservation, and inspire fear to render their existence secure.

No doubt moderation, justice and law are the true safeguards of society. But before this law and order can exist, the territory of a nation must be undivided, its frontiers unattacked and its nationality uncontested.

"The indivisibility of our territory for us is the first of all questions," cried the *Gazette de France*, in declaring that on the day that the national territory was violated it would call all its friends to arms, being sure that the dismemberment of the country would then be a possibility. And what did the Convention do but to place the safety of France and its integrity first and foremost, by means of the fourteen armies of the Republic? In 1793 the dismemberment of France was a much more likely event. Are not the conditions of the division contained in the congress of Pilnitz and the treaty of Pavia?

I had before my very eyes in March, 1794, the original of the partition treaty drawn up at Pilnitz, and signed by several of the allied monarchs, as well as a coloured map of France so divided. The nineteenth century will judge if the fears of the eighteenth century were justified.

A time will come when the public and private virtues
of nearly all the members of the Convention, their un-
assailable uprightness, and their beautiful devotion to
their country will be appreciated at their true worth.
Generations follow one another, and very fortunately do
not resemble one another ; thus does nature correct her
mistakes and nullify her calamities. France will one day
pay its great debt to the Convention for having devoted
itself body and soul to freeing the nation. In the nineteenth century the Convention will be thanked by public
opinion for having founded that unity of the French
nation which will never allow a despotism to efface it,
as heroic Poland was effaced by Russian autocracy.
The children of France will be grateful to those who
saved them from the yoke of the oppressor. At the
resounding voice of the Convention, a million citizen
soldiers rose up to drive the invading hordes back
across our frontiers ; France will then recognise the
right of such an Assembly to the prefix *National.*

The members of this body did much but said little ;
they were under arms and could not at the same time
conquer Europe and write books justifying their heroism.
The enemies of the Revolution have taken advantage
of this silence to overwhelm them with ingratitude, abuse ·
and proscription ; and the people who never judge for
themselves have submitted to the influence of these anti-
revolutionary writers. When the courage and devotion
of the Convention were no longer required, when all
the profit had been gleaned from their gigantic labours
and rich political inheritance, they were given over to
vindictive judgment. Under the Empire and Restoration
their enemies alone had the right to write the history
and portraits of the members ; biographies were paid for

by those in power with the sole aim of running down the Assembly that had established democratic liberty.

Some writers, during the period of reaction from 1795 to 1832, have accused the Convention of having imitated and travestied the republics of Greece and Rome, as if the Convention did not know that nothing in the world was less Spartan than the Parisians, less Roman than the French. These hired scribblers would have been correct if they had said that the Convention did not wish to imitate the aristocratic institutions of England, or the federal constitution of the twenty-five united states of America. Its members were lovers of unity, because it led to a compact nation and an entirely national army, and one capable of repulsing the invader. They were opposed to federation, because they did not wish to weaken the nation, attacked as it was on every frontier and in half the departments. They acted according to the needs of the times to preserve the integrity and independence of the nation. That was the only question in 1793 and 1794. It was the question of existence which depended on the chance of battles. There was hence no question of copying the ancient republics, who had virtues we have not: imitations are the work of presuming mediocrity. The disguise of English institutions, that the orators and law-makers talk of, are a fraud and deception. The Convention only imitated the disinterestedness and courage of the republics of old, which among the French are the virtues of dupes.

*   *   *   *   *   *   *

Although disinterestedness and honesty have become, in this over-civilised nineteenth century, useless virtues, at which the moneyed and influential jeer, one must yet name, for the sole benefit of posterity, one point of

stoic moral courage displayed by two members of the
Committee of Public Safety, two enlightened soldiers,
whose influence on the destinies of the freedom of France
was great.   These two citizens were Carnot and Prieur,
both natives of the same town of Dijon,[1] both engineer
officers of the same rank.   These men held the greatest
administrative and executive power that kings and ministers have ever had; they appointed and promoted nearly
every soldier who distinguished himself in battle for
forty years.   There was not one of these soldiers, who
afterwards became generals, marshals, dukes, and even
kings, but whose first commission was signed " Carnot,"
"C. A. Prieur."   Well, these ministers who were so powerful, and who created so many military reputations, each
kept to his modest rank.   All the time that they were
in power they never even used the right that their
seniority gave them.   These two men may well be called
antique heroes.

*   *   *   *   *   *   *

"Some great events never repeat themselves, at
any rate in the same manner," said Barère one day while
chatting with M. David, who quotes his own words to
me : " I should like to see a picture representing the
little room where the Committee of Public Safety used
to meet.   There nine members worked day and night,
without a president, round a table with a green tablecloth,
while the walls were of the same colour.   Often, after a
few minutes' sleep snatched from work, I would find a
heap of papers in my place; they were the reports of
our armies.   After reading them I drew up a report

---

[1] Barère is here in error.   Both were Burgundians ; but Prieur
was born at Auxonne and Carnot at Nolay.

that I used to read immediately from the tribune in the Convention. Our soldiers, with their woollen epaulets, fought the enemies of France, and when one of them did anything brilliant, they gave him a piece of paper on which was written the resolution of the Assembly that he had deserved well of his country.

"The Committee of Public Safety was the sublimest creation of the Revolution. This band of specialists was the only way to make France victorious, and it would have succeeded in fixing the Republic on a firm basis and in freeing Europe, if Robespierre had not interfered, with his insatiable ambition and his offended vanity, to thwart our work. I said just now that great events do not repeat themselves. So France will never have to fight the whole of Europe again, and the Reign of Terror will no more return than will exclusive despotism. Visconti once said to me : ' What the men of your age have done beats the deeds of the ancients. Demosthenes in his speeches struggled to make his fellow-countrymen repulse the seductive offers of Philip ; Cicero fought against Catiline ; but you fought civil war and a whole Europe in arms.' No doubt when all the material we left has been put in order, we shall appear giants."

The Committee of Public Safety went to work with a will. It was re-elected month by month by the Convention, and justified this extension of power by its success, when, as Barère says, in the interview we have just quoted, Robespierre came and thwarted their work. In combination with his two friends, Couthon and Saint-Just, he tried to be the centre of the executive power. The office for supervising the government officials, that Saint-Just had started in a modest way, was transformed

into a central police office by successive encroachments.
The members of the triumvirate controlled it in turn,
and their colleagues were hardly aware of their proceedings.

"He had such a good opinion of his personal
influence," says Barère, in his manuscript notes, speaking
of Robespierre, "that he laid claim to power he did not
possess, that of sending agents into certain departments.
He sent some to the Gironde and the Haute-Garonne
to keep an eye on the members on missions, and he
even arrested those that these agents considered suspicious, and denounced to the revolutionary committees.
M. Jullien was sent in this way to Bordeaux, where he
kept watch on the doings of Tallien and Isabeau, with
advantage to the public weal. Madame Taschereau, too,
was sent to Toulouse, where she caused a great number
to be put in prison, until the representative Paganel
forced this woman to say by whose authority she did
these things. She said she was on a special mission, and
showed Robespierre's full authority. Then she commanded Paganel to act in concert with her. But the
representative only replied to this strange order by
bidding the local authorities to lead this woman forcibly
out of the department. And then he set to work to
free a number of persons unjustly imprisoned."

The triumvirate endeavoured to get possession of the
whole power of the committee by encroaching on the
special duties of those members that it could not gain
over to its side. They wished to deprive Barère of the
direction of the military reports and give them to the in-
competent Couthon, but he gave way beneath the burden.
Saint-Just tried to oust Carnot from the War Office, but
was equally unsuccessful. As for Robespierre, he pre-

tended to look after things in general, perhaps to conceal his lack of business talent; and he was generally considered to have the same influence in the committee as he had in the Convention, thanks to the clubs; whilst in reality round that table, where men were measured by their worth, his domineering spirit met with stout resistance. He profited by his colleagues' cares of office, to which they were entirely devoted, to force his tactics in the party warfare of the time on them.

No doubt Robespierre was inspired with the wish to become dictator by no vulgar ambition, no mere lust of power. He thought that, as dictator, he could destroy the obstacles which stood in the way of the permanent establishment of the Republic. His pride also urged him to it, because he thought himself more capable than any other to carry out such an undertaking.

This last opinion of his has been favoured more of late than among his contemporaries. The Apologia of this man has been carried to the point of excommunicating all who opposed him.

Likewise the belief in the necessity of a dictator has increased among writers who judge the events at a distance. It was not so in Robespierre's time. Why a dictator? asked the republicans. To protect us against our foes? But our armies are victorious. Against the ambition of our generals? But there is not one who resists the orders of the all-powerful committee. But the factions at home! that was the chief cry. The partisans of a dictatorship concerned themselves more with the interior than with the exterior, to use a newly-coined phrase. But their opponents answered again: The army is devoted to the Republic—nothing to fear on that score. The royalists are crushed; perhaps even they have felt the strong arm too heavily. As for the few unworthy ones who disgrace the best cause, public opinion will always support their punishment. Let those proconsuls who set a bad example be recalled, the immense influence of the Committee of Public Safety will enable you to do it, as it has done before ; let these men be cast from public life. But if you wish to have another 31st of May, a 16th of Germinal, to start the national representation all over again, you will open a gulf in which all the defenders of liberty will be swallowed up one after the other, you will violate a principle which, if preserved, would shield the Republic.

However, Robespierre, who had crushed the Girondins, who had crushed Danton, wished to crush all his rivals. He seemed to know of no other means of establishing his power than the extermination of all powerful men. Napoleon, greatly his superior, could do without such expedients. But the ambitious know each other instinctively, and Napoleon did not hate Robespierre as his memory generally is hated. Let us listen to what Barère says :

"Napoleon, whom Madame de Staël, with the vain hatred of an intriguing foreigner, called a *Robespierre on horseback*, was in fact rather inclined to praise *Robespierre on foot*, because he thought he had views similar to his own, views of stopping the Revolution and creating a dictatorship in its place. Napoleon, who from time to time, in the midst of his glory and power, thought of Robespierre and his sad end, one day asked his Lord Chancellor as to the sad events of the 9th of Thermidor. 'It was a case judged before it was heard,' replied Cambacérès, with the acuteness of a legal courtier."

Barère, in his Memoirs, thinks he supplies this case

with an important piece of evidence when he quotes the letter, unknown till then, that Benjamin Vaughan wrote to Robespierre, a letter that the Committee of Public Safety seized on the 9th of Thermidor. This English-man, whom the committee thought dangerous enough to expel from France, told Robespierre personally of a plan of foreign policy which would have involved the re-duction of France to her former boundaries under the Bourbons, and which would have helped the conquered provinces to form a federal state. Barère supposes that Mr. Vaughan, a member of the House of Commons, was an emissary chosen from the ranks of the opposition to lull all suspicion, and that Robespierre had lent an ear to his proposals in the hope of supporting his plans of usurpation by external influence. Secret relations between a member of the French government and a foreigner suspected by that government were sufficient to constitute a grave accusation ; but does not the letter in question, up till now taken by itself, simply come from a man who throws his ideas broadcast? If this version is the true one, it is not surprising that the plan-maker, in preference, should write to Robespierre, whom rumour accredited with the chief authority. The newspapers, and even the foreign ambassadors, talked of the French armies as " Robespierre's soldiers," and the London pamphlets called him "Maximilian I., King of France and Navarre," either because they really considered him dictator, or to excite general distrust against him, or, in short, from hateful derision of France.

The document quoted by Barère does not, therefore, throw new light on the means that Robespierre reckoned on using to establish his dictatorship firmly. The fact that he wished to create this dictatorship for his own profit alone remains submitted to the judgment of history until fresh proofs supervene.

Let us now cast a rapid glance on the events, and especially on Barère's conduct.

The two camps were in view of one another. Robespierre having left the committee, not liking to measure himself with the enemy at close quarters, had taken refuge in the clubs, whence he launched his incendiary bombs. He did not dare to make a decisive attack, either from irresolution or, as he said sometimes, because he shrank from striking men necessary to the government, who were situated between himself and his personal enemies, so he had to fight two kinds of opponents.

The former represented the remains of all the conquered parties, stirred by revenge; behind them, monarchy and foreign rule were hidden with their aggressive agents. These were always weaving continual plots.

The others, animated by a spirit of moderation, but rejecting a dictatorship, had behind them all those who, wearied by an intolerable tension of revolution, asked to be allowed at last to enjoy the liberty they had bought so dearly. They hesitated between the desire of satisfying legitimate needs and the fear of producing one of those schisms, which destroy power and open the way to reaction. If they consented to shield some men, it was certainly not because they approved of their conduct; but the violation of the national representation appeared to them the greatest danger of all for the Republic. Robespierre himself, except for his threatening innovations, would have found protection in their eyes out of respect for this principle. In fine, nothing was more uncertain than the success of a premature attack, which, if it failed in the Convention, would have been turned to profit by their adversary, and have assured the triumph of his ambitious plans.

We reckon Barère among the men of whom we have been talking, for he was a sincere republican and had no vengeance to carry out; besides, the natural gentleness of his character would have prevented him doing so. Did he act the trimmer between the two sides, as has been declared? It has even been bruited that he had prepared two entirely opposite speeches at the moment of the crisis, in order to be ready for either result. We can only accept this tradition as a symbol of the part Barère is supposed to have played; as to the fact, it appears false in material points. The most probable version is the one Legendre gave during the sitting of the 9th of Prairial : " I remarked that Barère changed his speech according to the manner it was received by the Assembly."

Barère was always opposed to the idea of a dictatorship; he had resisted Saint-Just's motion on behalf of Robespierre, which was brought forward in the committee and defeated on the order of the day. He did not hesitate then between two opinions, but he hesitated, like others, to begin the struggle for motives we have just explained. " National Assemblies immortalise themselves when they write out the first declaration of rights, but they are ruined when they first bring an action against one of the representatives," Barère has said. Besides, he hesitated no more than others did, because his natural timidity urged him to be on good terms with everyone ; and if later he was aggressive, perhaps it was the fear of danger that drove him to it ; he was like a stag turning on the huntsmen.

Since the time that Robespierre and his friends had

been at variance with the Committee of Public Safety, the members of this committee had to think each day as the eve of another 31st of May, of which they would probably be the victims. But they did not stop work for a minute, and thus kept on till the hour of the catastrophe. It was only when the vague and astute speech of the 8th of Thermidor warned them that the arm was uplifted to strike them, that they charged Barère to draw up on that very night the proclamations and decrees to repulse the attack.

On the next day they were still at work, fully occupied with the urgent measures needed by the war, when they were warned that Saint-Just was reading their accusation from the tribune. They at once went to the Assembly Hall, where approving murmurs greeted their arrival. All the same, the Assembly was in a violent state of agitation and uncertainty, by which Robespierre wished to profit by mounting the tribune before the spokesman of the committee; many cried out for Barère, who was going to mount too. Robespierre insisted on speaking; the Mountain received him coldly, so he turned to the moderates of the Centre with flattering words and gestures. They were unmoved, and a voice cried, " Down with the tyrant ! "

It is then Barère's turn. He has little to say about the crisis, and he leaves the refutation of Robespierre's speech of the day before till later; but he protests against the military rule that prevails in the capital through the presence of a single commander of the forces, and he proposes the substitution of the old democratic organisation of the National Guard in place of this command.

Robespierre, who has only just left the tribune, and feels that the mainspring of his plans is broken in his hands by this clever decree of reducing Henriot, tries anew to make himself heard. Cries of "Down with the tyrant! Down with the dictator!" cut him short. The Centre sees that the Mountain has thoroughly made up its mind, and follows its example. Robespierre and his friends are overwhelmed, accused and arrested, and the Assembly, instead of at once following up its victory, adjourns, astonished at its own courage.

After the second struggle and second triumph in the evening, Barère was again charged with relating from the tribune the events that had happened in the Town Hall, and to draw up the proclamation addressed to the French nation by the Convention.

Robespierre fell a victim to a crisis that he had himself provoked. If, as some of his supporters assert, his only ambition was to consolidate the Republic, he could have put aside all personal views and frankly joined that section of the committee of whose disinterestedness and patriotism there was not the slightest doubt. Thus they would have been in a majority, and perhaps this majority, being possessed of a firm, recognised power, would have succeeded in relieving the overstrained situation, little by little, without losing its hold over it. But the illusion that France had of a little breathing time after Robespierre's fall, lasted a very short while. Reactionary passions, the results of hate and revenge, followed the revolutionary passions that had been generous and pure in their source.

We are assured that some of Robespierre's conquerors regretted afterwards that they had not seconded his efforts to purify the Revolution and to replace the committee by a Dictator of Public Safety. Billaud-Varennes is accused of such a change of opinion, although he

seemed the most unlikely of all the actors of the 9th of
Thermidor to do so. As for Barère, his appreciation of
the man seemed to grow more and more favourable with
time.

In 1795 or 1796, in a huge manuscript book, full of
reviews and reflections, in alphabetical order, which he
called, for no perceivable reason, *Vocabulaire littéral,* he
wrote :

"What a tyrant! without genius, without courage, without military talent, without political experience, without
true eloquence, without esteem for his colleagues, without
confidence in any enlightened citizen, without kindness
for the unfortunate or regard for the power of the
nation."

His Memoirs tell us what he thought of him twenty
years later.

Here is the picture he draws :

"Robespierre had a face wondrous pale and pock-
fretten ; the same mind that hollowed his cheeks with a
sardonic, and occasionally savage, smile agitated his lips
convulsively and lit up his eyes with hidden fire and a
sombre, piercing look. His speeches were always prepared ; his proposals appeared studied and sometimes
enigmatic, obscure, and tiresome, full of political threats
and distrust. His soul was of a strong, chilly nature ; his
temper was tenacious and obstinate ; his voice was deep
and occasionally terrifying ; his dress was very neat, in
spite of the habits and customs of the time, but his ges-
ticulations were rough and somewhat wild ; his distrust
of all the celebrated patriots, as well as of those who
were only hypocrites, he expressed undisguisedly in his
conversation and speeches ; his peculiar characteristic was
the pride he had in his popularity. Among true, en-

lightened and humane patriots Robespierre would have rendered great services to the cause of liberty; but he found around him none but men with exaggerated revolutionary ideas, who, having been educated among the lower classes of society, gave him neither wise views nor good advice. His fear and their flattery created for him a kind of guard composed of none but extreme revolutionary myrmidons."

In the notes composed for his own biography after 1830, Barère writes thus :

"Robespierre was always a republican, even in the days of the National Assembly which created the constitutional monarchy. During the Convention he continually upheld the cause of liberty and the rights of the nation. But his great popularity was mingled with a suspicious, wild and exclusive appearance. He was unmoved by riches, but, as every man is ambitious, he could act more freely after the death of Danton. After the month of March, 1794, Robespierre's conduct appeared to me to change. Saint-Just was to a great degree the cause of this, and this leader was too youthful ; he urged him into the vain and dangerous path of dictatorship which he haughtily proclaimed. From that time all confidences in the two committees were at an end, and the misfortunes that followed the division in the government became inevitable."

In 1832, during Barère's stay in Paris on his return from his exile, M. David went to see him and found him ailing. Violent asthma compelled him to keep his bed, which he called "living horizontally." They talked of Robespierre : "He was a disinterested man and a republican at heart," said Barère; "it was unfortunate that he wanted to be a dictator. He thought it was the only way of repressing the overflow of evil passions. He often spoke of it to us who had to do with the armies. We did not hide from him that Saint-Just, who was formed of more dictatorial stuff, would have ended by overturning him and occupying his place; we knew too that he would have us guillotined because of our opposition to his plans; so we overthrew him. I have reflected about this man since, and I see that his dominant idea was the establishment of a republican government, and that in fact he pursued men whose opposition impeded the progress of this government. It was lucky that there was at that time in the Chamber of Deputies one who denounced those who were conspiring against liberty. We were then on the battlefield; we never understood this man. He was of a nervous, bilious temperament; he had a contraction in his mouth; he had the temperament of great men, and posterity will call him great."

At the question, "How is the pension that Robespierre's sister received from Louis XVIII. to be explained?" he made an angry movement and exclaimed disdainfully: "Louis XVIII. was the greatest knave that ever lived. He was not able to tarnish this man's reputation in his lifetime, so he tried to do so after his death. This is the explanation of the pension which has caused so much talk."

M. David having spoken of his plan of making statues of the most famous statesmen of the Revolution, and having mentioned Danton's name, Barère sat up quickly and cried imperiously: "Do not forget Robespierre! He was a genuine, honest man, a true republican. His vanity, his irascible susceptibility and his unreasoning distrust of his colleagues caused his downfall. It was a great misfortune!" Then his head dropped on his chest again, and he remained for a long time wrapped up in his thoughts.

History will not fail to collect these important statements. But, also, in the interests of history, I ought to say that another contemporary, Carnot, never modified his severe judgment of Robespierre. He considered him a very average man, and his ambition for supreme power seemed to be based on little and to be dangerous for the country. This opinion he did not fear to sum up one day, in the very presence of the triumvirs themselves, in these words: "You are ridiculous dictators!"

Whatever may be the final judgment of history on the events we have just mentioned, everyone must regret their consequences. "Then," said Barère, "began that reaction which is not yet exhausted by the Consulate, the Empire, the two Restorations and the useless consequences of the Revolution of July; a reaction that has had its excesses, its Reign of Terror, and its bloody human sacrifices, as the Revolution that preceded it, but without making France free as its forerunner did. This reaction, which is still continuing in 1833, can only end with time and by the unforeseen events it brings."

To this reactionary spirit we must also attribute the extreme embarrassment which every honest man feels when he studies the French Revolution. The earliest histories were written with pens steeped in the bloody mire of this disastrous time, and one could never count how many lies have been told of the men and events. Unhappily these earliest histories nearly always form the basis of succeeding ones; rarely does a writer overcome his natural laziness that prevents him referring to original sources; and even if he did, where are these originals to be found? How many have been destroyed by men who feared them, and who were masters of the situation for so long? They are satisfied with first judgments, only recollecting their proximity to the events, without thinking of the passions that have distorted or blinded them. Would a serious, patient, just mind be successful in cleansing this dunghill, in seizing the thread of truth in this fœtid, deceptive labyrinth?

After the 9th of Thermidor Barère frankly entered upon less violent ways, which were more suited to his personal feelings. But this did not prevent him being attacked by the reactionaries.

The deputies who dared to stand on their principles and sit on the Left needed great courage, for the Assembly was soon led by men who, after having been the foremost agents of the Reign of Terror, strained every nerve to get up a reactionary terror, as if that was their natural element.

The first denunciatory attempt against several members of the committees was unsuccessful. It was started by Lecointre of Versailles, instigated by the reactionaries. It was declared libellous, and the Convention asserted that the committees deserved the thanks of the country.

" But," said Barère, "in France one has only to persevere in even the greatest injustice to be successful at last. Fréron and Tallien, who were corrupting public opinion in their papers every morning, kept stirring up Lecointre, and made him present his printed attack anew. This time the advice of Sieyès, who was secretly leading the reaction, succeeded in getting the attack referred to a committee of twenty-one members, who were chosen from the anti-revolutionists, among the personal enemies of the accused. All the same, Barère was acquitted by nineteen out of twenty-one votes. Sieyès again succeeded in getting this decree annulled, so that a ballot might be taken as to the accused as a whole; and Barère was included in a collective accusation.

The acquittal that Barère personally had obtained was not founded, doubtless, on the assumption that he was ignorant of the crimes with which Billaud-Varennes and Collot-d'Herbois were accused; but because the latter had not known how to make friends for themselves by their character. So they endeavoured to try the cases separately, and they sounded Barère on the subject of giving evidence against his colleagues, promising him an acquittal in return, but this offer he indignantly refused.

If Barère had not been the victim of ingratitude on the part of those whom he had served when in power, if the writers of those grateful letters which we found among his papers had dared to raise their voices, their powerful evidence would have prevented his condemnation. One of the seventy-three signatories of the protest against the 31st of May, Philippe Delleville, a good man, who understood that the victims of the Terror ought not to begin terrorising its authors, and who proposed the abolition of the guillotine on his re-election to the Convention, generously came forward and declared that Barère had saved his life. He had done the same for one of his colleagues on the 9th of Thermidor: "Do not come to the House to-day," he had said to David the painter, fearing lest he should keep his promise of sticking to Robespierre to the last, "you are no politician and will compromise yourself."

David used to like to tell this anecdote at Brussels. Contrary political opinions to his own were by no means a bar to his interest, and among the letters we were just speaking of, some contain political opinions whose frankness is as creditable to the recipient as to the senders.

The following fragment of a letter sent by Barère to his brother will show what his feelings were in the midst of such perilous circumstances :

> Paris, 2nd of Ventôse,
> .Year III. of the Republic.

MY DEAR BROTHER,

I write to you from the committee-room of the Twenty-one, who must decide our fate. I profit by D.'s journey near Vic to send you a dozen copies of my defence ; distribute them among my friends and relations. They will see that I have never swerved from that justice, humanity and honesty of which they have set me an example.

I am astonished at not having received any letters from you. You are easily frightened, and think much of solitude and life. As for me, my only fear is the violation of a principle or a lack of social virtues.

Some days after the arrest of Billaud, Collot and Barère, some officious people came and offered them passports and money to leave France. "The last," says an eye-witness, "was in such a rage that we should never have thought him capable of it, crying out that such a proposal was infamous, that life was not worth such cowardice. We shall go to the national tribunal to justify ourselves, to defend Liberty or perish with it."

The accused were protected by the great services they had recently rendered to the country, services that clamorous hatred could not so quickly efface; they were protected by the thought that a new mutilation of the national representation would only justify the former ones, and by the fear that a condemnation of the acts of the Government during the revolutionary disturbances would only encourage to a dangerous degree the enemies of that Revolution. The debates in the Convention appeared to be taking a favourable turn for them. Barère's defence, especially, met with continued applause from the Assembly. But their enemies suspended the sittings for four days, after which a riot, too opportune for its origin not to be gravely suspected, furnished a pretext to hurry on the judgment. Sentence was pronounced there and then on the 12th of Germinal, in the absence of the accused. Many other members of the Convention, of whom the reactionaries wished to rid themselves, were arrested at the same time, among them Lecointre, an honest man, who had gone over to the Mountain at the sight of the reaction.

Barère was still occupied in composing his defence when he was informed he had been sentenced to transportation. It was past ten o'clock at night. The next morning, at eight, a carriage came for him; other carriages contained Billaud-Varennes and Collot-d'Herbois.

But a threatening crowd obstructed the streets and uttered murderous cries against them. It was not, undoubtedly, the same crowd that the night before had imperiously shouted for their release. Did their enemies wish the rioters to kill them, as Barère thought? This prompt change of scene, and the enormous preparations employed for the departure of three persons seem to give some weight to his opinion, and what confirms it still more are the events that took place when Barère and Billaud had been brought back and placed provisionally in one of the rooms of the Committee of General Surety, their companion in misfortune having been able to pass the barrier. Tallien proposed in the Convention to change their sentence of transportation to one of death, to be carried out on the spot, but it was rejected with horror.

At midnight only could they be led through Paris

on foot under the escort of a formidable detachment of soldiers, from the Tuileries to the Montrouge barrier, when they again got into carriages. They were received at several points on the road by mobs, which they considered their enemies had assembled; this was notably the case at Orleans, where their lives were seriously threatened.

The castle on the Isle of Oleron, the former residence of Eleanor of Guienne, had been transformed into a state prison. There they were incarcerated and treated with shameful severity, being put on siege rations, without being able to better their lot, for the suddenness of their arrest had left them almost without money or change of clothing.

The events of Prairial formed a new pretence of persecuting them. Barère, in speaking of these events, declares them to be "a riot paid for by foreigners and emigrant nobles." Generally he pays very great importance to the plans of the enemies of the Revolution, in order that they should be hated for their excesses. Sometimes it is Marat, sometimes Hébert and Chaumette, sometimes Barras, Tallien and Fréron, whom he accuses as being instigators of royalism. According to him, English gold played the chief part in our crises. We can entirely overlook its influence, but when we see historians and artists attributing the majority of the acts of the Revolution to venal passions, we are tempted in our turn to believe in a conspiracy got up to degrade our national reputation. For Barère's part such an exaggeration is due to resentment of the cruellest injustice.

Billaud-Varennes and Collot-d'Herbois were ordered to be shipped to Cayenne. Barère, for motives we do not know, and which he himself seems to be unaware of, was not included in this order. He was transferred on foot by constables to Saintes Prison, where the criminal court was told to try him. Such a decision proved that he had not yet been tried—how then can the transportation of his colleagues be justified?

Those who ape the gilded youth of Paris in the provinces took pleasure in torturing their captive by giving him papers to read in which he and men of his way of thinking were outrageously insulted, and in paying people to sing in front of his door at night the threatening *Réveil du peuple*. The humanity of a warder and of the municipal authorities made his condition more bearable ; he was fortunate enough to see his brother.

From this place, without being able to get a look at his accusation, he addressed a summary of his defence to his constituents, which has remained in manuscript, and which has furnished us with more than one page of this biography. Here also, as we have said, a battalion of his countrymen, on their way to join the army in La Vendée, obtained permission to visit him in prison and present him with the national flag that Barère had confided to them in 1792 with his own hands ; a flag that was now riddled by bullets.

Barère devoted his enforced leisure in prison to his literary labours. He began to edit his Memoirs, and a few traces of this first attempt still remain ; and he made long extracts from the books he read, particularly from the correspondence of Jean Jacques Rousseau.[1]

---

[1] Extracts were a great part of his method of work. This reminds me of a curious page I found among his papers. It was written on the

He also composed some very bad poetry, which proves his calmness of mind at any rate. In the citadel of Oleron, worn by the ocean waves, remembrances of his native country occupied all his thoughts, and made him homesick, so he wrote a kind of novel to quiet his mind; the events are supposed to take place in the Pyrenees. It is his own story told under a very transparent veil. From this account, which shows us the inmost thoughts of the man, we can conclude that, although gifted with no deep passions, he had at least a lively imagination. Women seem called upon to play a part in his life, to fill a heart deprived of family joys, and to satisfy his taste for pleasure.

If the democratic attempts of Germinal and Prairial had been the pretext of increasing the sentences of the proscribed democrats, it seemed as if the triumph of the 13th of Vendémiaire over the over-impatient reactionaries ought to have led to some betterment in their lot. Far from that, their enemies were sufficiently powerful to cancel the order for Barère's trial before the court of

---

table of the Committee of Public Safety, half by Saint-Just and half by Barère. The two decemvirs, on one less busy day than usual, were arguing on literary matters, for which they both had a taste. The different manners of study furnished them with the text of an argument, in which the characters of the two writers are shown alternately in a curious way.

"The plan of making extracts is of very little use," said Saint-Just. "When you are struck by a maxim or by a train of thought, or by anything else in a book, read it twice and you will remember it; write it down and your memory will depend on what you have written; it will become torpid, and all your learning will lie in portfolios."

Barère replies :

"All the learning of the ancients consisted in committing to memory portions of the great masters."

Saint-Just adds and underlines these words : " *By heart.*"

the Charente-Inférieure, where they doubtless feared that public opinion would prejudice the judges in his favour, and they again passed the former order for his transportation.

At this news Barère, discouraged, interrupts his defence, and we read these words on the last page :

"Now the fatal hour of my transportation strikes a second time. But wherever tyranny may carry me, to the rock-bound coast of Africa or of Madagascar, I shall desire the prosperity of the Republic.

"I only regret one thing—causing misfortune to my family, one of the most patriotic and honourable in France.

"I much regret, too, my inability to continue the work of my civic justification. But for the past two months the grief of being expatriated and the troubles of imprisonment have weakened my health and almost blinded me. Ah! when shall I be able to rest where the wicked are powerless ? When will the tomb yawn between myself and envy, between the Frérons, the André Dumonts,

---

Barère : "Demosthenes travelled among the Egyptians to study and make extracts."

Saint-Just interrupts, and writes as a note : " I deny that."

Barère : "Tacitus educated himself by making extracts that he called *excerpta*."

Saint-Just again interrupts :

" This idea is good as far as translation rom oreign languages is concerned. Extracts from our own authors are rarely of use ; they increase our erudition without improving our understanding."

Barère continues in speaking of Tacitus :

" He saw all because he abridged all, which he had learnt by the habit of reading to a purpose. Maxims and good sayings are like engravings of which one keeps copies. They are portable libraries. They are like the portfolios of painters who go to study at Rome. Idleness alone can do without them. Genius uses them as Perrault used stones to make the beautiful colonnade of the Louvre."

the Sieyès, the Legendres, and the luckless object of
their spite? Long live France and Liberty!"

Then, after eight months of imprisonment, all hope
of regular justice being destroyed, the prisoner's patience
broke down, and his friends prepared a plan of escape
which he had refused up till then. This plan was carried
out on the 5th of Brumaire, the date of the prorogation of
the Convention. The representative of the people, having
again become a simple citizen, considered himself free
to do as he liked.

One must read in his Memoirs the account of his
imprisonment and his flight across the marshes and
forests to Cape Ambez, his joy at breathing the country
air and feeling safe from pursuit. A good farmer, taking
him for an emigrant who had returned fraudulently, put
him up in a large room of a mansion adorned with old
embossed leather hangings and damask-covered furniture.
A few friends of his captivity, a volume of Voltaire, the
ancient moralists, Young's "Night Thoughts," had escaped
the watchful ·eyes of his captors; but now he puts these
on one side to go in for shooting and walking freely on
God's earth, to live that life of physical exertion of which
his incarceration between four walls had so long deprived
him.

Yet he has such need to exchange thoughts with
others that solitude weighs on him at the end of a
fortnight. Besides, the police of the vicinity, having
received information of his flight and a description of
him, begin to be watchful. So he leaves his retreat and
takes refuge in a smack with two sailors; he reaches
Bordeaux; and there he finds an inviolable, refuge,
where he lives for five years.

This man, who a few months before had been one

of the chief arbiters of the fate and fortune of his country, then wrote to his brother:

"I am penniless. I am waiting for the 240 francs you sent to our old friend. He has told me of it. I am borrowing a coat, for I can no longer go about as a tatterdemalion. And as I ought not to be fed like a convict as long as I have something of my own, you must send me four hams for our pantry. They will be the chief dish at our meals for some time.

"To you and to my sisters I send my love. The one at Pau never writes a word. I suppose she is waiting till I am raised from the dead. Once more good-bye. Be equal to the dangers of our country; you will lose nothing by it."

Generous friends urged him to escape to the United States, and offered him the means of living there in peace, but he answered them : "I prefer to die in France than live in America. A foreign land would kill me with regret and weariness."

Poor patriot! who loved France so much, who refused to leave it in the prime of life, you will be compelled to bid farewell to your native land as an old sexagenarian, after having seen all you worked to build up cast down. How could those who had just come from the horrors of exile have the heart to inflict it on others? If they loved their country, they were very cruel.

Proofs of esteem and affection were showered on Barère during his imprisonment and retreat, but one satisfaction that he seemed to have sincerely desired was denied him—the clearing up of the misunderstandings that had embittered his married life. These misunderstandings had begun from the very first, a period when the faults are seldom on the woman's side ; a long absence

had perhaps increased the causes of disagreement; opposite political opinions and religious influences had their
share in widening the gulf; slander did its share, and
embittered the whole life of the married couple. Barère's
efforts and concessions to effect a reunion were without
result; his letters were sent back unanswered, and the
separation became irrevocable.

Barère was certainly more inclined to the pleasures
of the world than to those of home. Yet in the "Pages
Intimes," that we have already quoted at the beginning
of this historical account, he expresses his feelings in this
respect in terms which a biographer ought to reproduce,
and which prove that he did not perhaps deserve to be
deprived of these gentle pleasures.

"Since the Revolution, which changed the features of
social life in France, the relations of the sexes have become
nobler and more serious. Man has found that the happiness of society is but ephemeral and nominal, while
woman seems to prefer the real and lasting happiness of
home. The sanctuary of the family is now filled with
daughters, wives and mothers, whose minds have been
raised, whose hearts have been purified, and whose talents
have been utilised by a higher education.

"The wives and mothers are the priests of the family.
They give their children their first education; they teach
them religion and charity, they preserve their purity of
heart while stimulating and directing their intelligence.
Happy are those whose education has been directed by
mothers, who combine the virtues of their sex with studies
fit for them.

"A good mother is the basis of the family; she devotes
to it her care and tenderness equally. No one can better

know and apply what is necessary to the first stage of life, the physical and moral influence of which is so great on our after existence. A mother's watching is in no way irksome to a child nor troublesome to herself. This watching, which is one of her natural acts, is quiet and confidential, unceasing, yet almost unnoticeable.

" The children of tender, careful mothers are a picture of happiness, health and perfect union. Childhood is the age of pure minds, real affections, satisfied hearts and growing intelligences. How attentive a mother is to observe the first signs and still unexpected developments! A mother gives her child the first teachings of that divine religion which emancipated woman and assigned such a pure, useful, noble and necessary part in family life to her!"

In his long retreat Barère gave himself up wholly to work. He wrote much, and especially two works, one of which was published in Switzerland, the other at Toulouse. They were very successful, although the author was in exile. The first was a critical analysis of the Directory, under the title of " Thoughts on the Republican Government"; the other was called, " Montesquieu described from his Works," and was a study of the author of the " Esprit des Lois."

By these two works public attention was fixed on Barère just as the new government was entering on its duties. The electors of Tarbes, whose confidence had not been shaken by so many slanders and adversities, chose him as their member in the Legislative Council. The aim of this election was twofold, to give Barère back his civil liberty and his political existence. The election ought to have cancelled any sentence, if the rights of national representation had been respected.

But it was not so. Barère became the object of more furious attacks than ever. The Council of Five Hundred, whose reactionary feeling had elected Pichegru as their president, declared the election of the department of the Hautes Pyrénées null and void. Barère's friends, confident of the respect due to the choice of the citizens, had urged him to go to Paris and take his seat; but he had been better advised in not giving way to their entreaties, and in even redoubling his care to conceal his retreat.

The proscription of the royalists on the 18th of Fructidor in no way changed the situation, for the royalists had been conquered by the men who had brought about the 9th of Thermidor, who had no thought of pardoning those who had honestly served the Republic. The democrats who applauded this *coup d'état* were deceived in their hopes; and as for the power of the Directory, sapped in its foundations, from this day it became an easy prey to the future dictator.

All hope of deliverance being henceforth very distant, Barère returned to his studies. He finished writing a great work, in some part the substance of his numerous reports to the Convention on the policy of England.[1] One may say that on this occasion again Barère played the part of reporter to the Committee of Public Safety. One must honour the real authors of these broad, lofty views, of these generous thoughts for the future, which appeared so bold and new when they were republished in our days. The more one studies this period the more one admires it.

If one unchangeable opinion is found in Barère's life,

---

[1] "The Liberty of the Seas, or the English Government Unmasked." Dated, " From my retreat, 1st Ventôse, in the year VI. of the Republic." 3 vols. 8vo.

it is his hatred for England. He seems to have adopted the part of a French Cato, seeking to arouse a Scipio : "Where will the hero or the nation arise that will restore to the human race the liberty of the seas which has been usurped by the wealthy savages of the British Isles?" These are the words that he wished graven on his own book. This is his prophecy :

"One day the nations of Europe, terrified by the commercial tyranny, the political despotism and excessive corruption of the British government will realise Cato's vow : *This modern Carthage must be destroyed.* What will she do when all the peoples of Europe, enlightened at last as to this monopoly of wealth, this exclusive privilege of commerce, this appearance of political liberty that England boasts of so long, cry out : ' Let us break the sceptre of this Queen of the Seas, let them be as free as the land' ? " [1]

Already Mirabeau had called it, "A nation whose thirst for power and riches have produced such systems of oppression and crimes to ruin every quarter of the globe as would have revolted the Romans, those heroes of robbery, a nation that pursues liberty as a rival in all quarters, deserves to be conspired against by all peoples, if they were all free, and if the sublime philanthropy of a few men did not ask for pardon from the fierce patriotism of their fellow-countrymen." [2]

Barère's speeches against the British cabinet and nation served the Committee of Public Safety as war engines. England, who was the moral head of the coalition, made attack all the more dangerous as, while

---

[1] Report drawn up in the name of the Committee of Public Safety, August 1st, 1793.
[2] "Speech to the Batavians," p. 104.

pretending to fight against revolutionary ideas, she sought, above all, to destroy the resources of France. Barère, in feeding the flame of national hatred, kept necessary mistrust awake. In a manuscript note he thus justifies himself for once having cried, "War to the death to every English soldier!"[1] "Convinced of the ills with which the English government afflicts humanity, I wished to frighten, terrify and strike the cruellest enemies of the human race. It was to strike the war monster to the heart."

At the time that Barère had the idea of his book, the Directory was preparing for the expedition against Ireland, that Hoche and Brueys were to command. Proscribed and in hiding, he wished, nevertheless, to go on with his task, and to aid with his pen the cause he was not allowed to aid with his speeches. "And I, too," he cries, "have brought my patriotic offering to the invasion of England."

He dedicates his work to the expeditionary army.

"It will doubtless appear odd," says he, "to dedicate a philosophical work to an army; it is also something new to see an army with citizens for soldiers, politicians for officers, and philosophers for generals. The republican Greeks immortalised themselves at Thermopylæ, but they only fought for their homes. The free Romans distinguished themselves at Carthage,

---

[1] Sitting of the 7th of Prairial, Year III. England, who did not have the same grievances, did she not witness a similar action? "Posterity will shudder with horror when history relates that at the end of the eighteenth century, a member of the English Government dared to vote in favour of a war of extermination against the French nation." (Message of the Executive Directory to the Council of Five Hundred. Sitting of the 8th of Nivôse, Year VI.) The reference is to Lord Fitzwilliam, a member of the Opposition.

but they only fought for their empire. You, French citizens, republican soldiers, you have fought for your homes, your liberty, the rights of man, the independence of other nations, and the peace of the Continent, all at the same time. Now you are going to fight for the freedom of the seas."

This dedication is an appeal to all nations to ally themselves against a common enemy, a manifesto with bursts of eloquence in spite of its exaggerated colouring. The author reminds us of these hateful expressions of Pitt, restricting the right of neutral nations :

"France should be separated from the commercial world, and treated as if she only had a single town, a single harbour, and that this place was blockaded and besieged by land and sea."

To this he replies in the words of Montesquieu : "France should only have commercial dealings with England to the accompaniment of cannon."[1]

"The time has come," he continues, "for this terrible commerce to begin with this government estranged from the world, from Europe and from its own nation."

Barère's hatred was well repaid, if it is true as he makes out (but we prefer to believe that grief blinded him to the truth), if it is true that while he was imprisoned at Saintes, English agents came and stirred up men against him in order to provoke either a murderous riot or a hasty, iniquitous and cruel trial.

As for the idea of his book, it occupies too important a place in Barère's life for us not to briefly touch on it. This idea had served as his basis for drawing up the French Navigation Act placed before the Con-

---

[1] Montesquieu's " Lettres Familières."

vention in September, 1793; later he used it to sketch a plan of maritime legislation at Napoleon's invitation.

"Nature has given the sea to the different nations of the continents. It is a domain common to all, it is universal property.

"The naturalist calls the sea the boundary of different nations. The trader looks upon it as the roadway of every people. The sea is the theatre of commercial democracy."

Every nation has an equal right, therefore, to place its squadrons on it, to carry its produce on it, and to sweep its surface from pole to pole. It is the most powerful instrument given to man of making one family out of the multitude of families. The acknowledgment of the right of each is a guarantee of universal peace. This right cannot be transferred or monopolised.

Rome and Carthage were guilty of a double violation when they divided the empire of the land and sea between them to end the First Punic War.

Other nations have been more or less successful in gaining exclusive naval power; but it is the peculiar property of despotism to corrupt those who exercise it, and this is probably the source of the just reproaches England has deserved.

Cromwell laid the foundations of the English Navigation Act. No other power has possessed a connected persevering naval system; that of France in its best period was purely colonial, but continually impolitic, in turn weak and haughty. The system England pursues has every quality opposed to these faults: a sound basis of naval strength, a continuous direction of naval works and a theory on which the national mind works—all is connected.

"On land we are in the eighteenth century, on sea we are only in the sixth," says the author. The English government has still feudal rights over the sea, and considers itself its suzerain; it collects taxes and tribute from it.

"The commerce of every nation is subjected to a kind of toll to the English; their floating castles are on every shore, they demand homage from every state and people."

What trickery and crime the establishment and preservation of this supremacy has cost the English!

When the victories of Louis XIV. increased the preponderance of France, the British government exhibited the shadow of a universal monarchy to the nations of the Continent in order to hide its own encroachments. When the French Revolution came and proclaimed principles of equity and equality, it felt that the logic of nations would soon decide against its hateful despotism; so it frightened kings, it stirred up jealousy between nations and discord between citizens, it subsidised corruption in order to extinguish the centre of new ideas that threatened it.

As a matter of fact, many wars and treaties had pretended to establish the balance of power in Europe, and yet a Navigation Act, which monopolised the seas for one nation's profit, was endured without a murmur. Republican France was the first to open its eyes to this, and wished to establish the freedom of the seas. In working for the good of all, she made an implacable foe.

England disguises her ambition under the cloak of her insular position, which does not permit her to enlarge her territory. But she makes the sea itself her territory, and takes possession of it every day with her fleets; every day she extends her frontiers at her own goodwill.

Asia, Africa, America, Polynesia, these are her territories. This horizon seems too distant for the sight of our politicians, and when oppression is carried on far from us, it appears no longer an outrage.

Barère traces the history of the means employed by the English government to increase its colonial power, and pictures its conduct even in the heart of the British Isles. Few writers, one must confess, have better studied the subject. It is a cruel history, a revolting picture, but we must recollect that the writer is an enemy and wishes to arouse hatred. His conclusion is that such a government is incompatible with the interests of other nations.

Then he addresses each one of them in succession, and goes through the list of its grievances against England.

"There are two means," he says, "of attacking this power; one is immediate and decisive, and is entrusted to our brave army, the other is to shut every European port to English vessels, to seize English merchandise on every sea, and to shut it up in its island by peace on the Continent."

No one will be astonished at the favour with which this work was received by him who some years after established the continental system. We have just had its idea very clearly expressed.

Barère, who had voted for the decree of the 16th of Pluviôse, Year II., abolishing slavery in America, considers it an indispensable measure for preventing any naval power acquiring exclusive preponderance. The colonial system has changed, he says : with the ancients, a colony was only an extension of territory necessary to an overgrown national family. With modern people, a selfish mother country sends bands of slaves to work for her in distant lands. Colonies, formerly integral parts of continental states, must be cultivated by free men ; and this must be declared the law of nations.

Finally, his philanthropic feeling, rising to the most general point of view, dreams of a holy alliance of all peoples on the ruins of English despotism, which inspires this beautiful page.

"Europe has boasted much about the family compact which united two powerful dynasties to preserve the peace of the South. There is even a better compact to be made—that of the whole human race, of all nations, or at least of the European nations.

" Why should not this Continent, enlightened by the great minds of the eighteenth century and in revolt against the crimes of the English government, why should it not be governed by laws debated in a great central European Parliament, to which every people, state, power or government would send its representatives.

"Why could there not be a European parliament, as there is a French or a German parliament. In it every continental nation would swear eternal hatred to naval tyranny, and eternal allegiance to commercial and maritime liberty.

"Such a congress would be the finest sight our Continent could show the world. Such an august assembly would meet every ten years to settle the rights of nations, to maintain the freedom of the seas, treaties of peace, alliance, navigation and commerce. It would hear all complaints of governors and governed, and would judge rebels to the general will or to the interests of nations. Then would Justice, so long exiled from earth, unite with Peace to make this earth happy."

We do not think we have given too much space to

the analysis of this book, not only because it is Barère's principal work, but because it was of importance in its day. "England is on sea what Rome was on land when it fell on account of its might," said Raynal in 1770. Barère, in quoting these words twenty-five years after, adds: "The weight of its greatness must entail its ruin."

Since then the power of Britain has gone on extending, urged on by fate, for a decaying monopoly is certain of destruction. Is the accomplishment of the prophecy at hand? Will the new path that she is cutting out towards the East be the signal for the crash? In short, is not the weapon in her hands that will be turned against herself? Such is the question asked from one end of Europe to the other.

Will France, at least, cruelly taught by recent deceptions, understand that the state of her navy demands all her efforts, all her care? After having freed so many nations by her proclamation of the principles of liberty, will she bring about as well the freedom of the seas? Nigh half a century back the old member of the Convention, but recently dead, cried out to her, "France, *this* is the logical sequel, the worthy end of thy Revolution!"

Barère, in composing his book, had another, a personal object, that he makes no attempt to conceal. This was to make himself agreeable to the Directory by backing up its plans. But, instead of disarming stubborn hate, the book attracted attention anew to the author, and his enemies pursued him with renewed vigour, in order to carry out the sentence of transportation that had been pronounced on him. He had to leave his hiding-place for awhile, and again wander about in the country; then he took refuge in the suburbs of Paris, in the house of his friend, the Comtesse de Guibert.

His gratitude to the two persons who had generously shielded him was expressed in the most touching language.

On the last letter that M. Fonade of Bordeaux wrote to him, a few days before he died, Barère inscribed these words: "O Providence! after preserving me from the savage hands of my enemies, why have you torn from me this hospitable creature, who for five years and a half showered every kindness on me and reconciled me with this corrupt generation?"

And in his private diary we read: "I am writing my remembrances of Madame de Guibert with a pleasure mingled with bitterness. She was gifted with a truly heavenly soul by her virtues, her love of liberty, and her courage for succouring the unfortunate. I can say with Horace, '*Nulli flebilior quam mihi.*' She it was that sent me help during the first days of my exile, in 1795, in Saintes Prison; she it was who brought me further consolation when, having escaped from prison, I had taken refuge with a patriotic, generous merchant of Bordeaux. She it was who, on learning that the members of the Directory were still eager to arrest me, in the months of May and June, 1799, sent me money to travel, and offered me a safe refuge in her country house at Saint-Ouen, a league from the Luxembourg Palace, where my enemies met."

He lay in hiding there until the 18th of Brumaire, and even after that, for Bonaparte's real intentions were not yet known. Barère presented him with a copy of his book on the Liberty of the Seas, and the week afterwards he was included in a kind of amnesty which recalled a certain number of exiles.

This is his opinion of the Brumaire *coup d'état* and its consequences, not free from at least apparent contra-

dictions, and it was expressed several years after that
event

"The overthrow of the Directory had become a necessity for true lovers of constitutional government. The
Directory had made a practice of violating the constitution, and took pleasure in it. The way it was overthrown
was dangerous only because of the example it gave to the
army, which is very different from the people reasserting
their rights. But this necessary change in the State gave
rise to hopes. The Consulate was called a restorative
dictatorship by Lafayette and other republicans, as a great
occasion for washing away the outrages that the reactionaries had made them undergo. And yet the victor of
St. Cloud was popular for but a short while. His hatred
of the Republic and its defenders soon showed that
liberty, equality and a representative government would
not be fostered by the general of the Italian and Egyptian
campaigns. It was no good strongly warning the First
Consul not to turn the Revolution out of its course at
the very moment that it was going to make France happy.
The upstart soldier replied that he had only overthrown
anarchy and placed an imperial crown on his head—a
deed that only he and his flatterers desired.

"No party was satisfied. The partisans of liberty reproached Bonaparte for not working for them. The
emigrant nobility reviled him for not having worked
for Louis XVIII. The Council of Five Hundred did
not pardon him for having received the supreme power
from a section of the other council. The foreign princes
shrieked out at the usurpation in order to disturb France
afresh, already sufficiently divided, and to keep the victor
of Italy from power.

"In the eyes of contemporaries, the 18th of Brumaire

was but an intrigue of those upstarts the Revolution had created. For both the politician and the historian the 18th of Brumaire was a necessity. This is the real definition of this great event of the last year of the eighteenth century. On the 18th of Brumaire the indispensable man was General Bonaparte. Moreau was only a royalist soldier and an ignorant politician. Masséna, who had just conquered the Russians at Zurich, was only a brave, intelligent warrior. Bonaparte, without having learnt the science of civil government, had at least great political ideas, and if he had had wise, enlightened advisers, he would have made France the home of armed liberty and the centre of civilisation. When we know how to sum up men and things, when we clearly and honestly analyse the details and spirit of the time, we give Bonaparte credit for the extraordinary courage he must have had to overturn a constitutional government which from the commencement had taken some root in the nation. Bonaparte risked his head and his fame; the intriguers, who surrounded and urged him on, risked nothing.

"Liberty sat in front of the First Consul at the Tuileries, like remorse that disturbed the success of his *coup d'état* and the safety of his power ; so he directed all his attacks against liberty. He effaced the inconvenient word ' Republic' inscribed over the door of the Consular Palace; he destroyed the place of meeting of the Constituent Assembly ; he changed the hall of the Convention into a theatre, he even went so far as to cut down the trees of liberty that shaded the courtyard of the Tuileries. But these attacks on all the attributes and recollections of the Republic were not destined to enchain liberty for ever. Despots pass away, but peoples remain.

"The 18th of Brumaire was one of the most momentous periods of the Revolution : it changed its whole course, spoilt all its results, altered all its liberties, and destroyed the spirit of the nation. The great movement of the social regeneration of France and of the emancipation of European nations was stopped and paralysed by military violence, and confiscated for the profit of a bold soldier. The 18th of Brumaire has a discouraging and enervating effect on French and European patriots : it was the effect of civil rule crushed by military rule. The rule of force begins, and the sword is a bad legislator."

Madame de Staël fills her "Dix Années d'Exil" with regrets for the converse of Paris ; Barère seems to have written his Memoirs for the purpose of libelling the capital and its inhabitants, while proving on every page how dear he holds the life and habits of the great city. This love of society makes him exclaim in a more than artless way : " I forgot," says he, "in again taking up my civic rights that Bonaparte had attacked the rights of my country, and I only listened to my feelings of gratitude."

Hardly had he been granted his liberty than he hastened to present the Consul with the tribute of his somewhat gushing gratitude. The opportunity of proving his expressions soon arrived. At the invitation of Bonaparte himself, he refuted really cleverly a speech of the English minister, Lord Granville, and a pamphlet of Sir Francis d'Yvernois, both directed against the new government and especially against its chief.

However, Bonaparte was rebuffed when he. offered Barère the editorship of a *Journal de l'Armée.* He did so knowing the talents of the former reporter of the

Committee of Public Safety, and wishing to use them without giving him an important post in the government. "You are liked by the soldiers of France," said he to him; "they know how you used to excite their courage and celebrate their victories." But either because such a post seemed to be so inferior to the one he had held, or because he foresaw the use Napoleon would soon make of the national army for his personal advantage, Barère replied somewhat ironically, "The First Consul wishes to make a bard of me, but we are no longer in the time of Ossian."

However, he turned to journalism again, but for quite spontaneous patriotic reasons. The rupture of the treaty of Amiens rekindled his energy, and he thought that a press war against England would be a useful aid to the one the French government was preparing. Developing the idea of his book, he first thought of publishing a periodical with the title of "The Liberty of the Seas'"; but later the more frankly hostile title of "Anti-British Journal" was preferred. He submitted his plan to the First Consul, who approved of it, and promised him a subsidy, which, according to Barère, he never gave. Generally, Bonaparte's communications with the editor of the new paper, through the intermediary of Bourrienne and Duroc, were hesitating and diplomatically reserved. The reason for this is not quite clear, unless it can be explained by the consideration he had for the partisans of the *ancien régime*. Yet Barère was frequently consulted on points that the government considered very important, and his opinions seem to have been much prized. He was in the habit of furnishing information as to the tactics, the tendencies and members of the English parties; he was several times asked for notes on the organisation of the administration, on the legislation, navy, etc. Lastly, Napoleon showed his appreciation of Barère's political information and experience by writing . him the following note, dated the 9th of Floréal, Year XI., on hearing of his intention of retiring to the Pyrenees:

"The First Consul, having heard of Citizen Barère's coming departure for his own country, desires him to remain in Paris.

"Citizen Barère will make a report every week either on public opinion or on the progress of the government, or on anything he thinks the First Consul will be interested to know.   He may write quite freely.

"He will remit his report sealed to General Duroc with his own hands, who will give it to the First Consul; but it is absolutely necessary that no one know of this communication.   Should this happen, the First Consul will stop it.   He can also often insert articles in the papers to rouse public opinion, especially against the English."

"I will remain in Paris and faithfully and sincerely carry out what the First Consul wishes.   I can refuse nothing to him who has granted me the greatest of all benefits— liberty."   Such was Barère's reply on accepting this task, so unworthy of his position, as he himself confesses, but singularly well fitted to his talents.

Thus commenced a confidential correspondence of the utmost interest to the historian of this period.   Events are described and often foreseen, with remarkable sagacity, that the author had gained in the management of great matters.   Daily the changes in public opinion are very delicately shown; nothing is overlooked, neither the gossip of the drawing-room nor of the street.   Let us add, to Barère's honour, that the warnings and advice given by the old republican to the young dictator are inspired by patriotism as much as by experience. Barère was right in thinking that this correspondence, if it were made public, would produce a favourable impression of his reputation. By the Emperor's death he was released from his oath of secrecy, and he was taking measures for having it published at Brussels when the revolution of 1830 interrupted his plans. However, a few gentlemen saw these letters, which had become historical, among others by an author whose writings were thought much of under the Restoration, M. d'Herbigny, author of the *Revue politique de l'Europe en* 1825 and of the *Nouvelles Letters Provinciales*. M. d'Herbigny relates to Barère the impression he had on reading them in a letter we shall now quote :

" In this daily moving panorama the real spirit of France is depicted, rising rapidly from coldness to enthusiasm and dropping as quickly from enthusiasm to coldness, its quick, passing interest, followed by a desperate carelessness, its inconsistent admiration and contempt, its applause so quickly followed by groans, its confidence so near mistrust, and with lightning rapidity it passes from hope to fear and from joy to alarm, from ardour to despair, from praise to insult, from love to hatred. The whole of this picture is living and curious, above all, eminently instructive. It makes us know a people better than several centuries of its history. It shows the moral state of the nation, and they are the archives that tell posterity about the features and habits of their ancestors.

"In the midst of all these ephemeral, uncertain and hazy opinions, the clever politician picks out one, threatcuing, fixed and unchanging, that dominates all the others, and that obstinately attacks Napoleon's destiny.   It is the opinion of the old aristocracy, existing at first by reason of its fanaticism, upheld by unknown means, and directed by an invisible breath; it was an opinion that Napoleon despised, but which the clever observer thought important. Barère is always directing his attention to this rock that he disdains; he shows him this inflexible opinion uniting to the opinion of the Church, more hidden, but implacable, and both of them digging the pit into which they intend to fling him.   He warns him that these two fanatical opinions raised by him are no less inexorable against him; that their conspiracy is the greatest danger he has to fight against; that they do not forgive him for his victories, nor his power, nor his rise.   Napoleon thought himself out of danger on the pedestal he stood on; he despised both danger and advice, and his fall fulfilled the prophecies of the political seer."

These last sentences, which display the peculiar prejudices in favour of the liberalism of the time, prove that Napoleon's chosen correspondent wrote less as a courtier than as a citizen.

This explains the sudden stoppage of this correspondence, that lasted from the beginning of 1803 to the end of 1807.   Barère was preparing his 223rd letter when he received the following letter from General Duroc:

"I am directed, sir, to write and inform you that it is useless for you to continue sending me letters, as His Majesty's occupations no longer permit him to read them. If matters alter in the future, I will hasten to inform you."

Thus ends the history of Barère's relations with Napoleon.   It has been said that he fulfilled the duties of literary censor and editor of the *Journal Officiel.* He gives the lie to these two assertions in the most energetic and positive manner.

Henceforward treated with more than coldness by the Imperial Government, foiled by its agents in his candidature for the Senate, and by the Senate in his candidature for the Legislative Council, even persecuted on several occasions, Barère quickly passed from an excessive admiration for Bonaparte to the severe, rancorous, and often unjust opinions in which his papers abound. This malevolent frame of mind only gave way to a calmer, saner opinion after the final cataclysm of the empire.

In order to give an idea of this gradual change, we shall merely give a few of the titles that Barère chose for his proposed works on the life of Napoleon.

The first was, "France made famous and mighty by Napoleon." He urges him to become the "King of kings," or the "Emperor of Europe," in order to crush English tyranny. At this time Barère was translating the celebrated poems, by the Italian Francesco Gianni, on the capture of Ulm and Vienna, and on the battle of Austerlitz, as well as the "Poetic Garland composed for the glorious accession of Napoleon I. by the shepherds of Arcadia."

Later, from 1807 to 1815, the titles run: "Napoleon the Aristocrat," "Napoleon and the Liberty of the Press," etc.

After 1815 he is concerned only with a "History of Napoleon and his Reign," that he often regretted he never finished. An imagination like his could never remain unmoved by so much glory. So when, in 1840, the news of the return of Napoleon's ashes to France reached his mountain home, his old enthusiasm was rekindled and broke forth joyfully.

As Barère was classed among the suspected during the last years of the Empire, he avoided all political affairs, and lived the life of a man of letters. The results of his leisure were translations of Young (his favourite poet), of Tasso and Tyrtaeus, a "History of the Neapolitan Revolutions," the "Travels of Plato in Italy," and several other writings, some published, the others left in manuscript. He was often at the Théâtre Français and at the Opera, where his taste and learning were much valued by the actors. Lesueur, Dalayrac, Steibelt, Lays, Talma, and Larive were his intimate friends and appreciated his advice. He even wrote studies on theatrical art, especially on Talma, which are not without importance.

Barère was much run after in society by reason of his witty, graceful conversation. "You are the nicest of men," wrote Dr. Alibert, who was a judge of men; "after seeing you I am witty for a whole week." One day that he had been dining with Madame Récamier, he sat next to La Harpe, who asked his hostess after dinner the name of his neighbour, adding, "One can easily see from his courteous grace of manner that he is one of the old nobility; your republicans are all so full of the rough ferocity of their opinions." Madame Récamier merely answered, with a smile, "He is one of my husband's friends; there are so many of them that I cannot recall his name."

The events of 1814 interrupted the calmest, happiest period of Barère's life. At the approach of the storm, he had escorted the widow and daughter of one of his relations to the south, and he was there when the empire fell. The advance of the invading enemy drove him in succession from Tarbes to Toulouse, Cahors, and finally to Limoges, whence he returned to the capital in the month of April.

France had accepted the return of the Bourbons through very weariness, and from a hope of necessary repose after such shocks. The generation of the Revolution was not without mistrust, but Napoleon's despotism had weighed so heavily on it that it did not display any hostility to his successors; they on their side promised to forget all disputes. A political reform seemed to be imminent, by no means as rapid and complete as the one that despotism had stopped, but at any rate capable of establishing a public spirit by degrees; so the authors of the first reform frankly joined the second. Personally Barère had no reason to expect, and did not expect, any favour from the new government; he was satisfied with being left in peace, and took up his old life again. The few pamphlets that he wrote during the first Restoration merely express liberal sentiments, with no hatred for the present, nor regret for the past.

The return from Elba does not seem to have excited him very much, and his Memoirs prove it. But it is astonishing that he does not mention in them an act worthy of his courage and the perseverance of his convictions. On the 21st of March, the day after Napoleon's entry into the Tuileries, Barère wrote him the following letter that his biographers ought to quote. It will be seen what authority some chroniclers have had to accuse him of conspiring in favour of Bonaparte's return.

SIRE,—A man who will always place liberty and country before all the illusions of power and all the ambitions of fortune, owes it to himself to give your Majesty, reseated on the throne raised by the sovereignty of the people, the homage of truth. It generally has to force its way into the presence of ordinary kings, to-day it walks into Napoleon's palace by the strength of public opinion.

I prove my respect for your rule and for the power of the nation in telling you the truth. Those who seek by flattery and lying to obtain riches and influence outrage it.

Neither during the Consulate nor the Empire did I occupy any public office ; under your rule I lived in a permanent state of moral exile. My words, then, can be suspected neither by the French nation, whose rights I have ever defended at the risk of my life, nor by your Majesty, whose elevation to consular power I have twice supported, but whose authority I have never flattered.

Extraordinary events for several years past have made you the brilliant heir of the power of the French Revolution. You can preserve for ever its great principles that were destroyed under the Empire by the ambitious conquests which caused its downfall. Now these great principles ought to be proclaimed frankly and laid down with such firmness that they will always resist yourself and your successors.

The momentary restoration of the Bourbons placed, as it were, a century between your empire and the power which the army and the nation replace to-day in your hands You had become the conqueror of Europe, frightened at your successes and reverses alike. You will now become the preserver of France within its political and natural limits.

In less than a year Providence, who appears to be Prime Minister of France, has given kings two great lessons : your abdication of the empire and your return to the throne.

Public opinion, the sovereign who is never deposed and who overturns every throne and destroys every rule at its pleasure after having weighed it in its balance, the public opinion of a nation free though flighty, aware of its rights, although inattentive to them, had abandoned your Majesty a year ago, as it has just deserted the Bourbons.

Hence, Sire, let this great political experience be useful for once, and let your name, already known in all corners of the globe by the renown of your battles, be still more renowned in Europe as the name of a legislator who backs up laws by force of arms and public opinion by the power of the throne. Let the nation use its rights freely in all their energy and integrity. That is the real immortality of a great man.

The rough copy of another document, that we also found among his papers, will serve to confirm the reader's opinion on his political ideas at that period :

" France has escaped from the terrible *despotism of liberty* under which she was forced to exist from 1789 to 1800.

"She has escaped from the brilliant *despotism of glory* under which she lived from 1800 until the 30th of March, 1814.

"She has just escaped from the humdrum *despotism of heredity* under which she groaned from the 4th of May, 1814, until the 20th of March, 1815.

"Now it concerns her to escape from constitutional despotism, the most dangerous of all, for if a national constitution does not frankly ensure the rights of the people, does not guarantee all its liberties by a wise, strong organisation and by separating the different powers, we only get a despotism cleverly disguised under legal forms, and all the more fatal because it will be continued under colour of being the *general wish*.

"If the French nation only wishes to have, at this critical moment of imminent war, a *nominal and provisional constitution*—that is to say, the continuation of the imperial despotism with its bonds more firmly riveted, it may rest contented with the *additional clauses* to the constitution of the empire. But if it wishes to avoid new cataclysms, new efforts, new dangers, new sacrifices to assure its political and civil liberty, it must have the courage to demand a complete, definite constitution from the representatives of the nation, which should be drawn up according to the lessons of experience and contain the best points taken from the constitutions already accepted by our nation, adapted to the needs of the present day, and sanctioned by the experience of five-and-twenty years.

"The chief obstacle to a good constitution has always been the existence, the prejudices, the customs and the power of a previous government and those who have lived by it. We have experienced this under the Bourbons, who were brought up under other conditions; we ought not to experience it under Napoleon, born of the Revolution itself.   However this may be, a constitution is never a concession of the throne, but a conquest made by a nation of itself.   In the gross ages of barbarism and despotism, governments are like fortresses that have to be taken, or disguised, or made to capitulate in order that nations may enjoy a really free constitution; but in periods full of education and liberty they must be conquered by reason, public opinion and necessity, which is also a power, in order to proclaim the declaration of the national rights, and to ensure civil rights and the ascendency of law."

Barère continued in the path shown by the writings we have quoted.   Having become a member of the Chamber of Representatives, he never ceased to urge the drafting of a constitution, based on that of 1791 and submitted to the approval of the nation.   He even worked at the preparation of materials for it.   When the ill-starred *additional clause* was issued, which afforded such little satisfaction to the expectations of the country, Barère thought it his duty to refuse to sign it.   However, his opposition, entirely one of principle, was by no means cantankerous.

"If Napoleon," says he, "after the awful disaster of Waterloo, had had confidence in the representatives and had come before them like Varro, the Consul, not despairing of the safety of the country, they would have granted him soldiers and taxes, and his fatal abdication would not have taken place.   What a misfortune it was that France ever separated its destiny, either of its own accord or not, from that of Napoleon! If revolutionary liberty could only have counted on his sword, it would have been the surest weapon with which to triumph over Europe. France would have been undoubtedly saved by his presence at her head, although some politicians wished to save her without him."

" The events of the war became so pressing," says he in another place, "that the Chamber of Representatives was surprised in the midst of its constitutional labours, but it would not separate without having left a solemn declaration of political principles and rights to future generations. This was done on the 7th of July, 1815, at the evening sitting, on the eve of the day its powers were shattered by superior force. Several days previously Garat had brought in a bill of rights, which, although very short and incomplete, yet was supported energetically by Barère and Poulain Grand Pré, as sanctioning the flight of the Bourbons, just as the bill of rights in England had sanctioned the flight of the Stuarts. This bill of Garat's, amended by his two colleagues, was a kind of flag of liberty saved from the wholesale wreck. But as there existed a constitutional committee, charged with drawing up a complete constitution to be accepted by the King, whoever he might be, it was necessary to wake it up and hasten on its work by a simple declaration of principles. Barère first proposed one on the 5th of July, supported by M. Dupont de l'Eure, who also read another bill drawn up by an outsider, M. Jullien, of Paris. The Chamber referred these two drafts to a select committee of five, which made them into one. This is an instance of the political will of this assembly, that only lasted a month, but a month of energy, the most patriotic and national assembly after the Constitutional

and the Convention.   It foresaw too well the cruel reaction that the King and the lords would bring with them,
and so created obstacles for them, and it was generous
enough to fling itself between them and France, crushed
by a second invasion.   The almost unanimous decision
of the Chamber, the faithful, courageous representative
of the French people, was authorised by its origin in
the first assemblies and by the force of events to form
a constitution to take the place of the granted charter,
and to cause it to be accepted by this so-called legitimate
King, who was marching with foreign levies over French
corpses.   It was neither frightened by German artillery,
drawn up on the bridge opposite their House, nor by
the pretended omnipotence of Wellington, hastening
from Cambrai to Versailles, with halts at Louvres and
Saint-Denis for his royal marionnette, who entered the
Tuileries under cover of night.   It wished, at any rate,
to lay down the principles of liberty and nationality in
the famous pronouncement of the 7th of July, 1815.
In it are written for the benefit of a strong, free posterity
the undoubted conditions of that representative government for which the French have fought since the 14th
of July, 1789."

Barère spoke in the Chamber of Representatives with
a remarkable vigour and ease of diction.   I have seen
some of his audience, who expected a model of eloquent
demagogy, and who could not recover from their surprise.
His moderate conduct should have preserved him
from fresh persecution, but in 1815, as at every reaction,
the punishment of certain acts was a pretext for punishing
certain men.   Among the rulers of this period were to
be found those who ruled in 1795.

Barère, whose name was to be found in the list of the 24th of July, remained in hiding in Paris until the amnesty of the following 12th of January, which banished him from France. Then he took refuge in Brussels, the centre of a colony of French exiles, especially of former members of the Convention. Some of them had made their country famous by their knowledge, talents and courage, others had occupied the highest posts in the public service, and most had left these exalted positions poor, several even were in want of necessaries, without one of them ever compromising the dignity of misfortune. With difficulty did more fortunate colleagues succeed in fathoming the secret of their position, and make them accept slight help. There is a touching anecdote in Barère's notes with reference to this:

" Mons, Brussels and Liège were the towns where French refugees mostly congregated. Among the former members of the Convention several bordered on a state of indigence. The rich ones formed a society to help them. M. Ramel de Nogaret was appointed collector and distributor of the subscriptions, and he fulfilled this humane mission with great zeal and tact. One of them, named Savornin, had not been willing to make his distress known; he lived in an obscure corner of the old town on the remains of his few savings. Having fallen ill, his needs increased, and the Belgian woman in whose house he was lodging took care of him at her own expense. M. Ramel having heard of M. Savornin's bad state of health, discovered his lodgings, and placed in his room the help of the society. The poor old man now needed nothing. But finding out·how he had been able to exist so long without resources, M. Ramel learnt that his

generous landlady had pawned her own clothes and furniture to pay for the wants of the invalid. He hastened
to redeem her goods, and continued to look after his
former respected colleague. But illness and the misfortunes of exile had done their work ; Savornin died ; the
society paid his debts and his funeral expenses.

"Several other members of the Convention received a
fixed monthly sum from M. Ramel, and afterwards from
his successor, M. Oudot. These indigent refugees, whose
energy and devotion had saved France and her liberty,
were in a majority among the exiles. During this period,
Louis XVIII. was wasting the forty millions sterling in
Paris that France had to raise to reward those who had
betrayed her and fought against her."

Barére was not reduced to live on the charity of
others, honourable for them and glorious for the objects
of it ; but it was only by spending his modest patrimony,
already much reduced, and adding to it the fruit of his
literary labours that he managed to live. He had taken
up his former studies and habits and supported, resignedly,
the greatest trouble a patriot can suffer. The following
reflections, which we choose from several others among
his papers, prove the state of his thoughts :

"In an exile's life, there is a continual energy that
tyrants do not imagine, a moral energy that makes the
exile's courage greater than his misfortune.

"In the series of persecutions he experiences, there
are sublime moments when, by a desperate effort of his
mental over his physical nature, he conquers the violence
and refinement of tyranny.

"The exile takes refuge in Providence, the supreme

protector of the oppressed.   He alone can turn an inspired look towards heaven.

"The exile, in the midst of his troubles, has consolations unknown to his persecutors, he feels those incom-
prehensible impulses of the soul which can raise him
above material restraints and bodily sufferings.

"When I was exiled, I knelt on a stone in my prison
in the Isle of Oleron and at Saintes, and never has God
so granted my vows and accepted my prayers. Every
furious political party, every vile murderous passion was
aroused against me, alone, unarmed, and a prisoner.
God alone could protect me.

"Often had I in my mind those reassuring words of
Cato : that the struggle of a virtuous man against misfortune is a sight worthy of being regarded by God.
Cato's confidence had passed into my soul and consoled
me.   It was the hope of a Christian and the belief of
an honest man, who felt he had an irreproachable conscience."

We have purposely chosen these extracts because they
lead us to speak of Barère's religious opinions.

The intensely changeable and impressionable man
that we have depicted, who gave way so easily to the
influences of the moment and of his surroundings, never
gave way at any time of his life to bold or scoffing
irreligion.   We are not aware of a single word that fell
from his lips or pen that is contradictory to the religious
sentiments we have just quoted—that is to say, these
sentiments were deeply rooted.   Although a follower of
Voltaire in his studies and by the very nature of his
mind, Barère was too much of a democrat at heart not
to be just towards Christianity.   We find among his manu-

scripts a projected work with the title, "Christianity and Its Influence," in which he tells of the benefits of the *Lawgiver of Democracy*, which is the name he gives to Jesus. It is a singular fact that Grégoire also had the same idea his whole life long. He was ever collecting materials for a huge book on the *Influence of Christianity* from every point of view and considering every consequence.

Solitude and adversity make men think of God. Especially during his misfortunes did Barère's thoughts turn towards religion. He began a note-book during his first exile which he continued during his second, on each page of which is placed as a text a verse from the Psalms, followed by a short development applying it to the author's situation. This collection is headed : " The Words of the Psalmist; or, Religious Consolations on My Exile, My Prisons and My Return to France in My Old Age."

Although he lived far from his country, his heart did not grow cold towards her. His eyes, always fixed on her, followed all the details of a struggle to which he had helped to give the first impulse, whose end he doubtless foresaw. Pen in hand he filled the pages of his note-books with his impressions. He appears like an anxious parent in his fits of melancholy or hope, which appear alternately, at one time when he sees liberty openly attacked, at another when he sees it defended either by eloquent speeches from the tribune or by obscure conspirators resigned to martyrdom. Standing like a distant lighthouse, he points out the dangers of political navigation.

At one time, in April, 1823, the prosecution of the *Courrier Français* and the *Pilote* for treason reveals to his mind an attempt to re-establish the ancient parliaments.

"It is not an arrest, in the ordinary sense of the word, that we ask you for," the Attorney-General had said to the Royal Court, "it is a great measure for the public safety, an act similar to those carried out by the old parliaments, which to-day you are called upon to replace."

At another time, in 1824, the Septennial Act of the Elective Chamber appears to him like a new feudalism. "As soon as a man is a member for seven years, he will become the object of every servility and every ambition, his acquaintance will widen, his patronage become established, his gift of a few small positions will give him the reputation of great power; as soon as the member is familiar with the tactics of offices, he will become powerful by dismissals and promotions, the country magnates will have to reckon with him. The Septennial Act will strengthen the power of intriguers, they will be re-elected and become permanent; they will have every post, great or small, in their gift. Thus a legislative feudalism will be established, no less fatal than the feudal nobility of ancient times."

At another time he declares that the reduction of the land tax has a double aim—to favour large proprietors and to lessen the number of small electors.

Once again he unveils the tactics of the ministerial journalists, tactics not unknown in our own time. Some of them, performing the office of scouts, endeavour to accustom the nation to the violation of principles and to arbitrary acts; the others hold themselves in readiness to disown the former, if need be, should public opinion be too threatening in its revolt.

The same alternatives of hope and dismay are seen in the editing of these Memoirs, which then took up much of his time. "Twenty times," he says, "during

my exile has my pen dropped from my hands in thinking
of my contemporaries, of their natural ingratitude, of their
continual neglect. So I often stopped writing my Memoirs,
thinking this reactionary, servile, and venal generation
worthy of neither esteem, fear, hope, nor anxiety. I only
took up my work again in thinking of the young men,
the hope of their country and of the people—*i.e.*, the
lower classes, the true disinterested friends of public
liberty."

Purely literary occupations consoled him in his hours
of prostration, as they had always done ; to them we owe
the publication of the poetical works of Camoens and
several works that remained unpublished for the most
part.

The news of the Revolution of 1830 came and surprised him in the midst of this peaceful existence. In
October, 1829, he wrote in his note-book : " It would
seem as if Charles X.'s Government wishes to fill up its
cup to the full, it governs so much by proclamations.
All these preparations for the old order of things will
fall before the rampart of the national will." Ten months
later he cried, " Honour and glory to the men of Paris !
The heroic days of the 27th, 28th, and 29th of July
have recompensed public and personal liberty. Three
angry and courageous days have been sufficient to
destuartise France."

After his joy as a patriot, one of his first thoughts
was that he should be allowed to see his native land
again.

" My dear brother, my best friend," he writes to Jean
Pierre Barère at Tarbes, " at last the day of liberty has
dawned. I shall be able to look on you once more, to
kiss you and my family, to sleep 'neath the paternal roof,

and visit the beautiful Pyrenees again, whence I ought never to have strayed if I wished to remain happy and quiet.

"One thing alone worries me in the midst of my joy at the heroic insurrection of the Parisians, of whom I was far from expecting so much; it is your silence when these glorious events fill every heart with hope and happiness. How is it you never dreamt of telling me what was happening at Tarbes?

"You must have heard of the Paris Revolution on the 4th or 5th of this month, and now it is the 20th of August, and I have not received a line from you. Are you ill or has all this unhoped-for, marvellous work injured you in any way? I know not what to think or to fear!"

Jean Pierre's silence was explained only too soon.

One of Barère's first thoughts was to get at the cause of the events that had put an end to his exile, and to endeavour to celebrate it by an expression of public gratitude. This is what he writes from Brussels to M. Dupont de l'Eure, after having congratulated himself at seeing justice entrusted to such loyal hands:

"I must also give you the idea of getting a monument put up to the liberty of the Press by the new government: journalism has earned the gratitude of France and the human race in these latter days. A bronze statue should be put up in one of the squares of Paris to that worker of Mainz who invented printing in the time of Louis XI., one of our cruellest tyrants. You would dignify the industrial and working classes by such a monument, you would honour genius and great inventions, and you would teach the people by their eyes that the liberty of thought, of speech, of writing and printing is the most essential to maintain and defend. These monuments of public gratitude were much used by the ancients, who called them *the legislation of the senses.*"

As soon as he got to Paris, Barère gave M. David the same idea, which was later realised by the towns that saw respectively the birth and glory of Gutenberg.

We listened just now to the joyous exclamation the patriot made when he heard of the work of July, but even before he returned from exile his mind was disquieted by the news from Paris.

" [August, 1830.]—The Chamber of Deputies does not rise to the level of circumstances, it clings to legislative power without satisfying fresh wants.   It proposes to continue the anti-national policy of Louis XVIII.—his constitutional usurpation of the sovereignty of the people. The young citizens of Paris, more enlightened, collected round the Chamber to demand a new national constitution.   M. Lafayette promised them satisfaction to quiet them, but these political cobblers are in a majority; they are going to patch up the rubbish of 1814. . . . . The insistance of the young Parisians has made some modifications in the Charter—the sovereignty of the people has been recognised.   The deputies have acted like firemen at a fire — they have added fuel to the flames. . . . . Brave and good citizens make revolutions, cowards and tricksters then step in to reap the rewards.   A fortnight ago, the men who are now asking for posts were either in their beds or in their cellars.

"[September.]—Talleyrand's nomination to the Embassy of London has exasperated every patriotic heart. ·As if France was not tired for the last month of being betrayed, the diplomatic salesman of nations has been sent to the

one nation always willing to buy. The Government and
the Chambers have become entirely aristocratic, they are
afraid of liberty, they detest equality, they scarcely remember the people who were their saviours. The
Girondist Government goes on in its old ruts, and the
nation does not know where it is going."

Barère left Brussels towards the end of September to
return to Paris, where his imagination, as excitable as
when he was young, thought it would yet see the liberty
he had dreamt of for forty years. But his life, like
the lives of so many of his contemporaries, was doomed
to be a series of disappointments. This is one of the
first proofs of his new grief.

POLITICAL EMPIRICISM.

" Quackery preceded medicine as despotism always
precedes liberty. Governmental quackery precedes the
true benefits of emancipation.

"Charles X. began his reign with these words : ' No
more censorship, no more halberds'; just as when he returned in 1814 he had cried, 'No more conscription.' This
charlatanism was quickly unveiled. Charles X. only wished
to reign by the scissors of the censorship and by the
swords of his guards ; the people broke up the throne
and its supports, and the restored monarchy fell.

"On his election Louis Philippe declared to the people
that ' henceforth the Charter should be a fact and the
throne should be surrounded by republican institutions.'
The fact is that the Charter is violated, newspapers are
prosecuted, republicans are imprisoned, sentenced and
killed.

" But although the Charter is invisible to the citizens,
truth and liberty grow and republicans multiply.

"Who knows but if, one fine day, liberty should not come from the heads of the French, like Athene, who came fully armed from the head of Zeus ?   For the people is a powerful god, and liberty is the wisdom of peoples."

From this moment Barère's criticisms follow fast. We select a few at random from a huge heap, just to briefly show his opinions on men and things.   It will be seen to whom he attributes the greater part of the misfortunes that befell France.

THE ORLEANISTS.

"They are the Jesuits of European aristocracy, to-day tricoloured Jesuits, as formerly they were white reaction-aries.   Their character winds about in politics in a wonderful way.   Men devoid of generous passions them-selves, but clever to take advantage of the passions of others, they are royalists or quacks according to times and places, at one time courtiers, at another Liberals ; they take advantage of every ambitious, vain, selfish in-terest ; they recoil at no excess, no villainy, provided they think it necessary to their plans ; they fear none of the consequences of unpopularity, which is one of their state maxims ; they are in league with different parties and interests as long as they conduce to make their coalition majority more compact.   Officials of what-ever kind are to them nothing but political agents, if they have talent or boldness, or mere tools if they are common men.   The Orleanists are leaders and soldiers by turns, at the same time centre and motive power. They appear to be only a scientific clique, a set of political professors ; they are really a machiavelian gang of despots ;

they form a presuming party, full of hatred and censure of every free social institution; a sect of persecutors and enemies of every noble impulse of the age; a faction recruited from the upper and middle classes of society, helped eagerly but foolishly by the timid, the credulous, the ignorant and the fanatical. This faction neither believes in its country nor in freedom, it refuses to credit any moral or intellectual movement in France, and only hopes to reign by the silence of the tomb.

" This party pretends that it has nullified the Revolution of July, 1830, and has effaced every trace of the Revolution of July, 1789; to them the glorious days that shattered a dynasty several centuries old is but an accident, a catastrophe; to them the work of 1789 is but a usurpation of power; this party, cobbling at the Charter it has granted, wishes the Restoration to go on in spite of the popular victory that put an end to it, and to make the Constitution of 1791 of no effect; this party only sees as the goal of its labours the disposal of a budget of sixty millions, and considers the heroes of 1789 and 1830 as merely poor taxable material. Public opinion must pronounce judgment on these quacks, who have usurped every power and destroyed every right. Public opinion will judge them one day, for the dogmas of all these wise professors of classic despotism are but a return to tyranny and privilege."

UNPOPULARITY.

" The *progress* of the Bourbon rule cannot be denied. M. Pasquier, one of Louis XVIII.'s ministers, when asked in the House that the government should be impartial, artlessly replied that partiality was a necessity to a good government. M. Guizot, one of Louis Philippe's ministers, declared in the Chamber of Deputies in 1831 hat the first condition of a good government should be unpopularity.

"How blind those in power become! To proclaim unpopularity as a principle in the most civilised country of Europe, and to maintain that brute force, the inevitable result of unpopularity, is a means of government! This false, ignominious system has borne fruit in producing mistrust and disaffection, in exasperating party warfare, in perpetuating quarrels, in clashing with every interest, and in paralysing the efforts of commerce and industry by riots provoked by an unprincipled secret police force."

ARTICLE 14 OF THE CHARTER.

"This was pure despotism put in a constitutional disguise. The despot has no need to disdain laws, to interpret and twist them; he could do without them altogether, and put in their place his own will, his caprices and his passions. But this threatened veto, this sword of Damocles hung by royalty over the Charter, was no less perilous for him who used it as fatal to the nation. So the weapon turned against Charles X. when he wished to use it against France, the nation that feared nothing so much as slavery. His example should have warned his successors, if experience was of any use in politics. But ambitious pettifoggers, tricked out as ministers, discovered simpler tactics. They get to the same point without using Article 14. They perform revolutionary acts in the legislature and throw the responsibility and odium of their measures on the Chambers. These political adventurers are always talking of law, and they care not a fig for it; the only law they know is success."

PEACE AT ANY PRICE.

" This is the peace of Perier, banker and minister, a nominal, barren, illusive and even ridiculous peace. A peace on paper, governed by stock-jobbers, with its rises and falls, dependent on diplomatic concessions. It is a letter of credit for a long period, not open to protestation, drawn on the good faith of absolute monarchies. This peace, good for an idiotic, blind, credulous nation, has created universal mistrust, and has stopped commerce all over Europe, whilst it embitters diplomatic intrigues. The banker's peace, in the midst of great powers whose populations spend their time in military manœuvres, is an armed peace, kept up by regiments, and, in order to pay them, huge taxes and loans are needed, entirely out of proportion to the wealth of the nation. Peace at any price is a permanent state of hostility and warlike threats of two-thirds of Europe against the other third. This peace, credited in neither town nor country, at Court or in barracks, with its armies drawn up as on the eve of a campaign, this is the result of the famous ministry of the 13th of March."

THE FRENCH IN 1833.

" They possess freedom on paper, but not in reality.

" They have no constitution, but two charters.

" They think they are free, but are only mutinous.

" They possess a paper army, an army that has to be paid, but none in reality fit for fighting.

" They allow fortresses to be built to over-awe Paris, and those on the frontiers to fall to ruin.

" They are the Don Quixotes of Europe, and are not the defenders of France.

"They have neither peace nor war, but they take fleets and besiege citadels without having enemies.

"They cry out against the vile, oppressive treaties of 1815, and yet act as police to the Holy Alliance.

"They have a population of 33,000,000, of which 140,000 have representatives.

"The people are proclaimed supreme, yet election is in the hands of the few.

"The electors are registered by the record of the tax-collector, and ministers get themselves made chief electors by intrigue.

"In their empty civilisation they preserve barbaric customs, like the duel, and savage laws, such as capital punishment.

"They openly reward the victors of the Bastille, while the victors of the Louvre pine in prison.

"Among them are to be found men like Richepanse, Decaen, and Daumesnil, who gain victories, refuse money, and die as poor as Plutarch's heroes. The first places in the state are held by men whose thefts and exactions have made the name of France abhorred abroad.

"They are proud of the two revolutions carried out by the working classes and the younger men, and those who have kept aloof from them then step in to reap the advantages. The heroes are in the tomb, the place-hunters in power, reaction and ruin still remain the lot of France."

A sight that leads to such bitter reflections cannot be but painful, and one hastens to escape from it. This is what Barère did in June, 1832; besides, the life of Paris was too expensive for his modest resources, and, in short, his love for his native land was still green in his heart.

Before starting he wrote this passage from Ugo Foscolo in his note-book :

"I return to thee, sainted land, who first heard my groans, on whom I have so often rested my weary limbs, where I lived in obscurity and in peace, and felt the only true pleasures I have ever had, and to whom in my grief I confided my plaints and groans."

When he arrived at Tarbes he continued thus :

"On my return from exile, Paris and its turbulence appeared unendurable. I had no other thought but of returning to my native land, that I had never forgotten for a moment, but that had entirely forgotten me. I hoped to see my paternal roof once more, from which I had been banished for forty-five years by public affairs and their concomitant misfortunes. Disenchanted with this huge Babylon, whither every Frenchman comes to try his fortune, I only wished to end my days at my own fireside, in the midst of my youthful memories and of my few friends, if death had spared them during my long enforced absence . . . . My native land only holds for me the affecting remembrance of those good, honest contemporaries. Seven times did they elect me unanimously and confidently a member of the local or National Assembly, an honourable but fatal gift that cost me so much unhappiness, exile and outlawry.

"Having returned in my old age and after all these misfortunes and persecutions, I have found inveterate, ignorant enemies in the intermediate generation. The young generation, with its deeper beliefs, greater generosity and fewer prejudices, alone welcomed me and honoured my grey hairs with its approval.

"As for my parents, their tombs alone are left, on which, though over eighty, I weep in remembering their goodness and virtue, waiting to join them in eternal sleep."

Then he was compelled to add these bitter complaints :

" My family, during my absence, has devoured my substance ; and on my return to my home after forty-five years of storm and stress among strangers, it only welcomed me with long, unjust lawsuits to make me a beggar by legal means.

" I was forced, in order to gain peace from my three terrible sisters and their descendants, even greedier and more pitiless, to give up and sell my paternal home and to defend myself from the extravagances of an ungrateful brother and his fictitious creditors that he launched on me.

"Providence supported me in a most wonderful way during all these vexatious proceedings.   What I have preserved of my little property in 1834 I owe to the wise, enlightened magistrates of Tarbes.   But those at Lourdes deprived me of part of my estates."

These few lines display a wound deeper than any other, a blow all the more cruel because Barère had deep family affections.   Let us not gaze at the painful scene.   How ought they to reproach themselves who filled with bitterness the last days of an old man whom they ought to have surrounded with every care and con-solation !

His fellow-citizens elected him a member of the De-partmental Council of the Upper Pyrenees.   He felt this honour deeply, and fulfilled his duties assiduously until the year preceding his death.

" Being eighty-five years old," he writes, "after having undergone every trouble of a laborious public life, every danger of a long exile, I find, in 1840, that I must re-sign those public duties to which my fellow-citizens elected me in 1834, when I returned from banishment. I thought there should be an interval of rest, meditation and prayer between this mortal life and the life eternal. This moral need, so imperious in life's evening, seems unknown to the present generation. Yet, in this short period of repose from the troubles of the world and the vanities of life, the old generation gains that strength of soul, clearness of mind and calmness of heart in which religious consolation and hope arise, the necessity of our declining years."

All the same, Barère was not indifferent to the fate of his country and the freedom of nations. His last thoughts were on the "Future of Europe." He had for some time been preparing notes for a work with this title, and his dying hand placed a few more sheets in the portfolio that contained them. Although Barère's position in the government and the usual bent of his studies made everything he wrote on European politics of great value, yet the limited space of this notice only allows us to quote the last few pages his pen traced, in which he expresses his ideas on the events of 1840. From the heated ideas and expressions, one might easily imagine they had been written during his most energetic days.

FUTURE OF EUROPE.

"[June, 1840.]—Two governments are perpetually torn with usurpation, war and traitorous diplomacy— England and Russia. They are always talking of peace and only think of war. Peaceful hypocrites, they send armies all over the world. When they meet on the banks of the Oxus, on the boundaries of British India, the two giants of the North and the West will fight out their duel to the death and let Europe breathe.

"The English government continues to occupy Passage, in Spain, a second Gibraltar; it keeps a consul at Algiers who refuses to recognise the French rule; it has penetrated into Afghanistan, and wishes to reach Cabul; it has seized Aden, in the Persian Gulf, whilst waiting to seize the Isthmus of Suez; it endeavours to counteract French influence in Mexico, La Plata and Monte Video; it covets Egypt and Syria.

"The Russian government, which always keeps its cyclopean eye fixed on Western Europe, stretches its iron arm over Caucasia, Circassia and Persia; it does not lose sight of the long-prepared armed occupation of Asia Minor, of the European provinces of Turkey and of Constantinople. Although it failed at Khiva in 1839, and has been repulsed from the Chinese frontier, the obstinate, ambitious Czar is preparing another expedition to seize Khiva and the banks of the Oxus, if he is not forestalled by an English army taking possession of the important places of that country.

"These two governments watch and measure each other, they talk of alliances and trick each other diplomatically, without interfering for a moment with their warlike preparations. France, who has no ambitious projects on hand, is fully taken up with her war against the Arabs in Algeria, with England's efforts to take Egypt and Russia's to take Asia Minor. England increases her navy, Russia her army, whilst Austria returns to its *status quo* after its invasion of Italy, and Prussia keeps up its system of peaceful neutrality by economy, only paying attention to German custom duties and religious schisms.

"The situation can be summed up thus: a universal hypocrisy of peace and a real hostile feeling, an inevitable collision between two turbulent, ambitious powers—England and Russia. The inhabitants of Europe will be reduced to the old proverb : *Quidquid delirant reges plectuntur Achivi.*

"[July, 1840.]—England wants a railway through Syria as a short cut to India. The English government will sacrifice the safety of the Ottoman Empire and the peace of Europe to this selfish interest. This naval power spares nothing, and would set all Europe, Asia and Africa alight to preserve India with its 100 millions, who only work for a merchant company.

"The first care of the English government has been to prevent any friendliness between Mehemet Ali and the young Sultan. It takes care to warn the Porte of Egyptian ambition in order to conceal its own ambition to take advantage of the revolt of Syria to get possession of it for its own connection with India, the only feeder of English power.

"Its second care has been to get Russia interested in her old plans of the seizure of the Bosphorus and Asia Minor. The cabinet of St. James' will introduce the Russian armies into Constantinople as the price of her indulgence as to Syria. The Russian envoy, M. de Bronow, formed this gigantic plot at London with the Foreign Office; the cabinets of Berlin and Vienna have given their adherence, being reduced to mere military and political vassalage.

"Its third care has been to keep French influence out of Turkey and Egypt. And yet it has been difficult to act in a hostile spirit, France being the political ally of England. Lord Palmerston, who sticks at nothing that concerns extension of commerce or territory, or injury to France, has undertaken to start the Anglo-Russian conspiracy.   By his agents and his gold, he has made Syria revolt under the pretence of excessive taxation in order to get the Pasha into difficulties and to have the pretext of sending Admiral Stopford with a squadron from Malta into Syrian waters to support the rebels.

"Thus the attack on the Ottoman Empire has been begun by the English government and the Czar.   This is the future of Europe.   This English expedition into revolted Syria is full of political treachery and military events.

"[16th of July, 1840.]—Four nations have risked their peace, their honour and their armies on the weak belief in the Syrian insurrection.   On this English plot four nations have risked and compromised the French alliance after ten years of useful work.

"The most important question of the day—that of the East—has only been further complicated by this in-solent treaty that attempts to isolate France in order to crush her.

"How were enlightened ministers able to exclude France from a diplomatic question which includes, and may compromise, the interests of all the nations round the Mediterranean?

"How could they call in Austria and Prussia to dis-cuss the questions of this sea of commerce, nations that have nothing to do with it?   The sole aim is a league of the northern powers, who have always been the enemies of French liberty and of the Revolution and the rupture of the Anglo-French alliance, who are the real preservers of peace.

"But France has already defended her territory glori-ously and successfully, single-handed.   France is always there.

"[16th of August, 1840.]—The English government is like a huge fish that churns the water with its tail to screen the direction of its path. In the same way the cabinet of St. James' foments disturbances in Europe, Asia and Africa to hide the real goal of its insatiable ambition, and of its treacherous interference in all questions of policy.

"The disturbing preparations of a general war are necessary to England, so that in the midst of the confusion it can seize the isthmus of Suez and threaten Egypt.

"It wants Russia to invade Turkey to allow it to seize Syria and the Euphrates, a quicker route to India.

"It must give up Constantinople to the Russians, who will thus possess the finest site in the world by the help of England.

"On the altar of the infernal deities England will break its alliance with France and ally herself with Russia. She needs the confusion of a European war to succeed in her private wars.

"She wants Russia to be occupied with her projects on the Dardanelles, so that she does not pass the banks of the Araxes in Persia.

"Europe must be overrun by a brutal soldiery, so that England may be secure in Northern India and render herself mistress of Cabul.

"In short, England, secure in her ocean home, will deliver the Continent and the Turkish Empire over to destruction to preserve India, her real strength.

"What ought to reveal the treacherous and formidable policy of England and Russia to the rest of Europe is the method of these two powers, identical in its movements and results. In 1793 England took advan-

tage of the fret and fury of a *continental war* to seize
the French and Dutch colonies. In the same manner
in 1840 Russia wishes to concern France and other
states in a *continental war* to seize the provinces of
Turkey and Constantinople. These tactics, that have
a hidden source and an assured subsidy, are developed
by a coalition of four powers against one. They seek
to weaken and ruin continental countries to make them
powerless to prevent invasion and usurpation.

"The only thing to save Europe is a moral and
military league against this fresh Holy Alliance of despots. If the peoples of Europe passively resist these
allied governments the war will end for lack of com-
batants. If they claim their rights unanimously and
courageously, this cry of freedom will startle their kings;
Poland will arise from her ashes like a phœnix, Hungary
will recover her liberty, Cracovia will no longer allow
tyrants to protect her, the middle states of Germany
will form a more homogeneous and powerful confeder-
ation, Prussia will no longer consent to be the tool of
the Czar, Italy will free its nations from the oppressive
Teutonic hordes, and Great Britain will no longer go
unpunished for its naval tyranny, its usurpation of India
and its commercial extension.

"[25th of August, 1840.]—The age of coalitions
has passed. These political crusades no longer have
fanaticism to fan them nor English loans to subsidise
them. The four powers are penniless, and Lord Palmerston either cannot, or will not, make himself the
paymaster-general of the continental war as William
Pitt did.

"[4th of November, 1840.]—France has preserved
the integrity and independence of the Ottoman Empire

single-handed. France has twice interposed between Turkey and Egypt to pacify them. Lord Ponsonby has gained the ear of the Porte, and by bribery and intimidation governs Turkey in the English way—*i.e.*, by making war for his own benefit, by making conquests in Syria for his own profit, and in keeping Russia at arm's length.

"France has nothing to gain or to conquer in Turkey. Her interest is in the maintenance of the balance of power in Europe and in the continuance of peace. France only desires to preserve and defend the high position her power and moderation have gained for her. If France were the peacemaker between Egypt and Turkey in 1833 and 1839, her conciliation was at any rate frank and disinterested; she upheld law and treaties in the Pasha's favour. No European power can point to such an intervention nor offer such guarantees.

"France has been deceived, forsaken and threatened by the English government, who have been in secret treaty against France with her eternal enemy Russia; and this monstrous treaty threatens the freedom of Europe if the English nation does not disavow and punish its ministers. As a matter of fact, whether Syria becomes the hereditary fief of Mehemet Ali Pasha, or returns to the Sultan as its suzerain, is not worth the armies that would be wasted, the millions that would be spent, and the dangers that would be encountered should the war become general.

"The problem stated thus would have received a pacific solution but for the ambition of the English government, but for their desire to seize Adana, Candia, and especially the way to India through Syria. The cabinet of St. James' alone wishes to profit by the war begun in Syria with Turkish soldiers and Austrian mercenaries, carefully excluding its new ally Russia from all participation in Syrian usurpation and from any intervention in Asia Minor.

"[1st of January, 1841.]—The English government has made itself the absolute master of the Eastern Question by its naval war in Syria and Egypt. It governs the Porte, stops Russia's schemes, and is preparing to seize the valley of the Euphrates, to make capital out of British India, closed to all Europe and to Central Asia.

"Since the treaty of Methuen, this government has colonised the kingdom of Portugal to its own profit, except during the ministry of Carvalho de Pombal, and has now prepared means to recapture all its political and naval ascendency over this section of the Peninsula. It offers her immense commercial advantages on the Douro and Tagus, rivers useless to Spain since they flow into the ocean where England reigns supreme. Until the Passage Port was occupied by the English, at the time of the civil war during Queen Christina's regency, their government sided with the fanatical party in Spain to gain from the new Cortes of 1841 those commercial advantages that they seek everywhere, and which are the chief reasons for their intervention. So the Peninsula, forgetting its natural ally, France, will be exploited for the commercial and political advantage of St. James'.

"The English ministers will always oppose Portugal becoming a Spanish power, notwithstanding the plans of the Regency of 1841 and the military ability of General Espartero. Although France has every reason to back up Spain in this, yet she will not take the initiative against England, for that would leave the field open for Russia's advance in the East. France, not having a government able to follow a continuously firm line of conduct, will see her influence vanish in the Peninsula.

"The English cabinet, accustomed to their diplomatic supremacy, will decide the fate of Portugal as it has that of Egypt.

"[6th of January, 1841.]—The 15th of July, 1840, has borne fruit. England alone has benefited by it. She has gained the exclusive right of using the Syrian road to the Euphrates, so that she alone can reach India by this short cut.

"The cause of such great disturbances and the reason of the successive obstacles to the cessation of the dispute between the Sultan and the Khedive has been divulged. The English government quarrelled with Mehemet Ali because he firmly refused to allow a fortified road to be established between the Mediterranean and the Red Sea, to be used only by the English. *Inde mali labes!* The Khedive's refusal was really the cause of the war carried on with Turkish and Austrian soldiers by Commodore Napier, under orders from Admiral Stopford.

"England having gained her point, Lord Palmerston had made the three northern powers adopt a course that established the naval omnipotence of Great Britain. This opened men's eyes to the Czar's policy, imprudent through over-ambition. So the 15th of July, 1840, is called in all European states, the day of dupes.

"Peace has been concluded by the four powers between the Sultan and the Khedive. The isolation of France deprived him of all influence. She no longer afforded him her dangerous protection, and the Viceroy had the good sense to keep the hereditary succession of Egypt in preference to the perilous possession of Syria, in revolt against Ibrahim Pasha and secretly supported by the English government.

"Two letters of Admiral Stopford, dated the 2nd and 6th of December, 1840, to Mehemet Ali, proclaim the conditions on which the hereditary possession of Egypt will be assigned to him : they are the restitution of the Turkish fleet to the Sultan and the evacuation of Syria by the army of Ibrahim Pasha. These letters only grant three days' delay to Mehemet Ali, who hastened to send his submission to the Sultan on the conditions imposed by the four European powers. The ministry of the 1st of March had unwisely advised the Khedive to resist, and then retired from the discussion.

"So everything is suddenly changed in continental politics, under the insults of the English government. A telegram from M. de Nesselrode to M. de Pahlen, the Russian ambassador in Paris, was officially communicated to M. Guizot, the foreign minister, at the end of December, 1840. It is full of consideration for France. Czar Nicholas is no longer under any illusions as to the English alliance, so illusory and so treacherous. The conclusion of a Franco-Russian alliance, dreamt of by Paul I. and momentarily carried out by Alexander at Tilsit, would change the face of politics. The Continent, too often the tool of English ambition, would be preserved from playing that miserable part by the two continental powers, France and Russia."

Barère penned these lines a week before his death. We notice that, contrary to his custom (was it a presentiment?), he dated each of his writings during his last months.

For some time his family worries, and the loss of a

person who had faithfully accompanied him in his exile and who continued to look after him, had undermined his health. However, his appetite for work was seemingly returning when, on the 7th of January, 1841, a stoppage in his bronchial tubes accompanied by slight feverish symptoms obliged him to keep his bed. As he had similar attacks every year about this time, his condition at first gave rise to no anxiety. As the attack did not abate, and as his strength was ebbing, they proposed to call in a doctor. "Why ever should you go to a doctor?" he said. "I am an old machine; your cares are sufficient. As for the rest, I leave it to Providence!"

That was on the 12th of January. His people insisted. Then he told them to bring a sheet of paper, saying his loss of voice would prevent the doctor hearing him, and then, sitting up in bed, he wrote a very explicit explanation of his bronchial troubles, especially the pain in his throat. That was the last thing he wrote.

He passed a good night, and on the morning of the 13th he wished to put on clean linen to receive the doctor; but while they were getting it ready he had a sudden seizure that hardly lasted ten minutes. That was all his agony.

Two days later the inhabitants of Tarbes accompanied the mortal remains of their famous fellow-townsman to their last resting-place. M. Lebrun, the senior member of the bar, who had been the old man's counsel in his painful cases, spoke these touching words at his grave:

"Here, where every untrue word of praise would be a sacrilege, I can emphatically bear witness that never was disinterestedness purer, never was family feeling more affectionate, the love of arts more passionate, or the principles of sociability more honourable.

"It was a great consolation for the old man to be elected a member of the General Council of his department.

"It was also a great surprise for his fellow-citizens to see this old man, after his long and terrible hardships, preserve a noble, calm mind, a perfect benevolence, a clearness of mind and a freshness of imagination that youth might have envied; ceaselessly working to throw light on history, presenting it with priceless documents and important revelations. The pen only fell from his grasp at his last breath, at the age of eighty-five.

"Weak men that we are, let us be just and merciful at the edge of the grave.

"Citizens and Frenchmen, let us be grateful to those of our countrymen who broke our fetters, preserved our independence and founded our freedom at the price of their peace, their life, their fame!

"Old man, to-day, face to face with eternity, your country hails you, posterity listens to you!"

Barère was one of the last representatives of the generation that began the work of the Revolution. The longevity of many famous men of this time is a remarkable fact, and it is common to every political party. When the *emigrés* returned to France in 1814, they appeared like the shadows of a scarcely-remembered past; and when from day to day we read in the papers of the death of some member of our great assemblies, we ask ourselves in astonishment how any can still be left. Toil and suffering swept off all those of but ordinary strength very early, and perhaps there existed in both camps that strength of conviction that seems to make us tenacious of life.

That strength of conviction we cannot justly deny Barère possessed, in spite of the inconsistency and weakness of his character. We have tried to hide neither the one nor the other, but what hides them in our eyes is his invariable attachment to the national cause. The man who wrote the fine passage on the "Marseillaise" that will be found in his Memoirs, could not have been a faithless creature. Without any schismatic ideas, that were the cause of so many divisions among the republicans, and still cause confusion in their history, we have seen him fight every faction that was desirous of supremacy, for he was a sincere partisan of parliamentary government in every sense of the word—that is to say, government by the assembly of the representatives of the country. We have seen him oppose every approach to a dictatorship, even when draped *à la républicaine*. He deserves to be placed among those men who, in all the clash of passions, errors and interests, knew how to distinguish and serve the cause of their country.

Whatever the pretentions of those who claim the privilege of moderation for themselves alone, there are in every party moderate men and violent men. Barère incontestably belongs to the former class. Some of his phrases have unfortunately become famous ; the worst of them have been ascribed to him falsely, a fact we can prove ; others are simply terrorist gasconades, if we may be allowed the expression, the outcome of his head rather than of his heart, and these words are much fewer in Barère's life than his deed of humanity and personal service.

These same southern habits are still more clearly shown by the way he always puts himself in the front rank. He cannot help adopting a theatrical pose even when no one is looking, or help declaiming when no one is listening.

But, on the other hand, the southern sun often colours his thoughts; his pen describes startlingly bold and grand pictures;. there are few orators who have left behind them, in the minds of their contemporaries, a greater number of those sententious phrases which seem to live in our severely circumspect tongue.

We have stated that although Barère was fully imbued with the philosophy of the eighteenth century, he was no sceptic, that at a time when religion was so mocked, he had resisted the torrent, although such a slave to opinion and example, so ready to sacrifice everything to a smart saying. In his familiar confessions he shows his religion continually. It is a side of his character we must not forget; it contrasts with many weaknesses we have to reproach him with.

Barère was not a man of thoughts but of deeds. Every thought was at once put on paper. Hence a number of formless sketches, so many unripe plans. Politics, legislation, administration, history, religions, morals, literary criticism, fine arts, fiction and poetry, he tried all of them. But what deserves chief attention among his literary inheritance is a series of at least forty volumes in MSS. in which he wrote down his observations, his recollections and the result of his reading every day. "Senilia" is the title he gave to the last volumes of this precious library.

Barère co-operated in all the great acts of the Constituent Assembly and the Convention; in the Committee of Public Safety he worked hard to keep up the national spirit by his reports on foreign policy, and by his military reports to spread that electric enthusiasm that doubled the strength of our soldiers.

These facts will remain written in the life of Barère

and connected with his name; they mark his place in history.

In the composition of this notice, supported by autograph quotations, we think we have fully explained Barère's attitude and feelings in the most difficult circumstances of his public career. We have not sought to set him up like a Plutarchian hero, but to explain the mistakes he is accused of by human weaknesses that do not arise from a bad nature.

There were for ourselves two rocks to avoid : Barère being one of the men of the Revolution who displayed the least strength of character, was one of those with whom Carnot had least affinity; we had then to keep ourselves free from traditional prejudices. Barère has been the object of libels whose vileness was revealed more and more to us ; in letting our indignation have free scope, we might have been led into an *apologia*.

If, in spite of these rocks, we have succeeded in being truthful—which is all our ambition—honest readers will certainly reconsider some of their unfavourable opinions of Barère, and we can then congratulate ourselves on having fulfilled a labour of justice and rehabilitation. We shall also have done our duty in opposing systems or errors, by the help of which men have wished to decry the generation of the Revolution.

MEMOIRS

OF

BERTRAND BARÈRE

PRELIMINARY CHAPTER

I was born in the Pyrenees, that is to say, in the country of freedom, for the love of independence is the chief characteristic of these brave mountaineers, the descendants of the Gauls and Romans, living far from the corruption and slavery of capitals and large towns.

In my childhood I was brought up under the auspices of a *lettre de cachet*, by which my father had been proscribed for standing up for the privileges of the people in the Assembly of the States of Bigorre about the year 1762, under the reign of Louis the Well-Beloved (XV. of that name) and under the ministry of Saint-Florentin the Well-Hated.

My father, Jean Barère, having been appointed first consul of the town of Tarbes, was *ipso 'facto* the chairman or speaker of the Third Estate; this was the municipal privilege of the town of Tarbes in the States of Bigorre. He wished to carry out his duty and examine the state of the finances of the province; he knew the accounts of the treasurer were worthless,

he traced the abuses to their source, and he clearly
showed that the deficit in the budget of the province
was entirely due to the numberless privileges of the
nobles and their arbitrary exemption from taxation.
This made a great change in the expenditure and
put an end to the abuses the nobles practised in
reference to the taxes, the local rates and the finances
generally. This reform caused great complaints among
them, and they petitioned the royal governor of
the province, who obtained from the minister Saint-
Florentin a *lettre de cachet*, which prevented my father
from taking any part in the government of the town
or occupying any municipal office, so he could not
be re-elected to the States of Bigorre. Thus all
ages are alike; to-day in France the same injustice
prevails.

My master at school being much struck with my
work, he urged my father to let me go in for a literary
and historical competition, so that my thesis might
be dedicated to a Count of Gontault-Biron, whose
only distinction was the name of his ancestors, and
who was delighted to see his name and titles printed
on a Latin thesis.

I was sent to the famous legal university of Toulouse at the age of fifteen. I had to get a special
permit to matriculate, as their regulations made six-
teen the minimum age.

1772.—I came to the old capital of the Tectosages
at the moment when a despotic minister, the Chancellor Maupeou, had just destroyed the last traces of
public liberty, the *right of remonstrance* and the *right of
registering the laws of taxation*, rights that chance more
than the desire of the nation had handed over to the

parliaments, since the Bourbon Louis XIII. had, during the ministry of Cardinal de Richelieu, suspended the sittings of the States-General. Toulouse was in mourning for its celebrated parliament; everybody talked of nothing but the weakness of Louis XV., the despotism of the Chancellor, and the base eloquence of his private secretary, M. Lebrun, to whom was attributed Maupeou's famous phrase to the parliaments he was destroying: "You have nothing to do but to render justice; there your duties end."

[This is the M. Lebrun, a native of Dourdan, who, after having been Chancellor Maupeou's secretary in 1771, was elected a member of the Commons at the States-General in 1789. The remembrance of his share in the despotic dealings of Maupeou with the parliaments made his patriotism and liberal principles suspected in the Assembly. He never spoke on political subjects but only as reporter of commerce and finance. His style was clear, precise, and even ornate, as much as money matters could be so. He was the administrator of the department of Seine-et-Oise after the 10th of August, 1792; he was a member of the Council of Ancients in 1797 and 1798; he made the report in favour of the Hostage Bill and the Forced Loan that caused the downfall of the Directory. A zealous agent of the 18th Brumaire, he profited by it and was appointed the third consul under the auspices of Bonaparte, its leader. Afterwards he was made a Prince of the Empire, Duke of Plaisance, Viceroy at Genoa and Amsterdam. He was driven from the latter place in 1812, accompanied by shouts of "Long live the Prince of Orange"; and he was forced,

although a prince and a Bonapartist, to utter the
same cries. After the first abdication he passed
over to Louis XVIII., who created him a peer; and
after the second abdication, he still remains one. He
is one of those men useful to every government and
every king.][1]

In the midst of this universal hatred of a despotic
government and admiration for courageous magistrates,
who are the defenders of the rights of the people, I
passed my first three years at Toulouse, studying
Roman law, French decrees and laws, under the most
celebrated professors. At the same time, I attended
the sittings of the parliaments, where I heard the
speeches of Taverne, Gary, Monier, Duroux, and
other justly famous lawyers, with delight.

I had always loved the noble profession of the
law; the works of D'Aguesseau and Cochin had inclined me at an early age to adopt the courageous
profession of defending the weak from the strong, the
poor from the powerful. Even in my school days the
reading of Cicero and Demosthenes had kindled my
ardour, but when I read the speeches and the memoirs
of Loiseau de Mauléon and Elie de Beaumont, when I
heard of the eloquence of men like Gerbier and Target,
my mind was transported, and my only aspiration was
one day to be able to approach them in the defence
of some distinguished man or innocent defendant.

Political events followed one another quickly at
this corrupt Court; and one intrigue, in a short time,

---

[1] Added after the first edition of the Memoirs. These square
brackets will mark these additions for the future.

destroyed what another had effected. M. de Maurepas, a minister worthy of the French because he dealt lightly with serious matters, had just been recalled after the death of Louis XV. That King's youthful successor and his courtiers wished to soothe public opinion, whose awful effects they had seen at the secret burial of Louis XV. The first thing that the new ministry had to do was to recreate the parliaments and to re-establish all their rights and prerogatives, which were regarded as an obstacle to the despotism of ministers and the arbitrary increase of taxation.

It was at this period that M. Hue de Miromesnil, appointed Keeper of the Seals by M. de Maurepas, obtained a deserved fame by his justice and wisdom in this little legal revolution.

Everyone in France knows, and Linguet was not afraid of proclaiming it, that M. Hue de Miromesnil was appointed Keeper of the Seals by the Prime Minister for having acted the part of Crispin exceedingly well at his private theatre when he was in exile; and M. de Maurepas rewarded him thus when he returned to favour at the beginning of the reign of Louis XVI.

1775.—The rejoicings over the re-establishment of the parliaments were very brilliant at Toulouse, where the people, fired by their southern temperament, were much attached to their old institutions. The parliament brought life and lustre to the town and made the young men who were working for the magistracy, the bar and oratory, strive eagerly for supremacy.

On the 8th of July, 1775, in the midst of these rejoicings, I took the oath on being called to the bar. All the students of that day acquired, by a sacred tradition, a hatred for tyranny and a feeling that it was necessary by every means to put a stop to the arbitrary acts and excesses of ministers.

I worked at the bar of the Parliament of Toulouse with all the more perseverance because I feared to be obliged by my family to take up a magistracy in the seneschal's court of Bigorre, that my father had bought for me while I was still at the university. I had a natural aversion to a judgeship, in which so many men take a pride and delight. I preferred the lengthy, laborious work of a lawyer, because he is free, noble, courageous, and can attack tyranny and injustice.

To avoid being recalled to Tarbes as counsellor to the seneschal's court, I hurried on my studies and I hastened to work up a few small cases. After these first attempts, a precious opportunity arose of defending on appeal a young woman named Ribes, who had been accused of infanticide, and already sentenced to death by the seneschal of Limoux in Languedoc, according to the pitiless statute of Henry II., passed in an age of fanaticism and hypocrisy.

A copy of the proceedings is brought to me. I have to draw up a printed digest, to pay for the printing and all the necessary preliminary expenses. All this appeared easy at a time when the love of humanity is a passion, and the defence of the accused an honour and an enthusiasm.

Whilst reading through the proceedings against the young woman, in the midst of the agitation of public indignation, in a small town where fanaticism was mixed with the indignation such a crime should excite, I perceived that the judges of Limoux had paid no attention to the report of the surgeon who had been called to prove this pretended crime of infanticide.

M. Durègne, counsellor of La Journelle was the judge; he was severe, and did not wish any defence printed. I spoke to him with great entreaty, I told him it was *my first case*, and that considerations of humanity demanded a thorough sifting of the evidence, because the prisoner was innocent.

"If you are convinced of that," said he, "write your report and I will receive it; I give you a week."

I drop all my regular work and I hasten with the report to M. Villars, the famous professor of anatomy and surgery, with whom I had already had some business. After having read it he said, "This woman is saved, she is innocent; her child never breathed, he was still-born. The judge had no power to sentence her for infanticide."

The surgeon who had drawn up the report declared that having cut off a part of the lung and flung it in a basin of water, it sank at once and remained at the bottom. Thus the lung had never had breath in it.

This was a ray of light to me. I begged M. Villars to expand the facts and results of his observations in a medico-legal document that I added to the report which I had printed as quickly as possible.

The report and the medical opinion appeared publicly and were thought so much of by the bar that the parliament a few days after (1788) quashed the verdict against the poor girl and restored her to liberty.

I saw her on coming out of prison rushing to thank

me. "You should thank your judges," said I, "for the delay which allowed your defence to be printed." Never in my life had I such a true, pure pleasure. "What a splendid return are the thanks of a poor or unfortunate person!" the Abbé Arnaud used to say.

The deed is done; I am a lawyer for life. I am now one of the knights of the long robe, who fight in their own way. "*Militant quoque causarum patroni,*" said the Roman laws.

Having enlisted in this Ciceronian militia, I hasten to inform the author of my being of my first success. I had often heard him boast complacently of the talents of the celebrated lawyers of the parliament of Toulouse. My father replied by sending me, as a reward for my first legal success, a hundred louis with which to buy a small library. Alas! my father little thought that, by thus feeding my appetite for books, he was giving me a taste for legislation, public law and literature, which would result in my entering that wretched career of politics in which only slaves, intriguers and rascals succeed, and in which everything is against talents, patriotism and honesty.

I spent my happy youth in studying law and in cultivating literature. I gave up a part of my leisure to music and politics; one served as the relaxation from the other.

The Academy of the Floral Games proposed as the subject of a prize for oratory the Eulogy of Louis XII. —"the only king whose memory the people praise," as Mercier of the Institute said. I had always thought his reign the finest in chivalry, military and literary fame, in the midst of the gloom that enshrouded

France. Especially did I think his administration and public economy praiseworthy in an age when that science, which has created so many modern quacks, did not exist. It is true that if *the friendship of a great man is a present of the gods*, Louis XII. can flatter himself with having been so favoured, having had as his friend and chief minister the famous and beneficent Cardinal, George d'Amboise.

On re-reading the history of France, my mind is again kindled by this monarch's glory, and I start composing a eulogium to compete in the Floral Games. The Academy regards my work favourably, prints it in its transactions, but does not award the prize. However, that was my first step on an academic career, because I loved the fine reign, unequalled in our annals, of Louis XII., that generous prince who, after he had been shut up for three years in an iron cage at Tours during the reign of Charles VIII., spoke, on mounting the throne, to his brutal, vindictive courtiers those words, too often forgotten by later kings of France: "The King of France does not avenge the quarrels of the Duke of Orleans"; of that King who, when he had taken Genoa by assault, spared the con-quered, and entered the town after pardoning all the inhabitants. He used to carry a shield on which was a king surrounded by bees, and this motto: "*Non aculeo utitur rex.*" How petty and mean our kings appear who will neither learn nor forget, to whom pardon and forgiveness are impossibilities.

Shortly after the Academy of Toulouse had caused men of letters to remember Louis XII., the Academy of Letters of Montauban proposed the Eulogy of George d'Amboise.

I read over the history of Louis XII. afresh, and
wrote a eulogy of George d'Amboise, his friend, as
Sully was to Henry IV. My work obtained the prize
at the Academy of Montauban, which I had gained
the year before with a eulogy on Pompignan. The
famous works of Thomas, the member of the French
Academy, had stimulated my natural ambition for the
great men who had worked for the happiness and
liberty of nations.

However, I did not neglect my legal studies.
Though I was occupied while the courts were open
in making abstracts and holding consultations, I worked
up the difficult art of pleading, in which one is especially liable to defeat, because one fights alone, and
one's adversaries are talented, strong and solemn, which
handicaps one who is not accustomed to the imposing
appearance of a court with its large, well-informed
audience, accustomed to listen to celebrated judges
and lawyers.

The first chance I had was in a suit for annulling
a marriage on account of difference of religion. I
held a brief for the wife, and I had in my favour
all the maxims of the Evangelical religion, which
affirm the sanctity of the conjugal bond, in spite of
the difference of belief of the parties.

The influential clergy interfered, and I never made
my speech ; and the senior judge, who had promised to
hear my maiden speech, succeeded in persuading me
to take up another case, as this one might awaken
disputes between the Catholics and Protestants which
had only been too violent in Languedoc.

I awaited another chance, and I hoped that it
would arouse the interest of the public, or present

knotty points of law. One might say that women gave me fine opportunities for starting at the bar.

The daughter of a merchant of Beaucaire, of the name of Noailles, had been seduced and abducted by a Knight of Malta called Desroys. This man had led his victim into the county of Venaissin, and there, protected by the government of the Pope, he had married the young person he had carried off without the consent of her parents.

After a married life of some years, Desroys breaks his marriage vows in order to become the heir of his uncle, a Knight Commander of Malta, who would only leave him his wealth on condition that his marriage with this mere merchant's daughter was annulled.

The case had been judged by an official of the diocese, and an appeal had been made to the Parliament of Toulouse. The young, lovely, unhappy woman comes to me to defend her and get her marriage confirmed, telling me she would die of grief if she lost her dear Desroys.

What a fine occasion for a young lawyer — the defence of innocence and beauty seduced and betrayed! What rare opportunities for eloquence would be presented by a loving correspondence of several years preceding this marriage, brought about by love, but sundered by interest! I undertook to prove its validity and pursue the unworthy ravisher legally, if the judges declared him not her lawful spouse. This recreant knight, who cast off his wife after several years of married life under the empty pretext of inequality of rank, had had the further immorality to make her father intervene and demand the annulment of the marriage on account of the omission of paternal consent

rigorously exacted by law.   Thus was paternal authority
called in to violate the law of honour, to quash a con-
tract made before the altar, and to sacrifice the daughter
of a plebeian to the pride of Commander Desroys, who
could not allow such a *mésalliance* in his family, which
was more distinguished for its pedigree than its honesty.

M. Desroys came to Toulouse to rouse all the
neighbouring nobility in his behalf.   As he was a
nephew of M. de Bonfontan, he could stir up all the
sons of the municipal officers, judges, and old nobility
with the bend sinister in their arms.   It was a case
of the nobility against the people, of the prejudices
of pride against the useful professions.   I felt what
a powerful adversary I had, since I had to plead before
a court of peers of ancient or recent creation.   I went
on the line of invoking their honour, that idol of the
French peerage.

When I showed the two Houses the love-letters of
Desroys, much after the style of Héloïse and Abélard,
when I pointed out that the knight, in order the better
to express his passion and seduce the imagination
and heart of Mademoiselle Noailles, had opened a vein
and signed the promise of marriage in his blood : " Is
this," cried I, " the blood of that French nobility that
said in the reign of Francis I., ' All is lost save
honour ' ?   Is this the blood of those gallant knights
who fought for God, the King, and beauty ?   Is this,
in fine, the blood of those knights of Malta, so much
prized by the Desroys, in which these letters of seduction are written, these promises of a lawful union,
this language of an honourable husband ? "

I remember but dimly this piece of my speech,
but I well recollect the great effect it made, and that

the nobles on the bench trembled with indignation against Desroys, and blamed his conduct aloud. It was usual for the Upper and Lower Houses to unite to hear cases dealing with nobles. The Archbishop of Toulouse, M. de Brienne, who was an honorary member of the Parliament, wished to be present at the hearing, which had been discussed on all sides before being brought before Parliament. After my speech, the Archbishop invited me to his house and welcomed me most warmly, promising to grant me any favour in his power, either in Languedoc or at Paris.

I published a pamphlet containing the whole correspondence. The edition was soon bought up, especially by women, who were much interested in the case.

After several adjournments the case was judged according to the severe laws which preserve the paternal power. Consequently the marriage of Mademoiselle Noailles was annulled, but Desroys was condemned to pay her £1,200 damages, as well as all her costs, or be imprisoned in default. Lastly, the two chambers ordered Desroys to be prosecuted for the abduction and seduction.

This success greatly encouraged me, and a short time after I appealed in the high court against a papal bull, which had united a rich abbey of Vivarais to the episcopal revenue of Puy-en-Velay. I always worked for the oppressed against the powerful; my adversary was M. de Pompignan, the Bishop of Puy, against whom Voltaire had hurled so many diatribes and witticisms, but who, from his rare virtues, was a credit to the episcopal bench. He was wrong in wishing to unite riches with bishoprics, and in wanting

to dispossess the Benedictines who had enriched by
their work that part of Vivarais in which stood the
abbey whose existence I was defending.

A special pleader of the Parliament of Toulouse,
a nephew of the bishop, supported the ambitious piety
of his uncle by his credit and influence. In spite of
these advantages I gained my case ; the abbey of
Vivarais was not united to the bishopric of Puy.
A strange coincidence ! At the very moment that
I was speaking in the Parliament against M. de
Pompignan I was a competitor at the Academy of
Letters of Montauban for the " Eulogy of Lefranc
de Pompignan, author of ' Dido ' and ' Sacred Poetry.' "
I was rewarded with the prize by the honourable fellow-
countrymen of Pompignan, who were more particular on
the manner of appreciating and praising him than any
other town or academy in France.

After having gained these three prizes, at the age
of twenty-five I was received as a member of the
Academy of Montauban, which gave me great pleasure. I went on with my legal work in the usual
way ; I was engaged in several cases, I published
extracts of several others, and the *Journal des Causes
Célèbres*, then edited by M. Desessarts, very often
reported my speeches and abstracts.

About 1782, having made a trip to Bagnères, in
the Pyrenees, I made an excursion through the valley
of Campan, mentioned by every traveller and naturalist,
among others by Dietrich, Picot de la Peyrouse,
Ramond, and the Abbé Palassan. I went up as far as
Sainte-Marie ; I admired the slopes of the mountains,
wooded on the summit, and covered with grass lower
down, dotted with little farmhouses like Swiss chalets,

rich in flocks, and drained by a thousand clear streams cooled by the neighbouring glaciers of the Pic-du-Midi, one of the highest spots in the mountains. I then paid a visit to a well-known grotto, where several famous travellers have cut their names.

On my return to Campan, the chief town in the valley, I found Roman remains among the stones of the fountain in the centre of the chief square. A solicitor, M. Soucaze, took me to his house and showed me a small but splendid collection of Roman antiquities, excellently well preserved. That gave me a taste for such things, of which the country was full. I discovered several at the Campan gate of Bagnères in the walls of houses, where builders, who care little for antiquities, have built them in just as any other building stone.

By dint of hunting I succeeded in gaining possession of a Roman antiquity at the castle of Baudéan, which was all the more remarkable because several historians assure us that Cæsar never visited the mountains of Bigorre, and the independent people of these beautiful valleys never had the honour of a visit from this great leader, who conquered the Gauls and the Britons and destroyed Roman liberty.

This remain was a long stone of hard granite cut like a Roman votive altar. On the right side there was a well-sculptured sword; on the left side there was a cup—the symbol of sacrifice. On the front one could read these words, arranged as follow in large Roman capitals:

MONTIBUS
DICAVIT
CÆSAR.

Astonished at my find, I made a short description to show the place where I had found it, almost the highest spot in the Pyrenees. Baudéan is a fairly large village, situated at the foot of the Pic-du-Midi, which appears the highest point of the Pyrenees, although this honour in reality belongs to Mont-Perdu. I hunted up every author who had written on Cæsar's invasions ; some averred Cæsar had conquered all Gaul ; others asserted that he had never marched as far as the Western Pyrenees, having merely sent his generals there. I read my little paper before the Academy of Sciences, Inscriptions and Belles-Lettres of Toulouse, of which I was a member, although very young ; and this was followed by my offering this votive tablet of Cæsar to this learned society. I had it carried to Toulouse, and it was placed in a prominent position in the museum. Since the Revolution this tablet was taken with several other ancient monuments and scientific curiosities to the public museum established in the Convent des Petits-Augustins.

I hope the modest inhabitants of Paris, who esteem only the savants of their city and its suburbs, and who think there is but one academy in the world, the one on the banks of the Seine, will pardon me for having been a member of several learned societies in my early youth. They will be indulgent to this part of my Memoirs, thinking these are only little *provincial* societies and schoolboy successes.

The bar was however my only goal; literature and science were but recreations. I had fresh opportunities of defending the oppressed and innocent, and they gave me the idea of a society that is conspicuous by its absence at our chief law courts, where the lives, property and honour of citizens are judged.

In my thoughts this society should be to defend, in the different courts, the suits of the poor, the oppressed and the innocent, of the widow and the orphan. Certain noble, generous barristers, whose zeal I knew, did not refuse these unpaid briefs, but it depended too much on chance and circumstance, was almost unknown, and did not affect public opinion or justice.

I drew up a scheme and the rules of a charitable society, to be composed of twenty-five old barristers, chosen from the most famous writers and pleaders, and of thirty young barristers of over six years' standing. This set of lawyers of every age and rank in their calling was to meet once a month to share the cases and consultations among the fifty-five members and to hear the results of the cases undertaken on behalf of the poor and unfortunate.

To the honour of the lawyers of Toulouse, my plan of a charitable society was adopted unanimously, and the association was formed on the spot. The inhabitants of Toulouse applauded the institution and the choice of members. It did much good from the very moment it was formed. From the fastnesses of Gévaudan and the Cevennes came unfortunate peasants, who up till then had not been able to obtain their rights from their relations or oppressors because they were not rich enough to obtain justice at Toulouse, 300 miles from their homes. Among the thirty young barristers I especially remember the active zeal and generosity of a lawyer named M. Gex in this charitable work. Humanity also owes much gratitude to the memory of the old barristers who seconded the ends

of the society so well, and who often subscribed to
have abstracts printed by the poor litigants. I men-
tion here, gratefully, the names of D'Alberet, Sudre,
Ricard, Delort, Lapomarède, Lacroix, Marcard,
Viguier, Taverne, Melpel, Jamme, Gary, Duroux,
Poitevin, Veirieu, Gex and Faure.

Among the cases given me by the society, I had
the happiness to obtain the restitution of his goods
to a descendant of the persecuted Protestants who had
been ruined by the philanthropic religious laws of
Louis XIV. and his confessor, the Jesuit Letellier.

This unfortunate man, who had six children, and
was descended from a rich landed family, had been
obliged to become a tenant farmer, not being able to
even buy his farm. He lived in the Vivarais. His
Roman Catholic relatives were in possession of his goods,
because, during the Camisard War, his grandfather
had taken up arms in defence of his religious opinions,
and had been obliged to take to the woods, where he
had died, and his property had been confiscated by
the law of Louis the Great. This indigent father of
six had been sent to us by a lawyer of the Vivarais,
who had heard of the free pleading founded by the
lawyers of Toulouse. With tears in his eyes, he
showed me the ancient warrants depriving him of
his property and giving it to his Roman Catholic
relatives.

I got two abstracts printed and the results of a
consultation signed by the twelve most famous lawyers
of Toulouse. My efforts were soon crowned with
complete success, and my client, still clothed in rags,
was recognised the rightful owner of £1,600 a year.
We had to give him the money to get the warrant

executed, to get clothes, and to travel to the Vivarais. This case, with an extract from the papers, has been printed in the collection of cases published by M. Desessarts.

I divided my time between the academy and the bar. I had a valuable friend of ripe learning and warm sympathy, who was following the same career as I had chosen. His name was Taverne, and he was the son of a famous lawyer, and was already famous himself. He showed me the way in the higher paths of law. Every evening we made extracts from Tacitus and Montesquieu, from Beccaria and Machia-velli, from Gravina and Bacon. I gave up half my week to the study of politics.

I was far from foreseeing that this thorny and perilous path would one day be my one passion. I was still further from seeing that this science of politics would one day be the ruin of my fortune and the unhappiness of my life. Already my new study was mingling in my mind with a love of my country.

One day I found the prospectus of the Academy of Bordeaux: it offered a prize for a eulogy on Mon-tesquieu. The studies I had pursued in the "Esprit des Lois" since my call to the bar, the deep admira-tion I had for the author of the "Grandeur et Dé-cadence des Romains," the witty criticism of the "Lettres Persanes," all this persuaded me to compete for the prize. I could not at that moment (1787) appreciate all the excellence of the "Dialogue between Sulla and Eucrates," because I had only seen tyrants and dictators in the pages of my Ancient History. One must have passed through the horrible experience of the successive tyrannies of Liberty, Glory, Heredity, and Divine Right to be enabled to hate heartily both tyrants and tyranny. So in composing my Eulogy of Montesquieu I sketched but feebly all that belonged to what I had neither seen nor experienced. This eulogy, which was sent to the competition of the Academy of Bordeaux in 1787, can be read in the collected edition of my works, printed in Paris in 1806 and published by Crapelet in octavo.

Just about the time I sent my eulogy to Bordeaux, there was a vacancy in the Academy of Floral Games of Toulouse, to which I had often sent competitions for prizes. I had competed in the Eulogy of Louis XII., surnamed the Father of his People, and also on the question " Whether navigation had been more useful or hurtful to the human race."

The vacancy was caused by the death of a gentleman of the household of the Count de Provence (afterwards Louis XVIII.), to whom he had acted as reader. The Academy of the Floral Games gave me the vacant seat.   In its relations with me, the Academy has followed the lead of the Revolution : while I was in exile in 1795, it struck me off its rolls; when I was at liberty again in 1800, it put my name anew in its list of members, but it did not print my name in the collection of Floral Games by the side of the nobles who had competed.

I set off for Paris a few days after my reception, and from that moment my career became as unhappy as my youth had been happy in legal and literary successes and of all kinds of prosperity.

A lawsuit in which my father had been engaged for years before the Privy Council as to his feudal rights was about to come on for trial. My father sent me to look after it, although he knew well, since my studies at Toulouse, how unjust I thought these feudal rights, which had weighed for 900 years on the tillers of the earth in order to keep petty squires and tyrants, the hereditary descendants of military anarchy. I paid little attention to the suit during my stay in Paris; it was decided by the report of a former State councillor, whose secretary, a M. Lecoq, was a witty man. I soon got the suit off my hands by a kind of judicial transaction between the inhabitants of Vieuzac and my father. The hearing before the Privy Council, which cost me much money and worry, made me hate feudal dues even more than I had before.

I lost my father soon after, and thenceforward, lacking his advice and support, I felt alone in the world. What need I had of him in the new circumstances in which the extraordinary events of France were to place me! Alas! the author of my days had long foreseen the evils of a revolution. In sending me to Paris in July, 1788, he said to me: " You are going into a country that will become dangerous; the taxes are excessive, the ministers bad, the people discontented and the King feeble; the bowstring is too stretched, it must break." These were his very words, his political prophecy. As far as I personally was concerned, he added, " As soon as you arrive in Paris, I only ask you to be economical, precise and prudent; this journey ought to settle your life." My father was only too good a prophet. This first stay in Paris, in the midst of the bustle of public life, flung me into the whirlpool of politics, and was the cause of all my misfortunes.

All the inhabitants of Bigorre who knew his
strength of mind and his energetic common sense,
which had become proverbial throughout the country,
often heard him say the same thing, at this critical
point when the State was passing out of the hands
of a financial charlatan, like M. Necker, into those
of a squanderer like M. de Calonne.

These ministers of a day had by turns destroyed
the monarchy and led the way to the Revolution by
the increase of taxation, the persecution of the parliaments, the confusion of the exchequer, and the
depletion of the national treasury.   Twice had the
Notables been summoned merely to dissolve before
coming to any agreement; they had refused to make
the property of the nobility and clergy pay taxes. A
deficit of fifty-five millions was the only point that
was settled, and by seeing the terrible confusion of
the finances of every government of this period, it is
easy to understand how a deficit of fifty-five millions
could mount up, since several hundred millions have
since been spent on unjust wars and useless conquests.

I have edited the diary of my first visit to Paris
day by day, and have traced the successive development of events at this period of social crisis.   I have
called it " The Last Days of the Old Monarchy in
Paris."   It might serve as an historical introduction to
my Memoirs, or rather to the Revolution of 1789.[1]

Cardinal Brienne was Prime Minister when I arrived
in Paris.   The parliaments were threatened with revo-

---

[1] To fulfil Barère's design and to satisfy the reader's curiosity,
we give at the end of this volume extracts from this diary, which
is as original as its subject is important —EDITOR'S NOTE.

lution or fresh transformation. Maupeou's work was the type, others merely varied it.

A judge who did not bend to the winds that brought tempests and thunderbolts in their train, proud of his name, which was of little influence at a time when deeds were stronger than words, M. de Lamoignon competed with the Prime Minister to give us in place of the old parliaments a new High Court of Justice, which was ridiculed before it was founded, and was established forcibly only to fall immediately.

An administrator full of wit but lacking in tact and ability, practising a versatile despotism rather than absolute power, having liberal views in his proposals but never carrying them out, M. de Brienne knew neither how to bend to public opinion, listen to public needs, nor foresee the dangers of the future. He hated the parliaments through his ministerial traditions and made war on them. Above all, he believed in his genius for finance, while in reality he only knew how to take money from the treasury vaults. Public credit was destroyed, the fund holders were in terror, public honesty was forgotten and justice paralysed.

It was compulsory, then, to pacify the people of Paris and the provinces, to dismiss the Prime Minister and the Chancellor, who were objects of universal hatred. M. Necker was recalled to the Exchequer; he shows the King how many evils could be remedied, if only the Court and the two orders will help him. But the Court only wanted money, and not political reforms.

And yet we owe to the very folly of Cardinal de Brienne the first concession to the entire liberty of the press that ever happened in France. Hitherto we had groaned under the most iniquitous tyranny of thought, speech and printing.

We also owe to M. de Brienne the solemn promise of the King to restore the States-General to the nation. We were then under the despotism of the parliaments, which only warred against taxes when they touched upon their domains. The extreme tenacity with which the parliaments, twice summoned to the Assembly of Notables, had resisted every kind of sacrifice was vividly remembered.

It must be acknowledged that, on the 4th of August, 1788, the Parliament of Paris made a remonstrance to Louis XVI. to justify its refusal to register the disastrous laws creating still more taxation, and on this occasion it declared that the nation alone had the right of settling the taxation. The Count de Provence took the decree of taxation to the parliaments and the Count d'Artois to the Treasury. Public opinion ran very high against the taxes and those who took the decrees.

It was this cry of public freedom that M. de Brienne had the courage to welcome and consecrate by an edict. So Cardinal de Richelieu deprived us of our States-General and Cardinal de Brienne gave them back to us. Posterity ought to be very grateful for this political act that an odious Court disapproved of, but which the Privy Council thought necessary after the fruitless assemblies of the Notables and the eloquent remonstrance of the Parliament of Paris.

As soon as the Archbishop of Sens, the Prime Minister, had proclaimed, by reason of the urgency of matters, the promise of the States-General and the liberty of the press, two things entirely unknown to that generation, an astonishing change took place in public opinion and an upheaval of men's thoughts.

The French, electrified by the freedom of the press, knew no bounds to their wishes and pretensions. They attacked every abuse in writings, pamphlets and books, all of which appeared in great numbers.

Desenne's, the bookseller's in the Palais Royal, was perpetually full of the purchasers and readers of these thousand and one productions of the time. It was a freeing of thought and most active development of the intelligence, of which the bookseller's shop seemed to have become the headquarters.

I gave Desenne the extracts I had made of Linguet's Memoirs and Annals in 1786. He had them printed, and got rid of them quickly, so great was the indignation against the ministerial despotism of Versailles and such was the eagerness for civil liberty.

Cardinal Brienne, besides the liberty of the press and the States-General, had had another idea—to quietly regenerate the State, the government and the nation. It was to reconstitute the army by a completely new scheme which would assure political influence and a great military existence to France. With this object the Cardinal had formed a Council of War, and had appointed as secretary a talented and patriotic general officer. He was the author of an essay on tactics which had obtained for him the Cross of St. Louis at twenty-five years of age; he had reached the rank of colonel by his merit alone in an age of intrigue and at a Court where favour decided every distinction. This officer was the Count de Guibert, son of the famous and virtuous Lieutenant-General Guibert, Governor of the Invalides. Let us

honour the memory of Cardinal de Brienne, who was
wise enough to see the genius of the Count de Guibert and to make use of it. His principles of tactics
were tried at the camp of St. Omer, but the Prince
de Condé, who hated the Count de Guibert, made all
the movements fail, and thus decried the labours of
the Council of War.

The Count de Guibert, in 1788, drew up the reports
and orders of this council; the prefaces are remarkable
as the methods were intended to be useful and fruitful
in bringing the French army to its former high level.
Especially is this the case in his valuable collection
of " Reports to the Council of War," where we must
admire his political talents, his far-reaching views, his
military knowledge and his genius for administration
and tactics. This collection, which deserves to be
printed at the expense of the Government, is still unpublished and in the hands of the Count's widow, who
has piously collected them and put them in order.

At Guibert's death, on the 3rd of May, 1790, the
Count de la Tour du Pin, Minister of War, who knew
the value of his manuscripts, demanded them from his
widow in the King's name. His widow refused to give
them up, alleging they were the property of his family
and a dear remembrance of her husband. In his lifetime he had been flooded with insults, according to the
custom of every age and every Court, because he had
genius and foresight, because he loved his country and
wished to strengthen the army. All the military laws
made in the Constitutional Assembly by men like
Lameth, Menou and Dumas, were copied and imitated
slavishly from his reports, and especially his orders.

Political events helped the plans of the Prime

Minister's enemies. He had not had sufficient diplomatic foresight or sufficient military resources to prevent the King of Prussia's soldiers from entering Holland. The French alliance was despised in Europe. The minister disappeared with all his plans of the Council of War, of a Supreme Court of Justice, and of reconstituting the kingdom by an assembly of the States-General.

The Parliament remained masters of the situation. Numberless pamphlets ventilated the need of a great reform at Court, in the ministry, the law courts, the army, the executive, and taxation. Such was the state of things when M. Necker obtained an Act for the doubling of the members of the Commons at the States-General, which was necessary to enable the ministry to force the two privileged orders to bear their share of the national expenditure and to pass the reforms for the good of the nation.

It would be difficult to imagine the revolution caused in Paris by this Order of Council of the 25th of December, 1788, concerning the doubling of the members of the Commons and the means to be taken to convoke the States-General in another way from that adopted at the last in 1614, which was the method the Parliament of Paris held to strongly and exclusively in successive remonstrances. Everyone congratulated himself, rejoicing that there was at last a nation, that the French people were at last to be represented, and that Richelieu's despotism was at last revealed and happily done away with. Everything pointed to a new era in the new year of 1789.

The winter was exceedingly cold. Thirty-two consecutive days of frost had increased the misery of the poor. The remembrance of all the ministers dismissed, reinstated, driven out and recalled in so short a time without benefiting the State in the least had only irritated men and heightened the hopes of a new order of things.

1789.—I left Paris in the month of January. At the end of the month I arrived at the meeting of the States of Languedoc with M. de Puymaurin, the syndic of the States, and his relative, M. Darquier, a celebrated astronomer, who took me to Montpellier out of kindness. I was present at the public sittings of the States of Languedoc, which attracted a number of strangers. I heard an eloquent speech from the chairman, M. Dillon, Archbishop of Narbonne. This Irishman, gifted with a lofty mind and energetic delivery, spoke with the same kind of political eloquence that was admired in Mr. Fox's speeches. He showed us with a few broad, rapid touches the great works accomplished by the States for the past ten years, their plans, progress and administrative reforms. He then cast a piercing glance on the coming meeting of the States-General, the success of which he desired as a citizen, but the consequences he feared as a statesman.

I was seated by the side of the famous comedian, M. Préville, who listed with unusual attention to this kind of wit and eloquence, of which he had gained no idea from the masterpieces of the drama. On leaving the hall we surrounded M. Préville and paid him the compliments his celebrity deserved.

"Well, what do you think of this orator, this chairman of the States of Languedoc?" he was asked.

"My word," he replied, "he played his part magnificently."

Great actors only see comedians and comedies in everything. Everyone smiled at this smart reply and put his own construction on it.

Soon after I set out for Toulouse, and I arrived at Tarbes in the month of March, some time before the elections of representatives for the States-General.

Having been nominated as elector, I was, in the General Assembly held at Tarbes in January, 1789, a member of the Committee of Grievances according to the custom of the ancient States-General. I was one of the first to propose the abolition of feudal rights and the abolition of tithes. I spoke in favour of the equalisation of land taxes, whatever the nature of the property—land or houses. As I possessed a fair amount of property at Anclades, near Lourdes, and at Vieuzac, over which I also had feudal rights which extended as far as Aisac, Prechac and Ouzouf, my opponents at the elections circulated a leaflet pointing out the danger of giving the proprietor of feudal fiefs a mandate to abolish them. In spite of these underhand attacks, the electors, especially those in the country, spoke out bravely in St. John's Church, where the assembly was held, that I was the person they had chosen and they confirmed their choice.

The voting then took place. There were more than five hundred electors, and I was elected, defeating M. Pégé a lawyer, and M. Lanère, a patriot worthy of election. The second member was elected by the people of the valleys and mountains. I was looked on as the member of the plain. M. Dupont de Luz was my colleague. The nobility nominated the Baron de Fausseries de Gonez, a good loyal nobleman who despised the Court nobility, whom he called " brilliant footmen," but a staunch, warm partisan of the feudal system. He looked on it as the perfection of society, which, according to his ideas, ought to be made up of two classes—nobles and ploughmen. The clergy had the good sense to nominate one of the most erudite, honourable and charitable rectors of the diocese, and perhaps in all the surrounding dioceses. His name was Rivière. He saw that the good of the State depended solely on the reduction of the luxury and tyranny of the higher clergy, on the just amelioration of the lot of the minor clergy, and on the re-establishment of morals and religion. Of politics he knew nothing.

We set out together from Tarbes and arrived in Paris in the first week of May, the time for the opening of the States-General. All Paris was in a ferment about the Réveillon revolt. It was so called after a paper manufacturer of the Boulevard St. Antoine who employed several thousands of workmen. Demagogues incited them and made them strike work, so that there might be a pretext for calling in the military to quell these disturbances in the Paris factories. A personage in a high position was accused of wishing to frighten the members of the States-General in this way, produce a popular revolt, and thus render the assembly of the States-General impossible.

There had always been an intriguing party at Court that stopped at nothing to prevent the States-General from meeting, so that nothing should interfere with the royal power and authority, the pretended source of every power and every law by the grace of

God. So true it is that the French would have to go through much trouble, and experience much resistance and calamity and civil discord before the great unchangeable principle was recognised of the sovereignty of the people and of the national representatives. The first days of May disclosed for a moment this Court party, who desired neither States-General, nor right of granting the taxes, nor equalisation of land taxes, nor limitation of the privileges of the nobility or clergy.

A prince was at the head of the nobility as feudal prince of France, another at the head of the courtiers who wasted the property of the Crown. The King was alone with his deficit, his Chancellor of the Exchequer, and an apparent desire to put an end to the ills of France.

On my arrival in Paris I saw that public opinion was against the princes, that the hope of the people was turned towards the King and M. Necker, and that they wished to reform the ministerial tyranny, the arbitrary taxes and the abuses of the monarchy. On arriving at Versailles there was another horizon. There they were accustomed to a royal power without limit, revision, or even remonstrance. The custom established since the suppression of the States-General by Louis XIII., called the Just, was, that the King received no conditions from his subjects, to whom he conceded their own rights when he thought fit. The French of Versailles were indeed the most obedient and subservient subjects of the King of France. They received the fruits of this in a mass of abuses and positions, on which they lived.

And yet, in the midst of all this Court slavery,

the people of Versailles were not servile. There were ardent supporters and even enlightened propagators of the ideas of liberty and national sentiments among them. This was seen after the 14th of July, when they formed an excellent National Guard, one of the best in France.

PART I

FROM THE OPENING OF THE STATES-GENERAL, MAY 4,
1789, TO THE FALL OF ROBESPIERRE, JULY 27,
1794.

May 4, 1789.

THE opening of the States-General was a solemn
function, magnificent and religious alike. The three
chambers afterwards received the deputies of the several
orders, who were astonished to find themselves united
after a break or a silence of one hundred and seventy-
five years, then presided over by Cardinal Richelieu.

I was very young to form part of the finest assembly
ever held in France, so I set myself to listen and
observe. Two men attracted my attention more than
the others: these were, on the one hand, the Count
de Mirabeau, whose reputation as an orator, journalist,
and politician was well known to this meeting; the
other, M. Bailly, of the Académie des Inscriptions et
Belles-Lettres, was eminent for his social virtues, and
much more so for his scientific attainments and his
works on astronomy and his historic researches on the
Atlantic races. I made every effort to make the acquaintance of these illustrious deputies; my youth and
admiration for talent were my claim to their notice.
I conversed with Mirabeau whenever I could get near

him ; his conversation, at once striking, witty, amiable and profound, and always in good taste and good style, attracted to his side all who heard him. M. Bailly was reserved, although full of mildness and good humour ; he had, amidst his urbanity and goodfellow-ship, great austerity of principle, perfect rectitude of conduct and great intellectual energy. These opposite characteristics, these diverse qualifications were most valuable points for a young deputy to study. Here I was, so to speak, the satellite of these two planets, in the political perturbations found in the irregular system of the States-General, assembled for a minis-terial motive, but lacking any direction towards a national purpose.

This is what needed finding. The primary object of the debates between the three estates was the equality of the contributions or territorial taxes, and the necessity of subsidising the King to balance a deficit of thirty-five millions of francs.

Tactics of the two Orders of the Clergy and Nobility.[1]

The three estates did nothing for several days save observe, without progress, and dismiss deputations without a reply. The three estates followed the ex-ample of those armies which, before engaging, make *reconnaissances*, advance and retreat, and prepare them-selves by a course of continual drill. The clergy brought to their aid all the hypocrisy and worldly wisdom which have always characterised their want

---

[1] These headings occur frequently in the manuscript. We have, however, thought it necessary to add a few more to facilitate reading and reference —EDITOR'S NOTE.

of patriotism and their avarice. The nobility intrigued, canvassed and flattered the communal deputies in order to learn what they would be after, and decided to combine among themselves, if possible, to deceive and lead them, or to combine with the clergy, if the Commons put forth claims too high to suit the privileged classes. As to the Commons themselves, as yet they only wanted the sovereignty of the people—a term odious in the ears of the prejudiced, and disdained by the aristocrats; but, strong in the conviction of their rights and in the unanimity of provincial opinion, and that of the capital also, for the reformation of the abuses of the monarchy and for the equality of the taxes payable by all landowners, without distinction of rank and despite privileges, they quoted their precise instructions, of the unanimity of their records of grievances and of the necessity of knowing governmental action, of the security due to proprietors, of the payment of State creditors, and of the relief of taxation in the provinces.

The Commons adopt the title of the National Assembly.

All the deputations of the Commons to the clergy and the nobility gained nothing but derision, for their results were absolutely without avail, through the doggedness of the two estates in yielding nothing in abatement of what they called their immunities and privileges. Then there began in the Chamber of Commons a series of debates upon the form and the name of their constitution.

MM. Sieyès, le Chapellier, Barnave and Lanjuinais with Count Mirabeau spoke on the form of the constitution of the Chamber. Although one of the youngest deputies, I ventured to speak, and was much encouraged because I dwelt on the question of how to constitute the National Assembly.

After many lively and learned discussions, the Commons could find no other solution than that of reckoning the number of constituents they represented. This enumeration proved that out of a total of twenty-six millions of French, twenty-five and three-quarter millions were represented by the deputies of the Commons ; the last quarter of a million comprised the priests and monks, the nobles and the Castellans ; so the Commons were unanimous in resolving themselves into a National Assembly. This was only a right, but it was looked upon as a conquest, to be contested by the Court, by the clergy and by the nobility.

The effect of this first resolution was magical ; it electrified Paris, and was the source of that powerful public opinion of which the deputies of the Commons became the regulators by dint of their patriotism and energy.

From this I saw that the two estates were left in the lurch ; the bishops curried favour with the King ; the higher nobility intrigued with the two princes of the blood ; but a minority of the lesser clergy and a small number of prelates were inclined to join the National Assembly. Several of the most enlightened of the nobility, at the head of whom was a prince of the blood, the only one who possessed liberal ideas and was popular, were strongly inclined to join the party of union. These two minorities soon amalgamated with the great national majority, and France was saved.

[The most memorable and the most energetic of

the resolutions adopted by the deputies of the Commons, having as antagonists the two estates of the clergy and the nobility, the Court and the ministry, was to declare themselves a National Assembly. This step, as novel as it was decisive, to make that assembly the legal mouthpiece of the nation, in default of proper action on the part of the two privileged orders, produced a most imposing effect in the capital, and suddenly enlightened public opinion on the points of the States - General and upon the emancipation of the French people. This solemn deliberation of the Commons spared France a dissolution, which would have led to terrible disorders at this moment of general ferment and agitation, caused by the preceding assemblies of the Notables, the attempts and intrigues of the ministry, and the imperious need of the abolition of financial abuses and of social reform.

This constitution of the Commons as a National Assembly checkmated at one blow the wretched greed of the clergy and the arrogant attitude of the nobility, while, at the same time, it arrested the irregular and intriguing conduct of the ministry. Undoubtedly it did not check the backstair ways of the courtiers in the autocratic Queen's Austrian committee; but, at least, it abolished the humiliating attitude of the deputies of the Third Estate in the assemblies of the States-General, and destroyed, in the mind of the French nation, the glamour of those undignified records of grievances in which French subjects had to implore relief from the kings of France.

In the Chamber of Commons the partisans of M. Necker succeeded in forming a faction in order to divide the States-General into three chambers, to

conduct their deliberations and to vote by orders.
This was the only ambition of the two privileged
corporations. In order to effect this, they became, in
different ways, absolute fanatics. The nobility, arrogant and grasping by habit, *ordered;* the clergy, more
skilful and with a more free and easy policy, *negotiated;*
the nobility acted as a king; the clergy assumed
the character of an arbitrator. The debate with the
Commons might have been a long one, and its results
doubtful, had not the minor members of the clerical
party, vicars and priests with no chance of promotion,
given secret pledges in favour of the popular cause, and
only sought a pretext to join the deputies of the Commons. A small party of the order of the nobles, headed
by the Duke of Orleans, who had opposed, in 1788,
the King in person at a royal session held at the
Paris parliament, had evinced, in the Chamber of the
Nobility, such generous and national sentiments that
the Commons looked upon the members of this minority
of the nobility as well-wishers of good policy and of
the national welfare. These two minorities when
united with the Chamber of Commons, confirmed
and rendered its title as a National Assembly permanent.]

I leave history to relate the intrigues of the Court
and the rage of the ministry, how the place of meeting
of the three estates was closed by the military, how
the Commons alone had the courage to assemble in the
church of St. Louis, which was shut up the next day
by order; how, after, they gathered in the graveyard of
the same church, which in its turn was closed against
them on the morrow; and, finally, how they took to the

tennis-court, there to take a solemn oath never to separate before giving France a constitution.

I then edited, for the information of my constituents, a newspaper termed *Le Point du Jour*, wherein were reported all the memorable events and debates of the Constitutional Assembly, which was so hated by the aristocracy and so admired by Europe. I shall, therefore, in these Memoirs, only relate private facts which are either unpublished or unknown.

This journal forms a collection of twenty-nine volumes, and contains a report of the legislation and politics of this first epoch of National Assemblies, in which the public will was well known, and where the first principles of constitutions were discussed and established.

The celebrated painter, David, was so struck with the courage of the provincial deputies that he then sketched his admirable drawing of "The Oath in the Tennis-court," which has been etched by M. Denon, the present director of the Museum of Painting and Sculpture. David wished to include me in this drawing and represent me at the moment when, on my knees, in the shabby hall of the tennis-court, I was reporting the session of the taking of the oath.

M. d'Artois soon afterwards closed this court, which belonged to him; but the constitutional oath had been taken.

Preliminaries of the Royal Session of the 23rd of June, 1789.

The privileged orders maintained their division as separate chambers and their votes by order and not by poll. The courtiers persuaded Louis XVI. that the National Assembly would not occupy itself with the instructions and the works with which it had been charged by the communes. The ministers began to prepare the King's speech and the declaration of the royal wishes at a *lit de justice* to be held in the midst of the National Assembly. Thus the King was induced to commit the enormous mistake of declaring that he was the representative of the nation, even in the presence of the general and special representatives of the whole French nation ; the monarch assumed that he alone knew the desires of his people, better even than their deputies, although these desires were already deposited in writing at the various record offices of the provinces ; he also declared that he alone would carry out those reforms for effecting which the estates of the realm had been convoked. Thus the secret of the aristocracy and the only object of this royal session was exposed, and, after all, it was more fatal to the throne than threatening to the nation. The courtiers and ministers desired to render the wishes of the Commons abortive, and to adjourn the sittings of the Assembly by disorder or by armed force; they wished to veto the constitution and strangle it at its birth.

Royal Session of the 23rd of June.

The Court hastened to peruse the list of grievances and to open its famous royal session of the 23rd of June. It was during this *lit de justice*, held at the Hôtel des Menus, in the presence of the three estates, that it was sought to humiliate the Commons by allowing them to wait outside in the rain until the hall was opened, while the representatives of the two privileged orders had for some time taken their seats to prostrate themselves at the foot of the throne like the vile slaves who had repulsed the entry of the deputies of the Commons.

These two orders went before the King : the Commons remained seated. The two orders cheered lustily each speech and act pronounced or read in the Assembly; the Commons were silent.

When the meeting adjourned, the two orders, with the exception of the two minorities of the clergy and nobility which had already coalesced with the Commons, rushed to the doors by which the King was to pass in order to regain the equipages of the *cortége.* The Commons retained their seats. The King commanded the three orders to separate, and at once to repair to their chambers to vote, each in private. The master of the ceremonies (Brézé) had no need to advise the two orders: they had disappeared with the bodyguard and the royal procession.

The Commons, twice summoned by the Marquis de Brézé to obey the command of the King, retorted with the fine and energetic apostrophe of the Count de Mirabeau: " Go and tell your master that we are here by the power of the people, and that we shall not go away save at the point of the bayonet." The president of the National Assembly, M. Bailly, added that the Commons were going to deliberate upon what they had just heard, and that they would not leave the chamber until they were ready to publish the result of their debate.

During all this time, and just as the King had risen to terminate the sitting, the deputies of the

Commons (to the number of 600) put on their hats, and thus debated the annulling of the King's regulations and of the King's session, which had violated the rights of the French people. All this would be treated to-day as rebellion; but it was only through the courage of its representatives that the French could regain and preserve their rights.

The Count d'Artois and Louis XVI. (Episode.)

These events are undoubtedly known; but here are some that are not. When the King had got into his carriage, which stood in the grand avenue of the castle, M. d'Artois bent forward and told him that the deputies of the Commons refused to leave the chamber, and that they ought to be sabred by the bodyguard. The King, in these words, coldly replied :

" To the castle! "

M. d'Artois insisted more energetically :

" Give the order for them to be cut down ; otherwise all is lost."

" Go and do it yourself."

More insistance. The King, growing impatient, said to M. d'Artois :

"Go to the devil! To the castle, to the castle!"

I have these facts from one of the bodyguard, one of my countrymen, and from the King's private physician.

The Queen's Plan.

The events of the 14th of July, with their antecedents and their effects are known. What is less known is the plan conceived by the Queen to bombard

the Chamber of Deputies during the night of July
12th-13th, whilst an order was given to arrest those
deputies who were about to leave Paris during the night
of the 12th on the road to Sèvres. I was one of these,
and, leaving at nine in the evening for Versailles with
several colleagues, I was stopped before I got to Sèvres
on the bridge, first by some cavalry officers and afterwards by some artillerymen, but our energetic threats
caused our release; but we did not get to Versailles
until midnight. It was just when the Court was
busy in devising schemes to disperse all the deputies
of the Commons, to send them back to their provinces,
and to put into execution the reforms published at the
famous *lit de justice* of the month of June.

This project, started on the evening of the 21st,
did not succeed, in spite of the fervid wishes of
the Court. We had proofs that the Court party
wished to force the King to disperse the deputies and
arrest sixty-nine of them, of whom we procured the
list. These were to be imprisoned in the citadel of
Metz, and afterwards to be executed as rebels. This is
always the way of this Court and of this *famille*. The
Count de Mirabeau was the first name inscribed on
this order of proscription, with Chapellier, Target,
Barnave, Sieyès, Bailly, Camus, some Breton deputies,
and those who edited newspapers; on this last account
I had the honour of appearing on this list.

Marshal de Broglio.

The Marshal de Broglio thought it his duty to make
sure of the fidelity of the artillerymen who were drawn
up in the great park of artillery which occupied the
Queen's stables. On the 13th of July, about midnight,

he went to speak to the gunners and to ask them to take a fresh oath of fidelity to the King. The men were astonished at this request, and soon perceived that they were required to further some nefarious scheme to oppress the people; they therefore were unanimous in their refusal. The Marshal de Broglio was daunted, and dared not give orders to march on those deputies who were assembled for a continuous sitting; disappointed, he returned to the Queen, whose council desired to await events. On the morning of the 14th, they hastened to speak out. It was on this morning that two wives of gunners in the artillery assembled in the Queen's stables deposed to the facts of the proposals made by the Marshal de Broglio.

Session of the 14th of July, 1789. Deputation and Address to the King.

In the evening of the 14th, the events in Paris and the anger of its armed inhabitants changed everything except the projects and desires of the Court. In vain M. Charles de Noailles — who had been a witness of the extraordinary movement in the capital up to eight o'clock in the evening, and who escaped from Paris by a miracle—went to render an account of these events to the National Assembly; at the castle they refused to believe him. In vain this soldier, so full of loyalty, repaired to the Queen and related all that had taken place in Paris, all of which the courtiers had carefully concealed. The same incredulity infected the Court. But a numerous deputation waited on the King towards midnight with an address, which, as it included the positive state of events in Paris, unveiled the eyes of the King. I was among these deputies;

His Majesty kept his eyes firmly fixed upon M. de Mirabeau while the Count de Clermont-Tonnerre read the address from the National Assembly. The Bishop of Puy, M. de Pompignan, had been asked to deliver it; but he, being unable to read by candle-light, begged M. de Clermont-Tonnerre to do so for him. The King stood upright in the middle of the hall leading to his study. He was surrounded by all his ministers, with the exception of M. Necker, who, after having been outraged and insulted by M. d'Artois in leaving the council, on the evening of Saturday, the 11th of July, went away on Sunday morning, the 12th, after having sent in his resignation to the King.

After the reading of this address, the King replied with commonplaces, which showed, however, that he was disposed to accede to the demands of the Parisians and the National Assembly; but all this was uttered in a cold, dry manner, even when he added that he was about to confer with his council and would give us a definite reply. We waited in the same hall while the King retired to his study, the curtains of which, either badly fitting or carelessly closed, allowed us to see the play of the features of the ministers and the movements of the princes, who seemed to be inclined towards acts of severity. All the members of the deputation could see this political pantomime through the large squares of Bohemian glass which form the casements; and the well-lighted apartments let us see all this as if it were daylight.

At the end of half an hour of excitement rather than deliberation the King returned to the hall and told us that he would communicate more fully his proposals to the National Assembly. Indeed there was such an amount of indecision both among the courtiers and the ministers that it required all the zeal and devotion of the Duke of Larochefoucauld-Liancourt to unveil the eyes of the King, and to prove to him that the sole means of safety for the monarch, the monarchy and the whole of France was in his frank coalition with the National Assembly.

The King goes to the National Assembly.

It was not until nearly four o'clock in the morning that the Duke of Liancourt succeeded in deciding the King to take this step. He came in consequence to announce his intention to the permanent Assembly about five o'clock. So the King came on foot before seven o'clock, warmly applauded and sincerely believed in by the people, to utter words full of conciliation and attachment to the interests of the people and the National Assembly.

From the 13th the Assembly had ordered the despatch of a deputation of thirty-six of its members to calm the anxiety and agitation of the city of Paris. By chance I was nominated as one of these thirty-six deputies; and certainly in those days such a deputation was not without its dangers. But all our spirits were electrified to such an extent that all dangers faded before the interests and welfare of the country.

The events of one day turned this dangerous deputation into a brilliant embassy of peace and happiness. On the 15th of July it was decided that the thirty-six deputies, already chosen by ballot, should go to Paris to announce the approach of the King, and that the deputies would accompany him to the town-hall. The other details of this day are already known.

Reflections and Remarks relative to the 14th of July.[1]

When the French Revolution broke out on the 14th of July, 1789, it was the object of Europe's admiration and England's dismay. The enemy and rival of France, England only busied herself henceforth in attempts to hinder the progress of French liberty; she was eager to revenge herself on the Bourbons, who had favoured the independence of the United States of America, and she resented the great influence France would possess when armed with all the rights and means which liberty would give to a warlike, intelligent and enlightened nation.

At this period the Prime Minister, a Tory, a headstrong and semi-lunatic person, ruled England—one William Pitt—son of the famous Earl Chatham, who, in imitation of Hasdrubal, caused his son to swear eternal enmity to the French nation.

Pitt despatched diplomatic emissaries to frighten all the foreign cabinets at the great rebellion of the French. What was to become of the divine right of kings on the continent if this mania for reform was not arrested and condemned on principle? Plots were started by intriguing agents from England, and were for some time overlooked, until the time came when the Committee of Investigation nominated by the National Assembly discovered the cause of the

---

[1] The following fragmentary paragraphs, written at various periods, Barère suggested should be inserted in this place.— EDITOR'S NOTE.

disturbances in Paris and of the riots which disturbed the provinces.

The Cabinet of St. James' carried its plans of counter-revolution against this mainspring of liberty still further, and assembled a congress at Pilnitz, supported by the Bourbon princes who had emigrated from France. It was there that the partition of France was decided on, in imitation of the partition of Poland. To deprive a people of its nationality and of its territory was the radical policy of Pitt, the English minister, who found his model in the action of the three northern powers who partitioned Poland to prevent it being a nation or its people free. All these preparations for internal riots and for foreign wars were accomplished and subsidised in 1791, a period when the national constitution was just about to get to work.

This congress at Pilnitz, followed by the conference and treaty of Pavia, was the basis of all the coalitions of the kings of Europe against France and its liberty. It was a reaction which underwent changes of form and of leaders, but was constantly in opposition to France and her liberties. These cost the Cabinet of St. James' twenty-one milliards of francs, which formed its national debt from 1791 to 1815.

"Tros Tyriusve fuit, nullo discrimine habebo."

The French Guards in July, 1789.

The various party writers who have been occupied in distorting history to gratify their evil passions, have termed the French Guards revolutionists and counter-revolutionists in turn. The royalist writers say that the French Guards only marched on the 14th of July to retake the Bastille, which was stormed by the people, and to restore it to the King. The patriot writers aver that the people, in combination with the French Guards, attacked the Bastille together, and that the cannon pointed by the latter broke the chains of the drawbridge, which enabled them to gain admission into the fortress. However that may be, the Bastille once taken, despotism fell; and this fact is a vital one, because of its consequences. The French Guards thus gave the troops in general the example of serving the popular cause and of not lending themselves to overthrow national representation.

The counter-revolutionists of each period, from 1789 to 1833, all agree that it was necessary to avoid encouraging such sentiments, founded only in blind and brutal force. But this sentiment of the French Guards was noble and entirely patriotic; by refusing to proceed to Versailles and arrest the chief deputies of the Commons, they avoided overthrowing popular representation and the sovereignty of the people; they spared the King the effect of the crimes of his Court and the shame of the arbitrary judgments contemplated by the Queen's committee.

Danton's Motion, 1789.

In the Cordeliers district, the French Guards were approached and persuaded to reconstitute themselves under the same title, having shown their sympathy for the popular cause at the taking of the Bastille. In accordance with a proposition moved by Danton, it was desired to give them a commander whom they could not fail to honour (the Duke of Orleans); but the French Guards preferred to remain associated .

with the National Guard. Again, in reperusing the proposition made by General Lafayette, on the 16th of July, 1789, for forming the National Guard of Paris, and consequently of France generally, it can clearly be seen that the whole of the French Guards were to form but one body.

14th of July, 1789.

The revolution was not effected until the 14th of July, under the inspiration of civil and political liberty, and by the strong arms of the population of Paris and the regiment of French Guards. This revolution was consummated on the same day it was undertaken, and the whole nation ratified it as being necessary and conformable with its interests and rights. Without a popular insurrection, which accompanied and followed the taking of the Bastille, these generous efforts and patriotic resolutions of the Commons would have been useless, sterile, and even fatal, had not royal despotism perished on that day.

The Chamber of Commons having formed itself into a National Assembly, proceeded subsequently to swear (in the tennis-court) the famous oath never to separate before having secured for France a free and representative constitution. In this there were only the preliminaries of a revolution, and not a revolution itself. The deputies of the Commons protested against the royal session and the edicts of the 23rd of June, 1789, reversing and annulling all the proceedings of this royal session as being prejudicial to the rights of the nation; and this was one great step to actual revolution. The *coup d'état* aimed at by the royal session of the 23rd of June, by which the three orders of the clergy, the nobility, and the third estate were preserved, and so separated from the people that their privileges could only be curtailed by their own vote, a measure which rendered these abuses and privileges inviolable and everlasting; in fact, this *coup d'état* of Louis XVI. was nothing save a precocious counter-revolution, which hastened the true revolution of the people.

Thus the revolution was, before the 14th of July, only conceived and prepared for; it was the material fact of the unforeseen storming of the Bastille by the mob, which started and consecrated the French Revolution.

15th of July, 1789.

On this day Louis XVI. had no other alternative but to come to the National Assembly and avow himself a supporter of the rights of the nation. He announced that he was about to return to Paris, and requested to be accompanied thither by a deputation from the National Assembly, as a sign of mutual confidence and reciprocity.

M. de Lafayette, M. de Liancourt, and thirty-two deputies, among whom the ballot had included me, went with the King to Paris, where, before reaching the town-hall, we had great difficulty in suppressing the anger of the citizens exasperated at the grave causes of the insurrection. When we arrived there the King was received •with solemn coldness: an irritated and menacing people are little likely to flatter or to curry favour. M. de Lafayette then swore in the French Guards who had been instrumental in the taking of the Bastille and also all the troops in the capital;

they swore fidelity to the nation, to the King, and to the city of Paris, which now was absolutely the leader of the revolution.   Here was a revolution completed and entirely national; this example of 1789 and all the others has been in vain for Paris; so divided, Paris is no better than chaos.

Variations of a simple expression of a contemporary Deputy on the taking of the Bastille.

M. Gaetan de Larochefoucauld, of the Chamber of Deputies, said, on the occasion of the voting of gratuities to the conquerors of the Bastille, that he was the possessor of the manuscripts of his father, the Duke of Larochefoucauld-Liancourt.   After having asserted that the true revolution was commenced before the 14th of July, 1789, he quoted a manuscript of his father which states that Louis XVI., on learning of the taking of the Bastille, cried, " What a revolt ! " Larochefoucauld-Liancourt replied, "Ah, your Majesty, rather say: What a revolution ! "   But the narrator affirms that his father, in a moment of panic, only used the word " revolution " better to explain the King's danger.   He complained that his father's words were distorted in the Chamber of Peers, where his simple exclamation was changed into " What a great and glorious revolution ! "

General Lafayette replied: " The great secret, exploded in the Chamber of Peers, was repeated in the Chamber of Deputies.   It was desired to proscribe the revolution of the 14th of July, 1789, and, above all, the regiment which, by refusing to break up the Constitutional Assembly, was one of the principal movers in this revolution.   I prefer the subject treated

in this fashion; it is clearer and more definite. I did
not take part in the interview of M. de Liancourt
with the King, but I know that when Louis XVI.
used the expression, "What a great revolt!" M. de
Liancourt replied, "No, Sire; it is a great revolution." I never said he used the word "glorious";
but as to the other expression, I have it from himself,
and he has always accepted the compliments he received on this score. The King so thoroughly understood that the day—the 14th of July—was a *great*
revolution, that he hastened to call his new ministers
together, who counselled him to repair at once to the
National Assembly. Much as he thought of the
immediate danger, he did go, and there read the short
speech which they had drafted. (*Session of the 22nd
of April*, 1833. *Chamber of Deputies.*)

Night of the 4th of August, 1789.

I pass to another period, the night of the 4th of
August. The burning of the castles had already taken
place; and fear of robbers, who infested Paris and
the provinces after the 12th of July, had occasioned
the embodiment of the National Guard, which has
often defended and saved France.

I shall never forget the general excitement at
Versailles when the news of the burning of the
castles and other details from all the provinces came
to hand. The thought was: Did this agitation ori-
ginate from one source? Was it preconcerted in the
villages? The plan of the formation of the National
Guard which spread so rapidly, did not that also
emanate from the same mind, or from the same party
which desired popular risings in order to excuse

extraordinary legal measures ? All that I know is,
that I saw, several days before the 4th of August,
plenty of lobbying and influence exercised by MM.
de Pgd——, Ch. de No——, the Duke d'Aig——,
A. Lam——, and others. I well recollect coming
into contact with these gentlemen during the days
of the 3rd and 4th of August, and speaking to them
about the plan which several of the members of
the Commons entertained, of proposing the abolition
of the feudal rights, the privileges and immunities of
the two orders of the clergy and nobility. These
gentlemen deterred me from the plan and the message
with which I was entrusted as to these feudal rights
and the venality of the charges complained of. It is
necessary, they said, that the nobles should propose
the abolition of feudal rights, and that the members
should propose to end the sale of state appointments.
Thus the matter would have a better chance of
success.

I had never seen such reserve and low spirits
among the members of the two orders, who had
already joined the Commons, and deliberated in the
same chamber since the King had advised this step
after the terrible events of the 14th of July. This
publicity increased the insurrections in the country
against the proprietors still more; and their great wrong
in having refused an equal contribution to the territorial taxes caused, only too late, a bitter repentance,
and brought about fatal results to property and private
fortunes.

The session of the night of the 4th of August was
crowded : everyone wanted to know what had happened
in the provinces, the natural result of the great excite-

ment in the capital. The details of these almost general insurrections were heard in most profound silence; and after the report had been read, a generous feeling was universal. Some proposed to free the country from all traces of feudalism, others wished to declare the church rates abolished.

These decrees of abolition caused the issue of two remarkable works, remarkable from the names of their authors as by their disinterested character. One, written by the Abbé Maury, was entitled, "Return me my Eight Hundred Francs"; the other, by the Abbé Sieyès, was against the suppression of the smaller taxes, which formed the revenue of his abbey. The latter chose as the motto of his pamphlet, "They want to be Free, but do not know how to be Just."

These two protests showed the amount of patriotism of those abbés who preached either revolution or the cause of the monarchy, but who at the same time would much rather have retained their wealth and their livings.

This night is to be remembered for the transfer of property and for the generous abandonment of so many privileges which formed the patrimony of whole families. I myself, yielding to the enthusiasm, mounted the tribune to propose that the recklessness of Francis I. should be forgotten, for he it was who set the example of selling posts and official positions, and I begged the Assembly to accept the patriotic gift I wished to make to the national finances by resigning my position as magistrate, in the hope that the National Assembly would obliterate the shame of such venality in the disposal of judicial appointments.

In presenting to the national finances my post
of chief councillor of the *sénéchaussée* of Bigorre, I
relinquished the sum of 12,000 francs, at which sum
it was valued by the accountant-general. This was
a great deal in proportion to my fortune : it was too
much in comparison with the avarice of other magistrates, who neither gave nor offered anything to the
State. I was soundly blamed by my fellow-citizens,
who termed such an act a useless extravagance; my
family went further, telling me that not one of the
higher magistrates or wealthy deputies had made
similar sacrifices. However, I did not repent it. I
had done an act pleasing to my heart and agreeable
to my feelings for my country. Thus commenced
the diminution of my patrimony, a diminution which
always increased by the effect of the revolutionary
laws and the unhappy events resulting from my
proscription; while so many of my colleagues and
many others gained fortunes in the course of the
revolution. But I have never loved nor courted
riches : the future will be just to me, and that is my
real fortune.

I did hope by this patriotic act to excite a healthy
emulation among the magistrates, presidents, and coun-
cillors of parliament who were members of the Assembly; and this impulse, acting through the law courts
of the provinces, would naturally relieve the national
taxes. I soon found how much I was deceived : the
patriotic gift which I made was loudly applauded, as
all such sacrifices were at this period of impoverish-
ment of the treasury ; but not a single magistrate,
not one of the rich members of parliament, not one
of those wealthy chief judges or attorneys-general

cared to follow my example! It could be seen from that moment how much selfishness had worked its fatal way into French minds, and how completely the mother-country with us is an empty term.

September, 1789.

The month of September passed in debates on the constitution, and, above all, upon the Declaration of Rights, the initiation of which was due to M. de Lafayette, who had brought the idea from the United States, at the time when he gloriously fought for their independence. I was dining with M. Mounier, one of the Constitutional Assembly, who, like myself, had been invited to dine with the Archbishop of Bordeaux, M. Champion de Cicé, an able statesman, who could have done good service had the King created him a minister, an omission which at once was the abolition of the statesman and of a national policy.

Conversation with M. de Cicé.

After dinner, at which there were many disputes—for M. Mounier was a headstrong debater, although a very enlightened journalist—I talked with M. de Cicé, who asked me what my colleagues thought of the present state of France.

"They think," I replied, "that we are in mid-ocean, without sails, without helm, and without ballast. France can only be a constitutional monarchy. . . . The old abuses of royal despotism and the practice of absolute power on the part of ministers must be given up."

"But how can we remedy the actual state of

things?" said the prelate naively. . . . "The Court is irresolute, the country people are irritated, Paris is excited and discontented. . . . There is neither money in the treasury nor decision in public opinion."

"That is quite true, but greater efforts still must be made to remedy this state of things. . . . Pass a Declaration of Rights, more or less perfect, and cause it to be frankly and solemnly accepted by the King : this, at all events, will be a plank thrown from the shipwreck of public rights and of popular agitation. The constitution wants more time and a carefully-constructed organisation to produce good effects, and above all to be lasting. . . . Then pass this Declaration of Rights as soon as may be."

"But will the two chambers pass it ? . . . This would radically calm the two orders and the Court, who see their safety and their existence assured only in the establishment of two chambers."

"This is the political principle of a good legislative organisation ; but public opinion is a long way off such an institution. The imprudent and obstinate resistance of the two orders has caused the fall of the clergy and the hatred of the nobility . . . . Do not think for a moment to obtain the power to create two chambers, which, by their likeness to those of England, would re-establish the clergy and nobility and make them stronger, more influential, more reactionary and more aristocratic than ever."

Several days after, M. de Cicé said to me, in coming into the Assembly, "Your reflections have much struck me, and I have communicated them to the Constitutional Committee : these gentlemen have taken much pains to occupy themselves solely with the Declaration of Rights, and desired at the same time to pass three or four fundamental acts of the constitution."

5th and 6th of October, 1789.

Events changed their character every day in Paris. The dissatisfaction with the Court broke out everywhere. Was it, as has been said, a preconceived movement? The threat of going to Versailles to seek the King, of bringing him to Paris and keeping him there until the constitution was established, was this the effect of the manœuvres of a powerful clique which was accused of (1) having caused M. Necker to double the number of the House of Commons; (2) having prompted the events of the 14th of July in Paris, where the two busts of Necker and of the Duke of Orleans were publicly paraded; (3) having provoked, by the burning of the castles, the decrees of the night of the 14th of August? I leave to history the burden of clearly and impartially deciding on the value of the contemporary indictments.

It is perfectly certain that we learned, in assembly at Versailles, that the population of Paris were agitating, and that soon there would be another revolution. The members of the Constituent Committee were debating this subject, for from the beginning of October they were forced to obey the reiterated requests of the National Assembly, which desired to work out the constitution, well knowing that the opinion of the Parisians charged its members with a neglect of the work so essential to public tranquillity. M. Mounier was seen to come on the 2nd, 3rd and 4th of October to submit for discussion several pro-

positions, constitutional in character and declarative
of public rights.

Before five o'clock on the evening of the 4th of
October, M. de Cicé came to announce the first fundamental articles of the constitution to the King. The
King, having given his signature, and knowing the
agitation and excitement in Paris, went hunting in
his grounds near Satory. I saw him return about
. six in the afternoon of the 4th of October, on horseback, and escorted by four of his bodyguard. The road
to Paris was then crowded by people anxious to know
what was about to happen. A kind of deputation
from the rioters had come to the doors of the National
Assembly, which had declared a permanent sitting,
as it did on the 12th of July last.

I came from the Assembly, and was crossing the
road, to make notes of the day's session at home.
I was lodging opposite the Chamber, along the avenue,
in the apartments of M. l'Abbé Daram, one of the
chaplains of M. d'Artois, in the King's mews. As I
said, I was crossing the avenue, when the King went
by on horseback: the excitement was at this moment
so extreme that I saw some men among the rioters'
deputation from Paris fire twice at the two rear men
of the King's bodyguard. One of the bodyguard lost
his hat for a moment; I feared he was hit, and
returned to my lodgings overwhelmed with grief.

The Assembly soon learned that the King had
his travelling carriages ready for flight either to
Metz or Montmédy, where he could be surrounded
by faithful guards; that the Count d'Estaing, the
general of the Versailles National Guard, wished to
protect the flight or progress of the King; but the

guards themselves were opposed to this, and had shut the gates of the park, among others those of the orangery, through which the King's carriages were to pass. The night was awful. A crowd of people, armed in all sorts of ways, flooded all this avenue of Versailles as far as the palace railings, the gates of which had been just closed. Excited women were seated on the guns and even on the waggons which followed them. Soon the National Guard and several grenadiers arrived to swell the crowd that already had forced the first gate, and was storming that of the little marble court. Consternation and rioting, yells, jeers, threats, the explosion of firearms—these give a faint picture of this dreadful evening.

The night was worse: doors broken in, murders— but I stop, for it is for history to record these deplorable scenes of violence and cruelty. Several of the bodyguard, who courageously defended their posts, lost their lives. One of this bodyguard, a country- man of mine, well known to the Abbé Daram, with whom I lodged, and who was seen by him timorously running to hide himself, told us of the dangers he had escaped. We gave him shelter on the night of the 4th and all day on the 5th. On the 6th the rioters returned to Paris, taking the King with them. I shared in this good work, which was not solely to my credit, because the rioters never dreamed that one of the bodyguard would be found secreted in the lodgings of a deputy of the National Assembly.

The National Assembly in Paris.

I left Versailles with regret. Paris is not convenient for national assemblies; there exist influences at once corrupting, malevolent, chaotic and calumnious. It was not without reason that during the ancient monarchy—under the Valois, for instance—the States-General were held, in turn, in several provincial cities.

Thus in the history of the national and legislative assemblies we read of the States-General of Blois, Orleans, Tours, Roussillon, Rouen, Villers-Cotterets, etc.

Undoubtedly, were it not that the opinion of the masses was liable to corruption, if public spirit were not too often one-sided and created for the occasion, if civic virtue and enlightened patriotism always guided writers, journalists, authors and public meetings, as well as those cliques which have obtained too great an influence over public affairs: in that case it is clear that public assemblies would find a far more congenial home in the centre of the capital than in the provinces: simply for the reason that in the capital is found the home of public opinion and a richer gathering of enlightened men to rule the business and requirements of the State. But when will this desideratum be accomplished? When will there be more national feeling and backbone in Paris, and less selfishness in all its ranks?

Once in Paris, the deputies of the National Assembly sat in the Archbishop's palace. It might have been mistaken for a synod or an ecclesiastical council, rather than a political assembly, if one considered the stalls and decorations of the sessions-chamber; but one soon saw that it was the National Assembly in the exercise, by representation, of the sovereignty of the people, for the first question which

was there debated was to the effect: Was it necessary and legal for the nation to make public property
of the wealth, real and personal, of the regular and
secular clergy? This decree of appropriation has
been much criticised, although this is the fourth time
such an event has befallen the clergy of France.
Read Montesquieu, who says in "*L'Esprit des Lois*":
"Three times the clergy have succeeded in acquiring
riches and immense property, and three times have
they been deprived of them; yet the clergy go on
acquiring."

The Assembly was then occupied with the formation of several committees.

It had formed one called the *Lettres de Cachet* Committee, which comprised four members: the Count de
Mirabeau, the Marquis de Castellane, M. Fréteau and
myself. Our business was to inspect the registers
of the State prisons, to liberate all the prisoners, to
obliterate all traces of royal and ministerial despotism,
and to make a report to the Constituent Assembly
of the more remarkable facts and details of the subject
under discussion. The Count de Mirabeau said to us:
"Who would have thought that the prisoner of the
keep of Vincennes would one day have the charge of
liberating his fellows!" M. Fréteau had been confined
in the fortress of the Margaret Isles by order of Louis
XVI., before 1788, for having opposed the entirely
arbitrary augmentation of the revenue duty. M. de
Castellane and I did the greater part of the work;
M. Fréteau often helped us; Mirabeau lent us the
aid of his name and his great experience.

In four months all the State prisons were open,
and their occupation permanently forbidden. How

many poor wretches were restored to light, to free will, to public justice—that is to say, to liberty! This had been effected once before by the virtuous and unfortunate Malesherbes, whose name will for ever live in the hearts of the friends of France, of virtue and of liberty.

The Lettres de Cachet Committee appointed by the Constituent Assembly.[1]

After the taking of the Bastille, its darksome archives were found intact. The governor, thinking this fortress impregnable, took no care to disperse or burn them. This secret arsenal of despotism contained documents as curious as they were horrible, and pregnant with useful revelations.

The first care of the *Lettres de Cachet* Committee was to carry off the registers and documents of the Bastille, already given over to the corporation of Paris by the ministry of M. Manuel, its attorney-general, who had caused copies to be made for publications which he undertook some time afterwards on his own account.

Our investigations put us on the track of a certain Count de Créqui, a connection of the Bourbons, who had been confined in the Bastille, but whose fate was completely unknown, as his name did not appear in the list of deaths and burials of the Bastille. His family sought his arrest, and desired afterwards to lose all trace of him by arranging with the Prussian minister for his detention in the dungeons of Stettin, in Pomerania. In another place, I will tell how our

---

[1] Fragment interpolated.

committee managed to knock off unhappy Créqui's fetters.

We also found traces of the twelve Breton deputies whom the Archbishop of Sens, M. de Brienne, the Prime Minister, had thrown into the Bastille in 1788. It will be recollected that when the Breton nobility assembled at Vannes and at St. Brieux, where they represented twelve hundred of their members, they had delegated twelve commissioners to present to Louis XVI. a memorandum against the attempts made to the prejudice of the ancient laws of the kingdom, and to the prejudice of the Breton prerogatives and privileges, by the ministers and by the governors of that province. Consequently, the Counts de la Fraglaie, de Chatillon, de Guer, de Netumières, de Bec-de-Lièvre-Penhoet, with the Marquesses of Carné, Ferronière, Montluc, Bédée, Trémergat, Rouerie, and the Viscount de Cicé, repaired to Versailles to fulfil their mission. They requested an audience of the King, and waited in a trustful security, as deputies of an important and energetic province, for the day when His Majesty would please to receive them; when, during the night of July 14th-15th, 1788, they were arrested at their hotel by virtue of *lettres de cachet*, and shut up in the Bastille. At this news the whole of Brittany was aroused, as astonished as angry with this act of despotism ; and this staggered Cardinal de Brienne, who was forced to restore the twelve commissioners to liberty, and they returned to Rennes in triumph.

The most infamous feature in this arbitrary action which the *Lettres de Cachet* Committee discovered was the correspondence between the Prime Minister, Brienne, and M. de Crosne, lieutenant-general of police.   The minister ordered the latter to prepare quarters in the Bastille for twelve prisoners ; M. de Crosne replied that the place was overcrowded, and that he had no space at disposal.   Whereupon the minister issued new orders to the lieutenant-general of police to clear twelve dungeons for the new comers, and that the former tenants, so evicted, were to be sent to the lunatic asylum at Charenton.   This barbarous idea was carried out, and twelve Bastille prisoners were declared mentally afflicted, and received at Charenton as madmen.

Put on the track by this infamous correspondence between the Prime Minister and the head of police, we ordered M. Bailly, the mayor of Paris, to seek out these twelve unfortunate men.   The registers of Charenton were compared with those of the Bastille, and their identity was established.   The twelve prisoners were perfectly sane !   It is impossible to find in the sombre annals of European despotism as atrocious a trait as that discovered in 1789, for which reparation was then made.

The State Prison of the Bastille.

Aubriot, the municipal chief of Paris, and founder of the Bastille in 1370, desired the welfare of the capital, for which he founded essential institutions. He offended the clergy, who caused him to be accused and condemned to perpetual imprisonment in the Bastille on bread and water.

James d'Armagnac, Duke of Nemours, was shut up there, and condemned for State offences in 1477 ; his prosecution lasted two years.

In the reign of Louis XI. 4,000 prisoners were

confined in the Bastille for real or supposed political offences. Louis XI. had his private executioner, one from Toulouse; the King himself pronounced the verdicts and had them carried out.

Marshal de Biron was, like d'Armagnac, confined and tried at the Bastille, where he was executed. This was a shameful episode of the reign of Henry IV. It was a traitor, one Lafin, who betrayed Biron, whom Henry IV. had formerly pardoned during his stay at Lyons: this Lafin was one of Biron's staff officers. The judges condemned him under the pretext that his offence was one of fact, if not one of intention.

Cardinal de Richelieu crowded the Bastille, like a barbarous imitator of Louis XI. There he confined those nobles whom he persecuted, such as Bassompierre, Dryon, Count de Roussy, Count de Suze, De Mazargues, the brother of Marshal d'Ornano; Marquis Osegnies; the Abbé de Foix, Faucan-Langlois; Abbé de Beaulieu, Dorvat-Langlois, his brother; Vautier, chief surgeon to the Queen-Dowager; Chevalier de Montaigu, Marshal d'Ornano, Marquis Maupinçon; Fourlatton, a Scot; Mazincourt, Count Cramail, Count Charluz, Count Grancé - Merdaire, Marquis Assigné, Lupez, and the Chevalier Grignan.

Cardinal Mazarin, in succeeding to the power of Richelieu, set at liberty almost all the political prisoners proscribed by his predecessor. He substituted cunning for brute force, and treachery for barbarous treatment. Under his ministry there were but few prisoners in the Bastille.

But the reign of Louis XIV. was the grand epoch of imprisonment, proscription and *lettres de cachet*. Under this monarch the State prisons were always crowded. This infamous and cruel era of religious and political proscriptions dates from the period when a lieutenant-general of the police of Paris was appointed.

Fouquet, the Chancellor of the Exchequer, was for a long time confined in the Bastille, and finally died in the State prison of Pignerol, condemned by a special commission to imprisonment for life upon a vague indictment, very similar to that of Enguerrand de Marigny.

The nobles, the grand lords and ladies of the Court, who had tempted into crime three obscure priests, a page named Guignard, Davot, and two women—Voisin and Vigoureux—already condemned to death, only appeared at the Bastille in 1680 and 1692. They were soon acquitted by the Arsenal Chamber, although these nobles and courtiers were accused of poisoning—a crime then very common at Court.

Before and after the Revocation of the Edict of Nantes by the intolerant Louis XIV., the Bastille was not big enough to contain all the Protestant prisoners. Vincennes had the overflow from the former prison.

Under Louis XV. the Bastille was again filled in consequence of the proscriptions against the Jansenists and the Shakers. In consequence of the bull Unigenitus, issued by the Jesuits, eighty thousand *lettres de cachet* were issued.

The rigours of despotism only changed the victims and the causes, but the Bastille was the receiver-general of all proscriptions.

General Lally having triumphed over the English in India, it was necessary to get rid of him; having done what he could for the safety of the French colony, it was necessary to accuse him. He was thrown into the Bastille on the 1st of November, 1762. A decree, voted by a parliamentary commission in 1766, condemned him to capital punishment. A councillor of parliament named Pasquier caused him to come from the Bastille gagged, and he was executed in this state of enforced silence on the 9th of May, 1766. This decree was only reversed on the 15th of March, 1777, on the application of his natural son, M. Lally-Tolendal. *Quid cineris juvat ista sepultis?*

The officers of Louisiana—Mandeville, Grandet and Rocheblave—accused of having written to the prejudice of a tyrannical and arbitrary governor, M. de Kerlerec, were long, but unjustly, shut up in the Bastille. The Abbé Lenglet Dufresnoy was placed, under Louis XV., no less than four times in the Bastille, where, as a philosopher and writer, he passed much of his life. His crime was that he was a conscientious historian, who freely expressed his opinions. Tapin, an emissary of the police, was the man who four times led him to the Bastille. Mahé de Labourdonnais, governor of the Isles of France and Bourbon, passed eight years there.

On the 25th of June, 1769, eleven prisoners, forming the superior council of Cap Français, were sent to the Bastille upon the accusation of Louis de Rohan, because they refused to register an ordinance except with well-considered emendations.

La Chalotais and several members of the Rennes parliament were committed to the Bastille upon the motion of a Duke d'Aiguillon, governor of Brittany.

The provost of Beaumont, who had detected a lease granted for the purchase of corn by Laverdy, the minister, in the name of Louis XV., remained shut up in the Bastille and Vincennes for twenty-two years. For ten years his family did not know what had become of him, and he only gained his liberty on the 14th of July, 1789.

The State prisons were regarded by the governments of France simply as the strongest necessities of power, even if only exercised as instruments of inhumanity and caprice.

In the month of August, 1788, the Prime Minister, Brienne, archbishop of Sens, buried the twelve deputies of the nobility of the States of Brittany in the Bastille. And this was the last act of royal and ministerial despotism, so far as the Bastille was concerned.

The Royal Hunts, 1790.

Hunting was, in the eyes of the kings of France, a great privilege and social institution.

The rules of hunting contained regulations of order, precedence, of interior economy, and penalties, which would have been ridiculous had the system not been one of immemorial usage in France, and one of the oldest feudal rights, and one of its grossest usurpations.

During certain reigns, as one can see in the history of France, it was safer to kill a man than a deer or a boar. Thence originated the old chases, whose gamekeepers, as ferocious as their masters, had the right of life and death over men found on these preserves of animals and wild beasts destined to afford sport to princes.

These chases, to abolish which required all the vigour of a revolutionary reform, gave the royal family the exclusive enjoyment of sport; this exclusive enjoyment bristled with prohibitions and penalties, and covered twenty leagues of country round Paris.

These chases were so considerable and so exacting as to require fodder requisite for the nurture of wild beasts sufficient to furnish at once several hunting establishments. Game abounded everywhere, which was fed by the landowners; and the boars and deer devoured all the harvests, without any attendant recompense.

It was generally understood that of all these chases, of which the regulations were most severe and even murderous, owing to the barbarous immunity of the gamekeepers, Grosbois chase was the worst, which belonged, together with the vast forest of Sénart, to the King's brother, the Count of Provence, called at the Court *Monsieur*.

I was instructed by the Committee of Domains to make a report to the Constituent Assembly on the King's chases; and I worked hard to check the abuses and to curtail the excessive number of these savage pleasure grounds of the monarchs of a civilised nation. Louis XVI., who had been brought up as a hunting king, had a perfect acquaintance with his forests, the places of his meets, and of the statistics relating to his wild beasts and game of all kinds, which were there bred and fed with the greatest care and prodigality. The King was much more interested in the preservation of his hunting grounds and forests, which he had at heart, than in all the constitutional laws that he overlooked and never accepted.

As I had been long busy with other reports of the Committee of Domains, Louis XVI. incessantly

showed an impatient desire that the report relative
to his hunting affairs should be submitted to the
Constituent Assembly. He several times sent M. Ber-
thier to me to hurry me up with this report. He was
one of the King's aides-de-camp, afterwards one of
Napoleon's major-generals. Or he would send the
Prince de Poix, who was much attached to His Majesty.
Later, the messenger was M. de Talleyrand, with whom
I had then much to do, who often spoke to me of the
King's desire to have his forest and hunting rights
settled. This made me presume that Talleyrand was
the confidential adviser of the King, a fact hitherto
unknown, and which was afterwards proved by Talleyrand's correspondence, which was found by the minister
Roland in an iron coffer at the Tuileries in the early
months of the National Convention.

I therefore busied myself at this work, and subsequently read my report to the Committee of Domains ;
my proposition that the royal hunts should be restricted to the enclosed farms at Versailles was adopted,
and I subjected the King to pay fair compensation to
the landowners and farmers whose crops might be
injured.

The Constituent Assembly adopted my draft decree
thus presented to it in the name of the Committee of
Domains, and ordered it to be printed.

While preserving the royal hunts for a monarch
who clung passionately to his recreation, I sought to
remove all causes of discontent and ruin by suppressing
all the abuses that formerly were attached to these old
chases.[1]

---

[1] Close of the interpolated passages.

How the Breton Club became the Jacobin Club.

A short time after the National Assembly became settled in Paris, a club was formed, which became so influential, so celebrated, and so exclusive under the name of the Jacobin Club. This name was given it because it was held in the church of the old Jacobin monks in the Rue St. Honoré, towards the close of 1789. What was generally unknown was that the club already existed under another name, and with a less deliberative procedure, under the name of the Breton Club.

The Breton Club was founded at Versailles after the royal session of the 23rd of June. At first its members were the numerous and energetic deputies of the province of Brittany; afterwards, its members elected MM. Sieyès, the brothers de Lameth, Charles de Noailles, the Duke d'Aiguillon, Adrien Duport, and several other deputies. I was never elected to the Breton Club; it was only in Paris, a long time after it had been settled at the Jacobins', that my colleagues suggested I should be added to the deputies already there. There were then only the deputies and very few outsiders. Some months after, towards September, 1790, several deputies began to discover the club was becoming too large, too tumultuous, while increasing in power and influence; so some of its more distinguished members determined not to make a split, but to establish another club. This was to share the political influence of the Jacobins and guide public opinion by that spirit of opposition that does not destroy, but discusses; which does not burn down, but enlightens. Thus was formed at the two ends of the Palais Royal, near the Radzivill passage, the

1789 club. There the secessionists assembled to
read the papers and to dine on leaving the National
Assembly, and they comprised the Deputies Sieyès,
Mirabeau, Talleyrand, Jessé, Lafayette, Liancourt,
Castellane, and several others, who were wise and enlightened enough only to wish for revolution as a path-
way to a settled constitution ; they only formed this
club as a vestibule to regular and useful debate in the
National Assembly.   Several of the deputies belonged
to both the clubs, the Jacobin and that of '89· Sometimes they went to one, sometimes the other ; but those
of whom I speak generally frequented the latter.   I was
one of them, and the pleasure of hearing Mirabeau
in his more familiar talk drew me often to the
club in the Palais Royal. This ended in our establishing a regular discussion on the constitution.   Here
M. Ramond, who was a member, frequently discussed the constitutional articles submitted by the
debating committee of the National Assembly. This
was like a preliminary debate, and woke up everyone.   M. Rœderer, naturally disputatious and a
subtle casuist, sometimes opposed M. Ramond.   M.
de Bougainville, the famous navigator, was a warm
friend of public liberty ; and he never missed these
sessions for constitutional discussion, at which I sometimes spoke, but without the masterful and trenchant
style of Ramond and Rœderer.

Meeting at Madame de Genlis'.

It was about this time that I was introduced to Madame de Sillery-Genlis, in whom were combined a literary celebrity and advanced ideas. At Belle-chasse she directed the education of the young Orleans princes, and that of *Mademoiselle*. The young princes were most promising. They were carefully brought up in the best principles of morality and policy. They understood the history of nations thoroughly, and they belonged to a country, scarce in the experience of princes, which believed that the people existed for themselves.

I found in the conversation of Madame de Genlis information combined with wit, good sense mingled with a most profound experience, vigour in speech, graciousness of spirit, absence of prejudice, clear perception, conclusions full of judgment, and a subtle appreciation of talent. She received the deputies every Sunday. Matthew de Montauran, Alexander Lameth, Barnave, and the famous painter David, intimately connected with the Pole Myris, the young princes' professor of drawing.

I also saw there MM. de Talleyrand, Alquier, the Viscounts de Beauharnais, de Volney and de Sillery.

The eldest of the princes struck me as being grave, full of sense and learning, a good citizen, a fervent patriot, and a lover of wit and sparkle in conversation ; appearing to possess all that could characterise a wise, thoughtful and humane prince. His second brother, the Duke de Montpensier, was the image of his father—much more like him than his elder brother, whom he also somewhat resembled. He had the same carriage of the head, the same disposition, and an air of amiable dignity. M. de Beaujolais was a fac-simile of Forbus' picture of Henry IV. in the Palais-Royal gallery—the same vivacity, the same disposition, and a gallant air, at once striking and animated.

What delightful days I passed in this aristocratic society, where my title of deputy was my only introduction! Sometimes we spent the evening in Mousseaux Park, sometimes in Great Raincy Park. I was overwhelmed with the thoughtfulness and kindness of Madame de Genlis and of the young princes, whose memory will always be precious and honourable to me.

Sometimes on these evenings I met the Duke of Orleans, whose colleague I was in the Constitutional Assembly. He amused himself by chatting to me on the course of public affairs, and more often on the policy of England, with which he was intimately acquainted, as he was with the character of the French and the manners of the English. The Duke of Orleans concealed under an appearance of levity and recklessness the power of deep thought and sensible conclusions. They said he was far more fitted for company than politics; but he was misunderstood. He was timid, although a great personage; he was a citizen, though a prince; and had he been able to conquer his natural indecision and his political fears, that were taken as flaws in his character, he might have proved fit to reign, and redoubled the part of Louis XII., also once Duke of Orleans, who had been calumniated, misunderstood and persecuted at Court as he was.

The Duchess of Bourbon, sister of the Duke of

Orleans, sometimes visited Madame de Genlis in the evening. She talked in a lively way, like her brother, but with less reserve and more force upon public affairs, on the causes and progress of the Revolution. I continued to enjoy the advantages of this circle, so distinguished for many reasons, until the close of 1791, when I left for Tarbes.

One day Madame de Genlis, hearing me describe the Pyrenees and the patriarchal life of their inhabitants, asked me to write a detailed account of my experiences. In consequence I wrote her the following letter, which she inserted, two years after, in a pamphlet entitled, "Explanation of the Conduct of Madame de Genlis during the Revolution":

MADAM,—You appeared to me favourably impressed with my feeble sketch of the pastoral manners of the Pyreneans. What would they be if you witnessed them—you who, born with exquisite sensibility, have learnt the art of adequately describing the great yet simple beauties of nature? I will repeat the little I told you of the country in which I was born, and of which I constantly recall the happiest recollections of my life To talk to you of this is to revisit my native place, and I owe you this pleasure.

The constitution of our mountains is entirely pastoral. Nature has decreed this, and it has been accepted by a hundred generations, which have passed in these beautiful valleys, where man is philosophical without knowing it, and fully happy without envy.

The only enemies of this pastoral constitution are the floods and the bears. One deluges the fields and the other destroys our flocks which browse there. But nature soon repairs the inevitable ravages common to this smiling country, and faithful dogs drive off the animals of prey, which, since the mountaineering population has increased, have taken refuge in most inaccessible spots and in the dark fir forests, where they live without annoying their neighbours. Our men, living thus between nature and mankind, have preserved the benefits of the one and the advantages of the other.

Thus one sees amongst them domestic customs which make

both ages of society meet, where one comes fresh from the hands of
nature, and where one adapts oneself to the usages of society.

A child is a shepherd as soon as he can follow that employ,
and leads his flock to the common pasturage grounds; he feeds them
with care, shelters the sheep from the sun, leads them in the
evening to the well and the fold; he makes butter and cheese,
thus carrying out his youthful career. Soon increasing strength
calls him to harder and more important work: the constant
cares of agriculture, the little transactions of commerce and of
the markets entirely occupy him. The elder ones find a legal,
though unjust, method of marrying with undue advantage: a
companion shares their labours, and the home is repeopled with
fresh shepherds, who, in turn, become agriculturists and fathers.

At last the one who has built the cabin, who first saw
the increase of his children and his flocks, approaches senility.
A relative or a deputy takes over the domestic cares, and
the subsequent proceedings interest the veteran no more. His
age protects him from household cares, and his patriarchal
life recalls him to his first employ as a shepherd, but not the
shepherd of his earlier days. The flocks he has to tend do not
leave the fields around the house. On his return the young
ones tend the sheep. The old man at the close of day retires
to his peaceful fireside, where he finds consolatory care, respect
without constraint, and that peace of mind which is more particularly the meed of a naturally spent life.

But I will admit that the first time I saw those old shepherds—grandfathers reduced to the employment lowlanders only
give to servants—I saw an affecting contrast between an honoured
age and the head of a family, and the little-esteemed position
of a shepherd among agriculturists. Their state of servitude
and insignificance vexed me, and I inquired of one of these
patriarchs whether he still possessed any happiness in life. He
undeceived me directly by telling me it was only right that each
one in his turn should bear the household cares and the field work.
I asked him if he got tired of being all day alone, and among the
fields he had seen so often. I soon saw by the simplicity of his replies that *ennui* is the malady of the rich, and that the grand beauties
of nature never tire or surfeit the heart of the mountaineer.

I stop. You only wished to know this particular feature in
the pastoral habits of the Pyreneans of Bigorre; and I have
told you all. I only wish my shepherds could find themselves
next your pupils, although they date centuries before the Declaration of Rights! . . . .

I have the honour to be, madam, respectfully your most
humble and obedient servant,   B. B.

Since then the events of the Revolution developed so rapidly, what with the 10th of August and the National Convention, that Madame de Genlis, who had first retired to Belgium in 1793, thought it more prudent to take refuge in Hamburg. It was there, in 1796, at the time of the Executive Directory, that Madame de Genlis printed and circulated in France a pamphlet entitled, " Details of the Conduct of Madame de Genlis since the Revolution." I here subjoin an extract from these details concerning myself, although this lady, after having heaped kindnesses on me, now loads me with the names of " scoundrel," " monster," and other amenities, which, in an emigrant, may well be excused.

On the first line of page 24 can be read:

" At the commencement of the year 1790, one of my acquaintances spoke to me in the most flattering terms of a young deputy who came from the depths of the southern provinces, and who, it was said, was passionately fond of my works, and was anxious to be introduced to me. I thought that, since he liked my works, he possessed those principles which give tone to manners and respect for religion. I was confirmed in this idea by the fact that he was himself a literary man, author of two works which had competed for the prizes given by the literary Academy of Toulouse. These two books, which bore his name, although they had been published two years, were little known in Paris. Their author sent them to me. One was, 'A Eulogium on Louis XII., Father of his People and King of France,' and, with a panegyric on this Prince, contained, 'A Eulogium on Monarchical Government and the Love of the French for their Kings.'

The other book was 'A Eulogium on the late M. Lefranc de Pompignan,' and contained, at the same time, a touching defence of religion and a well-founded satire on modern philosophy. These works were badly written (and the author has not, up to now, matured his style), but one found in them wit, good reasoning, ingenious argument, and excellent morality. I consented at last to receive this deputy: he was the execrable Barère!

"This curious anecdote would have taken this monster to the scaffold if I had recollected it in Robespierre's time; but my silence and the thorough oblivion into which these two eulogies had fallen gave impunity to an author who committed the *enormous crime* of displaying humane and religious feeling in these first productions of his pen, but which were otherwise quite insignificant. This is the way in which I made this rascal's acquaintance. He was young, enjoyed a good reputation, joined to much wit, a plausible character, an insinuating manner, and ways that were lofty, calm and reserved. He was the only man I have met coming fresh from the provinces with a style and manners that are never out of place in society and at Court. He was not well educated, but his conversation was always amiable and attractive. He evinced great sensibility, a passionate taste for art, talent, and a rural life. These soft and alluring tendencies, joined to a lively wit, gave to his personality and character much that was interesting and really original. Such he appeared to me, and doubtless to others also; cowardice alone made him a sanguinary ruffian. For the rest, my connection with him (as with other people I have only known since the Revolution) was never intimate ; he only came once a week, on Sundays, which was my day for visits. I wrote to him but once in my life to ask for details as to the manners and customs of the Pyrenean shepherds. He replied in a three-paged letter, relating solely to this subject. He wrote to me once since, at the close of my stay in England, to ask me to return ; and in this epistle, which I have preserved, he added that he could easily imagine the terrible scenes that had happened in Paris had utterly shocked and terrified me ; that he did not advise my return to Paris, but offered me a refuge in his house in the Pyrenees, where I could stay until the troubles were over ; that I could live there retired and peaceful in the midst of those pastures of which I had so well sketched the manners and customs, and so on and so forth. The remainder of the letter was simply complimentary, and was dated the 1st of October, 1792. I made no reply, and never since have written to him."

Divisional Committee.

At the National Assembly I took a large share in the discussion against the modern system of dividing the provinces and slicing up the nation into a thousand insignificant parts, and thus give them over, in detail, to an oppressive administration, with the pretext of governing them more easily. It was in this committee, justly termed a divisional committee, that the various deputations discussed this subject. It meant no less than to break up the old federations which made France; to take from these provinces their distinguishing traits and character without touching the principle of general federation. In a word, our journalists of the day wanted what they called a clear course, or rather to smoothe the way for despotism the moment liberty ceased to exist among us.

The Abbé Sieyès was credited with the idea of splitting France up into small departments, and we called this project the " Departmental Draughtboard." Many deputies, rightly attached to certain great advantages resulting from the federative system as a means of resisting as a State body both the arbitrary acts and governmental corruption, would not agree to departmental division ; each department seemed to them too small to baffle despotism of whatever kind— for has not liberty its own despotism ? Other deputies feared the risk which would be run by liberty and the newly-constituted corporations, as powerful as were the states of Languedoc, Burgundy, Provence, Dauphiny, and Brittany.

They saw nothing but incitements to civil war in these large confederated provinces, while others saw nothing but incentives to despotism and political servitude in small unresisting departments, without an armed force, with a sparse population, and with no powerful influence on public opinion or protection.

In the midst of these debates I found the majority of the deputies, eager for novelties, blindly adopting the plan of departmental division. They hastened to decree this in principle, desirous to break the federative ties of the provinces under the pretext of abolishing their mediæval immunities and their dangerous privileges.

The provinces were abolished, and thus lost all they could lose; the elective counties could but gain, as they were relieved from the stern despotism of the *intendants.* We resigned ourselves to hoping only to see a return to the federative system, like that of the United States of America, when France had experienced all the calamities attached to revolution, all the dangers of political novelties and the loss of liberty, through the means, too, of these weak, disunited and powerless departments, which would throw themselves by their very weakness into every excess, into every extreme, even into the arms of tyranny, to serve it as tools or nourishment.

Under these circumstances, I thought it well to confine myself to the preservation of my little province of Bigorre, which scarcely possessed the population or extent required by the decrees of the National Assembly to form a department. The deputies of Béarn and Navarre desired to absorb our province of Bigorre, which is richer, better situated, and more cultivated than their own country; they insisted in the divisional committee that Bigorre should form two districts of the Béarnais department, one mountainous, the other of the plain.

They did not fail to lay stress on the fact that Béarn had been a kingdom which governed Bigorre under Antoine d'Albret, the father of Henry IV., so Bigorre would naturally form part of the department of Béarn. I thought differently, although the Béarnais were very desirous to carry out this idea of reunion.

My only means of acting was to write a descriptive history of my country, describing its staples, its population, its thermal springs, its customs, its agricultural and pastoral character, its peculiar institutions, and its administration, which was in the old states days always independent, resembling that of Béarn. I printed this essay, on which I spent much care, and wherein I clearly demonstrated the necessity of creating a department at Bigorre, under the title of the Hautes Pyrénées. I took a copy of it to Mirabeau, asking him to read it, and, if he thought it reasonable, to support its cause. He received me with his accustomed grace and urbanity. In the course of conversation, he told me he was overworked with his letters to his constituents and to the *Courrier de Provence;* that he would willingly join the *Point du Jour,* of which I should always be the sole editor, and that he would write for it several articles weekly. I have always mistrusted mixing with lions, so I replied, in a manner calculated to soften my refusal and to flatter his incontestable superiority : " The sheep of the Pyrenees do not herd with wolves; you are a power which would soon crush the humble editor of the *Point du Jour.*" He smilingly said, "I will repeat my proposal another time." He never failed to testify great kindness and even friendship for me. We used to dine twice a week at the Marquis de Castellane's in those days.

The Province of Bigorre created the Department of the Hautes Pyrénées.

I caused my essay to be circulated among the members of the National Assembly, and when the decree relative to the department of the Hautes Pyrénées came before the House, a very able and impartial reporter, M. Gossin, insisted on the many points made in my work. I was lucky enough to curb the ambition of the Béarnais deputation, while I secured for my province:

1. That it should remain intact as a department.

2. That the neighbouring country, known as the Quatre Allées, which was desired by the department of the Haute Garonne to add to the district of St. Gaudens, should instead be added to our department, which was already under-populated, and that thus all the institutions which are attached to each departmental division would console my fellow-citizens for the loss of their administrative power under the states system, a loss they regretted for many reasons.

The deputies of the town of St. Gaudens had also shown a desire to create a department by joining the states of Bigorre to the states of Comingeois ; but I succeeded in baffling the St. Gaudens deputation as I had done that of Béarn. Thus my country remained a department, and possessed the self-government it had exercised as the province of Bigorre.

In all my work as representative, the most agreeable and most useful to my reputation was that of obtaining the creation of · the department of the Hautes Pyrénées. For this I received the most flattering and continual testimonials of the gratitude of my countrymen, and whenever there was an election I was invariably elected deputy. Their votes repaid me for my trouble, softened the evils of my proscription, and have proved to several governments that a people or a department beyond their corrupting influence follows solely the impulse of their own will and that of their own gratitude. The celebrated D'Aguesseau would have found in the Pyrenees the truth of one of his maxims : " In its suffrages a free people glorifies itself and never sells them."

Indeed, patriotism rules in the Pyrenees ; but in

populous districts crowded into a few square miles of
land, it may be said with that heroine deserted by
her family, " I have no fatherland." Rome was
patriotic; and this is only so in a town where the
population knows everyone, and is united in the defence of its country. The Roman empire, made up of
a crowd of nationalities, without either a connecting
link or intimate connection, was nothing but an
aggregate of men astonished or irritated at finding
themselves under the same yoke. Sparta and Athens
were like Rome in their adoration of patriotism, and
for the same reasons; but when Philip had cor-
rupted them, and when that madman Alexander had
incorporated them in the Macedonian empire, patriotism
fled and slavery commenced. And so it is in France.
It is always chimerical for Parisians to talk of patriotism.
The Provençal and the Alsatian are really patriotic;
but not in Paris, which is simply the general cara-
vanserai of Europe.

I shall leave it to time and to the onward march
of moral and political corruption to prove this sad
truth. I take up the progress of events, in which,
unhappily for my fortune and peace of mind, my life
has been entangled since 1789. I pass over the intrigues of the ministers of Louis XVI., who, towards
the middle of 1790, endeavoured by means of prompted
and paid agitations in the departments of the centre of
France, to cause the Constituent Assembly to endow
the King with his old authority. This authority, they
said, was necessary for the suppression of the riots
caused by the peasants, who rose against many feudal
and fiscal rights, which they declined to pay, especially in the departments of the ancient Quercy,

Limousin and Poitou. Saint-Priest, the Minister of the Interior, was the one who started these agitations, with the purpose of giving the King his original power, so much desired by his courtiers.

The Assembly ordered a circumstantial and exact report of these agitations to be laid before it, which should state their true origin, their results, and the legitimate method of repressing them.

A remark of Mirabeau's, annotated by himself.

It was about this time that the great question as to the liberty of the press was discussed. Several fly-sheets had been circulated in the Assembly defending this right, to be subject only to the repressive laws against libel and the discussion of political events, and that their infringement should be decided by juries and not by the ministerial police. It fell to Mirabeau's genius to define the limit of liberty and license, and to defend this palladium of civil and political liberty with energy and judgment. It was then, in a burst of eloquence, while asking that a fixed day should be appointed for the discussion on the liberty of the press, he said: "Each deputy should bring to bear all his intelligence upon this important question. I appeal, in the name of liberty, to one of the most enlightened men here to give us his opinion: the silence of M. Sieyès would be a public calamity."

These words gave a certain elevation to the reputation of the Abbé Sieyès. That day several deputies, M. Frochot and myself, went to dine with Mirabeau in the Rue de Mont Blanc. We repeated this speech which unduly flattered the polemical talents of the vicar-general of Chartres. Mirabeau laughed in his sardonic way, saying: "Let me alone; I have given this abbé such a reputation that will take him all his time to support."

An Autograph Letter of Mirabeau's.

When the national tribune was deprived of the genius and statesmanlike eloquence of Mirabeau, M. Aubriet, a barrister, one of my friends who was intimately connected with him, called to sympathise with me on the loss of this great citizen. He avowed that for some time he had had grave presentiments. Mirabeau had among the Lameth party inveterate enemies, both envious and implacable; and he only saw when too late the fate which awaited him. "There was no longer time, in the latter days of March," he wrote to his friend, M. Aubriet, "to feel oneself alive," and he added, "were it not for this, I should be off, and that sharply." When he wrote thus, on the 26th of March, poison was then in his veins. But M. Aubriet, suspecting nothing, did not warn him of the danger of rival ambitions and of political immorality.

"I leave in your hands," M. Aubriet said to me, with tears, "I entrust you with these last words of a great man, whom you have honoured with a splendid funeral, and whose debts you have caused the nation to clear off." I cannot make a better use of this epistle, written by the almost dying hand of Mirabeau, than to insert it in my reminiscences.

COPY OF THE LETTER ADDRESSED TO M. AUBRIET, FRIEND OF MIRABEAU, DATED SATURDAY, THE 26TH OF MARCH, 1791.

Sometimes one's clock is fast, and sometimes slow. I did not go out this evening until ten minutes past six; I did not leave my den this morning until one. If your last nights had been as unhappy as mine, we should have met. I want to see you; I want . . . . .[1] but I cannot do the impossible; and I must feel myself alive, or I should be off, and that in quick time. As to the rest, I shall be in Paris very early on Monday.

It was curious at this time to note the agitation and the efforts made by all the nobility and the priests of the Right to effect the re-establishment of the old royal prerogative, and to put it in going order before the inauguration of the constitution. I have heard them say, " Maury and Cazalès are quite prepared to speak strongly on this subject." Indeed, these two champions of the old despotism spoke most vigorously, and even with eloquence, upon the necessity of restoring this conservative and repressive power, of this time-honoured authority, which is the foundation of public peace. But this eloquence was to order : these two speakers had their speeches by heart; nothing was spontaneous. They repeated harangues prepared long ago. True royalists as they were, they were in no way enthusiastic; everyone could see they were under orders.

This second - hand eloquence and these official speeches from the mouths of these two knights of the old monarchy had little or no success. The ministerial intrigues were laid bare and entirely checkmated by the just and wise measures which the Constituent Assembly itself decreed, instead of returning, as was desired, all the requisitions of the departments or provinces to be settled by the executive power. It is well to emphasise in contemporary reminiscences this abuse of authority, these ministerial intrigues, this

---

[1] Here the letter is torn; the lacuna is marked by dots.— EDITOR'S NOTE.

Machiavellism of Courts, to warn the people and their
national assemblies against similar traps.

Soon after, a very extraordinary proposal was made
by M. Matthew de Montmorency to abolish all nobiliary
titles, a motion which was only developed and supported
by gentlemen like De Lafayette, De Lameth, De Virieu,
Charles de Noailles, the Duke d'Aiguillon, and De
Broglie.   Mirabeau was the only one who did not speak
on this question, which, however, induced him to bear
his surname of proscription and glory, of hatred and
renown, no longer; they called him Riquetti simply,
which, as he did not conceal, was not to his liking. But
had not M. de Mirabeau published his excellent treatise
on the "Order of Cincinnatus," in which the useless-
ness and danger of the institution of nobility is discussed with so much eloquence and depth?

Undoubtedly France, in spite of the power of the
decrees of the Constituent Assembly, would have found
much difficulty in sweeping away this feudal caste, this
nobility of the Castle and Court, which was constantly
springing from its ashes; like all our superstitions and
prejudices, they crop up again, even in this enlightened
century.   Nobility is abolished by the constitution,
but it remains through our customs; it is banished
henceforth by our code, but it is with us always by
our habits.   Nobility will always be to a State what
rust is to iron.   Nevertheless, when the decree abolishing nobiliary titles and denominations was published,
public opinion enthusiastically endorsed it; but who
can tell the future of the French?

Repeal of the Laws of Louis XIV. against Protestants.

I had been instructed by the Domains Committee

to make a report on the repeal of the atrocious laws of Louis XIV. against Protestants, and cause the property confiscated by the King and administered officially to be restored to them. With what satisfaction I took up this work!

I issued a decree that the descendants of those fugitive sectaries and proscribed families caused by the revocation of the Edict of Nantes should return to France and receive all their civil and political rights.

I also caused it to be ordained that the descendants of the proscribed families should enter into possession of their unsold or unadjudged estates now being officially administered.

Had not the nation been most impoverished by the depredations of the preceding reigns, it would have given the descendants of these proscribed families a much more generous indemnity than was the one allotted to the emigrants.

Fugitive Religionists under Louis XIV.

" In 1790 Barère, a member of the Constituent Assembly, proposed and carried a decree for the restitution to the descendants of proscribed and banished Protestants of their confiscated estates, which were then under official control. But the unhappy wretches whose goods had been seized were not voluntary emigrants." M. de Montrol, in his "History of the Emigration," published in 1825, reports this legislative fact, in recalling the persecutions they underwent at the hands of the Jesuitic power which now, as then, dominates France. The unsold estates were restored ; but as for the others which had been

sold or given over to the rapacity of the courtiers
of Louis XIV. and Louis XV., the word "indemnity" which was so frequently and complaisantly pronounced by the emigrants when they became legislators, the word was never used by the reporter who
drafted the law of 1790 in the Constituent Assembly.
And yet, had not the unhappy religious fugitives,
who had been oppressed and despoiled for so long,
as valid rights as the anti-constitutional and anti-
national emigrants?

As soon as this motion was carried, a large
number of wretched families of these religious fugitives, and of those who had remained in France,
reduced to the lowest depths of misery, applied to
me and presented several requests, either as to those
Catholic families who had been enriched by the
plunder of their unfortunate Protestant relations, or
upon the various concessions which the barbarous
extravagance of the governments of Louis XIV. and
Louis XV. had granted, by way of recompense, to
claimants not related to the families of these fugitives.
I had the pleasure of seeing the good effects of this
law of restitution.   A large number of inquiries
came from Prussia, England, Switzerland, and, above
all, from Holland, and members of those families which
had been proscribed by the bigotry of a despotic king
came too.   No law was ever so beneficial.   It brought
hope and welfare into hearts and into families which
had known neither for a century.   Eventually I caused,
through the Committee of Domains, sundry clauses
confirmatory of the law to be drawn up, which had
the effect of smoothing over difficulties raised by
the courts on this subject.

Protestants in France.

Assassinated in France by Charles IX., besieged and exterminated at La Rochelle by Cardinal de Richelieu, under Louis XIII., persecuted wholesale by the dragonnades of Cévennes, under Louis XIV., expelled by the Edict of Nantes, which had assured the crown of France to Henry IV., the Protestants regained some of their rights only in the first years of the reign of Louis XVI., during the ministry of Turgot. An edict of the new King in favour of non-Catholics gave them back those rights of which the revocation of the Edict of Nantes had deprived them. The Constituent Assembly crowned the work of tolerance and justice commenced by Louis XVI. in recalling these emigrants to France as citizens, and by restoring to them all the property still remaining in the possession of the crown. We have here a brief recital of the miseries and of the recall of these Frenchmen, who were at once so estimable and so long unhappy.

The work of the constitution progressed slowly, because the Assembly, justly distrustful of the ministry, became imperceptibly burdened with the entire public administration, and because this kind of deliberative government, continually issuing decrees, became encumbered with litter, offices, and correspondence, becoming what I called "a government by pen."

This nuisance of papers and crowds of boxes has been one of the greatest drawbacks of the governments since 1789, and will for a long time be the same in France, where there exists a race of administrative officials who carry out the national administration badly.

It was not until 1791 that the work on the constitutional laws was accelerated. The population of Paris, accustomed to novelties, thirsting for revolutions, required a change of scene and fresh political actors.

At the door of the Constituent Assembly was sold about this time a wretched pamphlet, which had a great run, entitled, "Return us our Eighteen Francs, and sling your hook!" The licentious style of this libel against the Assembly, and the reproach of the miserable pay of eighteen francs a day roused the opinion of Paris against the Assembly, and increased the foolish impatience that existed to see the end of the representatives. One would have thought that it was the Parisians alone who paid the miserable stipends of the deputies; for it is the mania of the population of the capital that all France is contained in Paris.

The people seemed to fear that they would never see the constitution formed and agreed on. The Court feared the close of these labours of the Constitutional Committee, which would oblige the King to accept this new *régime* of politics and hard and fast law.

The Year 1791.

Everything, therefore, was done to hinder this acceptance in 1791, as everything had been done in October, 1789, to prevent the King giving his assent to the first articles of the Declaration of Rights. The Court tried by delay to gain all their ends; the better to obstruct, it sought to get up strife in the palace. The National Guard often found itself contending in the Tuileries with a courtiers' guard, which had for title "The Knights of the Dagger." This was composed of squires and gentlemen culled from Brittany and the south of France to defend the King and his authority, which was said to be more threatened than ever. The scenes which happened in the Tuileries were more farcical than terrible, and ended this exhibition of provincial loyalty by the disarmament of the "Knights of the Dagger," and their expulsion from the palace. The name of one prince, who was one of the knights, gave rise to a riddle which enlivened the scene, and concluded this sort of chivalric play in French style.

Flight of the King on the 21st of June.

The month of June offered a fresh excuse for the acceptance of the constitution by the flight of the King and Queen, with their children, to the frontier towns of the north, while Monsieur, the King's brother, also took flight to another part of the frontier. M. d'Artois and his family had left France on Sunday evening, the 12th of July, 1789, and had taken refuge at Coblentz.

The first news of the departure of the King and his family during the night of the 21st of June, 1791, caused a general impression of astonishment, to which succeeded a feeling of anger at the violation of the royal promises and of so many pledges to form the constitution. But, little by little, public opinion was reassured, and by midday nothing survived but universal joy. Everyone felt delivered from what was then called "the evil of kings." A republic was not called for, but the people had republican sentiments without knowing it.

The same day M. Achille du Châtelet, an enlightened and honest patriot, printed and placarded an
address to the people, in which he incited them to
decree a republic, since the King, by his flight, had
shown his own estimation of the monarch and of
monarchy. This publication produced no little effect
on public opinion ; but one side looked upon a republic
as impossible, the other as premature. As to myself,
I thought then as now, after the various phases of
the revolution, that a republic no more suits the French
than an English government would suit the Turks. I
therefore joined the majority of the National Assembly,
which only wished to profit by the light of the age
and the force of events so far as to establish a constitutional monarch or a constitutional monarchy.

The spirit of the age was for democracy; the spirit
of the Jacobins was for a republic; the feeling of the
National Assembly was solely for a monarchy.

The calm attitude of the Constituent Assembly
contributed much to that shade of public opinion which
congratulated itself upon the departure of the King, as
having delivered us from a fatal hypocrisy, of which
hitherto we had been the dupes.

One might see at the bar of the Assembly all the
generals, officers of all ranks, nobles, knights of the
various orders, and public officials : some to give up the
cross of St. Louis, others to tender their devotion and
services to the country and their support to the Constituent Assembly. The Viscount de Beauharnais presided at this session with such dignity and with so
much nobility of feeling that history has recorded these
notable words: "Let us pass to the order of the day,"
which he uttered after the Assembly had concluded its

discussion on public order and the flight of the King. Unhappily for France and for Louis XVI., the *fracas* on Varennes bridge caused the recognition and arrest of the King. He was led back to Paris in the midst of the shamefacedness of the captives and the indignation of the spectators.

When the news of the King's arrest reached the Assembly a profound depression ensued. It was felt that the royal yoke, till then believed to be broken, would again weigh upon all, and the enforced return of a fugitive King at once annoyed the nation, which blushed at it, and the Assembly, which found it embarrassing.

Two days afterwards, when the King and his family, whose dress and following are as difficult as annoying to describe, reached the Tuileries by the revolving bridge, a raging crowd surrounded the carriage with awful hoots, cat-calls, yells and execrations. The Assembly, being advised of this, and fearing lest some fatal accident would happen, immediately sent thirty deputies to escort the carriages of the King and his family through the garden to the palace, and to repress the fury of the populace.

I was one of these deputies. Our duty was a dangerous one, owing to the exuberance of popular feeling; but we thought the mob still maintained confidence and regard in and for the National Assembly. We were not deceived. The moment we arrived before this huge enraged crowd, which more than ever hurled oaths and reproaches at the Queen rather than at the King, its ranks opened to let us reach the carriages of the King and his family. We had only to give our names and show our medals, which acted like a talisman. Meeting the King and his family, who had hitherto been escorted from Varennes by four deputies sent by the National Assembly, we surrounded the carriages. But when they reached the terrace of the palace to put down the King and his family at the central or clock gate, the rage of the crowd broke out anew with such violence as to make me tremble for the King's life, and still more for that of the Queen, on whom the imprecations poured with terrifying unanimity. Another deputy (M. Grégoire) and myself then determined to take charge of the young Dauphin, and we carried him indoors. Then the King got out, surrounded by fifteen of us; the other fifteen remained with the Queen, who earnestly implored their help.

After having seen the King to his apartments, we rushed to find the Queen; we found great difficulty in getting to her carriage; it was almost impossible to penetrate the crowd and keep one's head in this tumult, where one heard nothing but strident voices and furious yells from those who would not let the Queen enter the Tuileries. Half an hour elapsed, when the deputies closed up and formed a double rank from the carriage to the door. The Queen got out, much frightened and in tears. She was at last rescued and led by us to the King. It was a grand sight to see the deep feelings of gratitude which the Queen now evinced to us! These demonstrations of regard redoubled when she saw the King and her children again. The King desired us to thank the National Assembly for all the zeal they had shown to rescue them under such difficult circumstances. We waited until the crowd in the Tuileries had somewhat diminished and popular feeling calmed down, so that when we had gone the King would have nothing to fear.

We returned to the Assembly, where much uneasiness existed as to the issue of our mission. One of us made a satisfactory report, and the Assembly went on with its work.

Flight of the King, 1791.

The country was really in danger from the events of the 21st of June, 1791, as it had been from those of the 12th of June, 1789, because of the military movements around Paris. However, in 1791, by the time that the constitutional decrees had been discussed and approved, the interest of the nation, the supreme law of the popular welfare, and of the constitutional laws, protected the throne as with a veil, in order that the representatives of the nation should not seek for an offender there. The law was silent, and the prince was led astray by his courtiers, guided chiefly by the Austrian clique.

The National Assembly was obliged to be prudent, all the more because it included the powerful party of the two Lameths, Barnave, Menou, Laborde, Talleyrand, and some other deputies of the Constitutional Committee, who were still inclined to keep Louis XVI. on the throne, in spite of his glaring desertion. The Assembly was therefore obliged to assume the attitude that imperious circumstances imposed on it. The King was not declared in fault, and a committee was named to revise the constitutional decrees, to enlarge the royal prerogative, and to take away the causes of the protest written by Louis XVI., which he left behind on leaving for foreign parts or

for some stronghold on the frontier. Public opinion
was against the ideas of this revision ; there was
great perturbation of spirit, and all appeared desirous
to move the Constitutional Assembly, by petition,
to declare the abdication of Louis XVI.

The Society of the Friends of the Constitution (under
the name of Jacobins) excited the people the more
by propositions tending towards a fresh revolutionary
rising, of which no human foresight could predict
either the extent or duration, especially with representatives flouted by calumny and wearied with a three
years' permanent session.

It was unwise to expose France so lightly to a
change of constitution and to a new form of government, as the predilections of the French had forced
the National Assembly to continue the monarchy in
spite of its feeling and of its democratic laws.

The Jacobins carried their pretensions so far as
to rise against the National Assembly and its decrees
by various motions and discussions. But, under
these circumstances, it was very dangerous for the
interests of public peace that popular societies should
oppose the law and thus give fatal examples to the
citizens, so the deputies ceased to attend the sittings
of the Jacobin society, and confined their deliberations
on the welfare of the country to the Assembly.

Several placards demanding a republic had been
stuck up in Paris, even on the doors of the Constituent Assembly. Indeed, republican ideas were
no strangers to the feelings of this courageous majority
of representatives, who had established liberty and
equality, had abolished feudalism, aristocracy, nobility,
and parliaments, and had restricted the power of

the clergy. But they thought monarchical forms could preside over democratic institutions, provided the royal authority was very limited, and severely circumscribed by the Constitutional Act and the authority of ministers and other officials.

Nevertheless, the mob was very excited, and collected in the Champ de Mars in order to sign, on the altar of the country, a petition to the National Assembly in order that the abdication of Louis XVI. might be proclaimed. The royal party in the Assembly had elected as president for the fortnight M. de Lameth, an old and crusted aristocrat in a democratic mask. He it was who received from that section, which had been termed by Mirabeau the Thirty Voices (in allusion to the Thirty Tyrants of Athens), the secret authority to give Bailly, the mayor of Paris, and Lafayette, the commandant of the National Guard, orders to expel the petitioners of the Champ de Mars by armed force and to fire on the people.[1]

The National Assembly would not have permitted this; any such measure would have been rejected with indignation. It knew nothing about such a step, and only learned of its existence by its results and by the yell of public indignation. So, in order to palliate this step, false and exaggerated reports were made on the hidden intentions of this meeting, which was represented as a fanatical onslaught on the republican form of government.

This sanguinary event on the Champ de Mars

---

[1] M. Charles Lameth has been so strangely *naïve* as to boast in the tribune of the Chamber of Deputies, in 1832, of having given an order in July, 1791, as President of the National Assembly, to fire on the people.—NOTE BY BARÈRE.

opened a path to the cunning authors of the revision of the constitutional decrees, who joined the members of the Constitutional Committee to alter the existing decrees and enlarge the royal prerogative, with the intention of causing Louis XVI. to accept the constitution and conquer his repugnance to divest himself of the ancient authority. This is the cause of the outcry raised against the Constitutional Act since its birth; an outcry which caused much trouble, and brought about the events of the 10th of August, 1792.

Revision of the Constitution.

Since this deplorable and only too memorable time, two great objects occupied the thoughts of the deputies: the first, to settle the various constitutional decrees so as to form a political machine of them, a social mechanism capable of securing public order and the prosperity of the nation; the second, to decide to what royal person could be confided the execution of these constitutional laws, which would constitute a great and delicate innovation on the customs and government of France.

As to the first question, we resolved to codify all the various constitutional decrees and separate them from mere acts of procedure. This end was not attained; and what was then called the revision was gone on with, and, under the pretext of revision, they reformed, mutilated, and left the constitution without form or harmony, that is to say, left it deprived of that political vigour which alone makes for progress and solidarity. They mixed up too many acts of procedure with others purely constitutional; they imposed too many limits on the mistrusted royal authority;

they weakened it, and thus being impotent it only conspired for more power. The truth is, in organising political powers, the executive has naturally such strength that, if not adequately endowed with power, it only seeks to extend its sphere; if you render it powerless it usurps. The National Assembly absolutely failed as regards its section on royal and executive powers.

Who would have thought that among the seven hundred deputies who formed the majority—in other words, the Left of the Assembly—there were only thirty-five of us to oppose the revision; that is, this small but influential and working number which had promised to reseat Louis XVI., notwithstanding his flight to Varennes, and endow him with greater power? What could thirty-five deputies do against a mass of seven hundred, headed by the Constitutional Committee and by several skilful intriguers? We did obtain, by our opposition, the amendment of several sections and of several constitutional enactments more favourable to public liberty, but the revision itself produced a constitution without vigour or balance.

As to the second question, that of selecting a royal person to whom to confide the administration of the constitution, the Assembly had many ideas. One of these was to continue the King's authority, in spite of the occurrences of the 21st of June, and to avoid the Queen's regency during the minority of her son. Another one was to found a National Council of regency over the young Dauphin, and only to leave the King a handsome income, with a palace and hunting grounds, and leave the Queen the simple care of the hereditary prince. Nobody thought of the Orleans branch since the occurrences of the 5th and 6th of October, 1789, although that branch comprised three young and well-educated princes, constitutionally inclined, whose principles seemed to promise the country more stability and more attachment to the new *régime*.

When a regency was spoken of, the deputies saw in this contingency merely a vast area for constitution-makers and for clever intriguers at the Court. Possibly the Assembly, as a whole, possessed too much honesty and patriotism, as, by a solemn and unanimous decree, it permanently deprived its members of all ministerial functions. The same disinterested feeling and of dislike of ambition caused the rejection of a regency. It was requisite, therefore, to stand by the King, who had convoked the States-General; and, in the doubtful state of affairs, this selection was probably the most just and inevitable.

The only requisite was that Louis XVI., to secure a happy reign and strengthen the fresh legislation, should have good ministers, a wise, sincere council, and public functionaries taken from those men who had compiled the constitution.

Intrigues of the Lameth Party.

The art of stirring up revolts in the Constituent Assembly is due to the Lameth party. The discontent of the populace of Paris had been excited on the subject of the flight of Louis XVI.; on the 21st of June his abdication was called for; a petition to this effect was to have been signed on the altar of the country in the Champ de Mars. This cabal was organised, and the National Guard was to have been its docile instrument. M. Charles Lameth was elected during this July as fortnightly president of the Assembly. He it was who, of his own accord, gave the order to M. Bailly, the mayor, and to General Lafayette to clear the Champ de Mars by armed force. The order was only too ruthlessly executed. The National Guard fired upon the mob, and many were killed or wounded.

The National Assembly did not share in the movements of this martial indignation, but it found it would be impolitic to censure it. The Lameth party profited by this inaction ; it had instigated this attack on the people by the guard established for their defence and for the support of constitutional decrees.

Consequently the Lameth party demanded to be named as assistant members of the Constitutional Committee, in order to proceed to a general revision of the constitutional decrees, with the object of putting them in accord and codifying them in one statute.

Thenceforth the committee with its assistants had no other object than to reform those decrees which had settled and limited the royal prerogative. They increased it in several of the attributes, under the pretence of thus securing its adoption by Louis XVI., who had, since the 21st of June, 1791, when he fled from the Tuileries towards the northern frontier, expressly protested against the constitutional decrees.

The decrees were revised, toned down in parts, and augmented by fresh resolutions ; and Thouret brought a compact edition, under the title of a constitutional statute, before the National Assembly, in the name of the Revision Committee.

It was vehemently opposed and modified several times by thirty-five deputies, who declared themselves discontented with this partial revision. These were

Pétion de Villeneuve, Buzot, Rœderer, Barère de
Vieuzac, Robespierre, Bouché, and some others whose
names do not occur in the debates on the revision,
collected in the *Moniteur* and other journals of the end
of July, and of August and September, 1791.

This untimely and insidious revision was the
apple of discord thrown into the National Assembly
by intriguing royalty. The patriotic party kept aloof;
the revising party, profiting by the weariness of an
Assembly which had held a permanent session of
three years, was both blamed and attacked by the
Society of the Friends of the Constitution, sitting at
the Jacobin Club. The revision caused the Assembly,
which in reality was the most patriotic, the most
rational, the most reformatory, and the wisest France
had ever seen, to be grossly calumniated. The revision also depreciated the constitutional statute in
public opinion, and the Constituent Assembly disappeared without causing any regret.

The King accepts the Constitution.

At last, in the month of September, 1791, the
constitution was accepted by Louis XVI. with a
solemnity and an abnegation to the wishes of the
nation which seemed to forebode a happy future.

Why, then, accuse the French nation of being
neither generous nor confiding? It ignored all the
obstacles put forward by the court and the ministry
to hinder the work of the constitution and the
establishment of public rights, and invested the King
with royal authority afresh. At the public demonstration given on the day of the acceptance and
promulgation of the constitutional laws, was seen

the spectacle of a people intoxicated with joy, enthusiastic as regarded their King, and begging him to enjoy his own again, after a three years' revolution.

The French were then far from suspecting that the King's ministers were seeking to grasp a more absolute power than that with which the constitution had endowed them; that fresh deputies in the Legislative Assembly would nullify and reverse the new constitution instead of carrying it out; and that from this blind and fatal alliance of the Court and the Legislative Assembly would spring a terrible sanguinary revolution, destructive of national prosperity, and lasting several years. There was not one good citizen, not one wise person, who did not desire, in 1791, that the Constituent Assembly should resolve itself into a Legislative Assembly; itself to administer its constitution, to elevate its mission by wisdom and moderation, and give the people and the King a solemn example of obedience to the laws emanating from national sovereignty.

But these wishes of the enlightened public and the true friends of liberty were not realised. The Assembly wished to show itself generous: it was only imprudent; it committed suicide by its own disinterestedness; it destroyed the constitution by giving it over to grumblers, who hated all that did not emanate from themselves, and thought themselves better legislators than the Constituent Assembly.

On the Constituent Assembly; from 1789 to September, 1791.

The Constituent Assembly has been accused, half a century after its existence, by men who profited by its work, and who, in 1834, would have been nothing if it had not enriched the land with liberty, and over-turned the old pillars of servitude and despotism.

Was it nothing to have uprooted the feudal tree which covered France with its sinister shade?

Was it then nothing to overthrow the aristocracy, born in the time of feeble kings, and formed into a military caste from Louis the Débonnaire to Philip Augustus?

Was it then nothing simply to have abolished this seigneurial nobility which left royalty but a name, and the nation but serfs?

Was it then nothing to sweep off that absolute monarchy created by Louis XI. and continued by Cardinal de Richelieu until Louis XIV.?

Was it then nothing to demolish the autocracy of Versailles under Louis XIV., and the ministerial despotism under Louis XVI.?

Was it then nothing to limit royal authority, to found the responsibility of ministers, to create a national representation, and to proclaim the theory of the people's sovereignty?

Was it nothing to publish a declaration of the rights of man and of the citizen, and to pass a constitutional decree with guarantees for liberties and rights?

Was it nothing to maintain a general peace in the midst of a sudden and radical revolution, whose results affected all the states of Europe, and warned the absolute powers of Europe that bounds must be put to their procedure?

Was it nothing to proclaim that free France was opposed to all ideas of war and conquest?

To effect a complete and thorough revolution in the course of three years, with liberty of the press and freedom of discussion, in the face of oppressed nations and armed despots, was the real miracle of the first Revolution.

It was the Constituent Assembly, at once courageous, united, and disinterested, that struck off the fetters France had borne for fourteen centuries, that founded national unity by abolishing the peculiar privileges of the provinces, that re-established and handed over to the people exclusively the right to levy taxes, that destroyed the abuses and venalities of justice, and that has endowed the country with the tutelary institution of juries.

The French Revolution on its appearance produced upon Europe the same superstitious terror which the apparition of a comet did in the middle ages. The aristocracy feared it, the people did not understand it. Armed fear and credulous ignorance seemed united against the Revolution and its disciples.

Scarcely understood by France, the Constituent Assembly was entirely misunderstood by Europe: the French swept away factions and parties as obstacles to liberty; Europe formed armed coalitions to overthrow it.

Consequently, the French Revolution had to devote more time to fighting than to progress. The Constituent Assembly having concluded its duties of reform, the social regeneration could neither be continued nor developed usefully even by the nation which had undertaken it. For a revolution to succeed, it requires a nation to have the strength and will to act with a feeling for its rights and liberties. It is only by these united means that it can obtain the force of numbers which must aid moral force.

Intelligence breeds revolutions, and the progress of
the human will develops them, while men of integrity,
talent, and conviction utilise them; but public opinion
and justice alone can secure their duration. It is for
love of country and of liberty, for men of courage and
disinterestedness, and for heroic nations to conquer,
defend, and preserve their rights.

Such was the invaluable and sublime legacy which
the Constituent Assembly left to the French people,
and, in their name, to Europe at large. This legacy,
long contested by despotism, autocracy, servility, and
corruption all allied, will sooner or later be utilised
according as progress and resistance may determine.

The life of nations is counted by centuries, and as
yet we have but experienced half a century of revolutionary action, mixed with many anti-revolutionary
reactions—half a century of systems and political
variations, of civil and foreign wars, of exceptional
legislation and oppressive doctrines.

Time alone leads to truth and liberty.

EXTRACTS FROM A MANUSCRIPT ENTITLED "THE LAST DAYS OF PARIS UNDER THE OLD RÉGIME."[1]

CHAPTER XIV

A National Event.

THE 17th of April, 1788, closed the exile of the Duke of Orleans. He had been banished to Villers-Cotterets and Raincy for having expressed his opinion too strongly since the royal session of the 19th of November, 1787. There were fireworks at the Palais Royal to welcome his return. There was much talk then about the remonstrances the parliament was about to make as to the suppression of the order made after the royal session of the 19th of November and of the impropriety of placing these orders on the register. But, two days after, there came a very

---

[1] This work, until now unpublished, was written during the year preceding the French Revolution, a circumstance which gives it a unique value. It is made up of a large number of chapters capriciously placed one after the other, and is remarkable less for its plan than for the vivacity of its details. It resembles the journal of a young traveller just come from home, and to whom all Paris is new. This young traveller always follows the course of events, which are destined to foreshadow a great era of regeneration, with interest, and more so because he himself is destined to play an important part in the drama on which the curtain is rising. "The Last Days of Paris," like his Memoirs and like his whole political life, show Barère as two persons: one animated by national and patriotic sentiments, the other without fixed ideas, at the mercy of

forcible answer from the King, which was read to the prince-peers and the magistrates who had been summoned to Versailles, the King being in hunting dress, whip in hand. A coming change in the magistracy was expected, but I let them talk of politics: I was only in Paris to see the sights and study the manners of the capital.

———

CHAPTER XV

The King's Review (3rd of May, 1788).

REVIEWS of military forces by kings form imposing spectacles: the drums and bands strike sonorously on the ear; the arms glitter, and imposing uniforms fascinate the eye; while the idea of royalty inflames the imagination. This is what I said to myself while thinking I should see the King's review on Sablons Plain. I went there. Nothing more resembles the excitement of the Parisians at these spectacles than

———

every wind that blows, and heaping contradiction on contradiction. This artistic variability betrays his weak side as a politician from the start; at the same time indulgence is felt for the citizen, not born for stirring events, who has, nevertheless, the courage to face all perils when the safety of France is at stake. One sees that Barère often made mistakes, almost whenever he came across great intellects; one sees also that he never lacked patriotism, and that he was capable of much devotion. One sees, after all, the principal cause of his faults came from natural imperfections which he did not perceive.

Tied to space, we have confined ourselves to those passages which more particularly concern political matters, because these form a useful supplement to this first part of the Memoirs.— EDITOR'S NOTE.

the flight of the inhabitants of a besieged town or one taken by assault. One would have thought the English were taking Paris through the gate of Saint-Antoine, and that we had no refuge but the Bois de Boulogne. I rushed with this hurried crowd through a blinding dust, which the wind rendered almost insufferable.

At noon the drums announced the arrival of the Princes; the Queen came after them with a brilliant *cortège*—eight horses, covered with feathers and plumes, drew the Princess's carriage at a walk. The King appeared next, mounted as usual on a white horse, and surrounded by his Court. After having inspected the Swiss and French guards, he placed himself in the centre to see these two regiments march past. To me this sight at first was imposing, then monotonous, and finally childish. I saw the King with pleasure, because I feel all Frenchmen like their sovereign— that is our special patriotism. I saw, however, that he was treated with much indifference. I went to the Maillot Gate to see them go back. He passed through a large crowd in the deepest silence. Two or three lemonade-sellers cried, " Long live the King! " But these venal salutations led to no others. Hearts were cold and spirits were iced. What a good lesson, I thought, for a sensible king! How eloquent this silence is! Oh, great Henry! what would your great heart have said if this cold silence had confronted you in the midst of your people? You would have wept tears of blood through fear of having merited it.

CHAPTER XXVI

Public Affairs, May 7.

CONSTERNATION was general. The contests between the parliaments and the royal authority, the threat of arbitrary taxes, the fear of having to fight against despotism, gave to all a touch of sadness, and gave such an aspect of public mourning as accounted for the deep silence with which the King was received.

Everyone knew that we were on the eve of a revolt of the magistrates; a revolt which the whole nation deprecated. The proposals of the ministry had made a terrible commotion among the people. On the 5th of May a decree of parliament appeared, by which decree the members of this ancient tribunal solemnly engaged to resist every innovation in the profession of the magistracy to their last breath. This decree staggered the ministers, and the *lit de justice* appointed for the 7th of May was put off till the morrow. But already, by five o'clock, a summons (called *lettre de cachet*) was served on MM. d'Esprémesnil and de Goislard, counsellors-at-law, who had vigorously supported the proposals embodied in this famous decree.

These summonses, served at four in the morning, were eluded by the flight of these two magistrates, who rushed in disguise to take refuge in the law courts. There the chambers, which were soon assembled, were besieged by fifteen hundred soldiers of the French guards, who encamped in the middle of Dauphin Square and the quadrangle of the law courts.

After two days and one night passed in the law courts with this military force, M. d'Agoult, an officer of the French guards, was sent from Versailles with strict orders to arrest the persons of MM. d'Esprémesnil and de Goislard, wherever they were. This rigorous order was rigorously executed. M. d'Agoult arrived with his troops in the law courts, and, proceeding to the Great Hall, he asked for M. d'Esprémesnil. "We are all D'Esprémesnil," said one of the magistrates. A second summons was made in vain. Finally, a third. M. d'Agoult calls an usher, and orders him, under pain of death, to point out to him in the hall the two magistrates he has orders to arrest. The usher goes along the benches twice, and says he does not see them. M. d'Agoult threatens to have the usher locked up. At that moment MM. d'Esprémesnil and de Goislard got up from their seats and gave themselves up, with the remark they did not wish a good man to suffer for their sakes. They added, they did not fear death if it were for their country's good.

These two magistrates were taken away in silence and through a secret door to a cab, and thence to the lieutenant of police, M. de Crosne. There they received the orders of exile. M. d'Esprémesnil was taken to the Saint-Margaret Isles in Provence, and M. de Goislard to Pierre-Encize—that is, according to public rumour. As they were taking away these eminent exiles, the best people in Paris were busy consoling Madame d'Esprémesnil with every mark of sorrowful sympathy. Loud murmurs were heard in every public place in Paris at such an arbitrary act, which the Fronde, among all its horrors, never attempted.   It was talked of as an act which tarnished the reign of Louis XVI.   What other monarch would have dared to violate the sanctuary of the law, and execute an arbitrary order in the presence of the guardians of the citizens' liberty?

———

CHAPTER XXVII

Lit de Justice — Grand Political and Legislative Act — Conspiracy against the Laws, May 8.

THIS was only the prelude to a *coup d'état*, rendered most important by the sequel.   The next day the King convoked the High Courts of Paris, for a *lit de justice* to be held at Versailles.   The parliament was to meet at eight o'clock, the audit officials at one, and the inland revenue at five in the afternoon.   An order as to the administration of justice was registered. These new resolutions reformed many real abuses of which the people had long complained.   They raised the petty courts in order to crush the intermediary powers which despotism dared not destroy or attack without being openly unmasked.   Virtually abolishing the parliaments, they crushed the seigneurial justices, who were the sole remains of feudal power.   Formerly pleaders had the option of appealing to the King.   Thus they seemed to respect feudal law and the rights of property; they appeared to preserve the parliaments, at the same time ignoring the only two courts which were not in the hands of the King.

Many people were deceived by an appearance of public welfare, and by the popularity of the system

of M. de Lamoignon and the Archbishop of Sens;
but it seemed to me, at a first glance, that despotism
could not make greater strides in two hundred years
than it had made in the two days of the 8th and 9th
of May. It was the establishment of the Plenary
Court that showed this up best.

CHAPTER XXVIII

The Plenary Court.

WHEN a monarch desires the welfare of his people,
he does not destroy those courts which defend public
interests. When he desires to effect vital reforms,
he does not choose a period of disaster and trouble
to bring them to a head. It is during peace that
men taste the price of happiness; it is during the
calm of empires that one resuscitates them. Why,
then, should the sovereign of a people naturally
attached to their rulers reverse the precedence of the
magistracy at a time when this honourable body was
protecting the nation against arbitrary and onerous
taxation? Good effected in this fashion presents
itself under forms of fiscal intrigue, which at once
degrade and sterilise it. It was only after vainly
proposing a territorial subsidy and a clear five per
cent. that the King, or rather his ministers, changed
the monarchical constitution under the pretence of
re-establishing it.

For the future a Plenary Court alone will register the taxes and laws of the whole kingdom; it is
composed of men tied to the King by their appoint-

ments, and even more so by their ideas. The members
are elected for life, and can only remonstrate; the will
of the King alone makes the law. These words need
no commentary; that is the way of Eastern princes.

However, if circumstances compelled the people and
the judges to accede to this plan which had been conceived by the Court, the new tribunal might at least gain
vigour and exercise influence over the body politic. It
might amend its constitution, as a kernel may produce
fine fruit. The States would regain their position, the
provinces might send their representatives, the Commons might fall in line with parliament; we might
one day be worthy of liberty, and at length we might
profit by our frequent intercourse with England without
being led to turn out such rebellious and cruel subjects
as those haughty islanders.

Sensible people always think that such revolutions
never have beneficial results, and that intermediaries
are necessary between the people and the throne. The
welfare of the people mingled with those of despotism
in these new laws would be disturbed in being entrusted to the assembled nation; that is, at least, the
happiest view to be taken of the situation. What
could one hope for from a Plenary Court composed of
courtiers? What have popular representatives to do
in an Assembly where the King's will makes the law?

CHAPTER XXXII

Versailles—The King—The Court.

HERE I am, proud as a peacock. I have just seen
the King of the most ancient monarchy of Europe in

his palace. To go to Versailles seemed to me a sur-
passing joy; and it is the hundredth time in my life
that anticipation has been better than reality. Whit-
suntide is notable for the assembly of Court flunkeys,
decorated with an ell of blue ribbon on this occasion.
I fly to Versailles. A magnificent triple avenue, glit-
tering with lights, leads to the dwelling of the sovereign. I approached this palace to which all who
live at Versailles are attracted; an inquisitive crowd
hung round the portico. I followed the crowd, and I
saw men who were once the peers of the King mingling
with the sightseers. The moment the King's levée
was announced, all these peers and princes rushed to
the royal chamber.

While they went to prostrate themselves at the
feet of the monarch and beg for a look, I was admiring
the pictures of Lebrun, whose genius had served to
reproduce the battles of a prince who would have
been so great had he not been a conqueror. This
celebrated artist has only painted for us battered
towns, devastated provinces, or vanquished cities begging for peace or carrying humiliating tokens of their
defeat to their vanquishers. Although a Frenchman,
I could only admire the painter; to me the subjects
were horrible. Let others boast of warrior kings—as
for me, I hate them; the misfortunes of humanity
extort only tears and cries of terror from me. What
wasted time and genius! I thought; and I left this
great awe-inspiring gallery to collect my thoughts
by looking at that part of the park where the green
turf and the canal are. The aspect of the greenery
and the water refreshed me and soothed my excited
feelings. Here at least I could praise the effects of art.

Suddenly a herald exclaimed, "The King!" At this the attention of all was aroused, and every eye was directed to the spot where Louis XVI. was about to appear.

The King is about to pass, I thought. This man, of the same nature as myself, can cause the happiness or misery of twenty-four millions of people, human like himself.

The Keeper of the Seals came first. The revolution that had been introduced within the last few days in the old constitution of the country and in the magistracy made me curious to know him: I was impatient to see what physiognomy was possessed by the descendant of the estimable Lamoignon, the author of a conception so strange and so destructive. I saw a hard, disagreeable, and even uneasy, face. Did circumstances make me look on him thus? I do not know; but I had more pleasure in looking at the tall D'Estaing and the fat Suffien, the heroes of the American Revolution. The appearance of M. de Breteuil frightened me; his face is austere and hard, and I thought he carried in his hand the royal or ministerial thunderbolt, as does Jupiter's eagle. I was struck with the appearance of Monsieur, who passed, rightly or wrongly, for a popular prince—a mild man, and a friend to literature and humanity.

The King followed. He looked festive. My eyes rested with curiosity upon his handsome face, which to me looked open and noble, although his eyes were cast down. They consider him good, I thought; but they are deceived; this man is bound to make people unhappy if the truth is kept from him. Who knows what they tell him or what they hide from him, and what calumnies they repeat to him about the parliaments?

Behind Louis walked the Archbishop of Sens (formerly Archbishop of Toulouse), Loménie de Brienne—one would have taken him for a king, and rightfully; for he has the power without the title.

The sight of this prime minister reminded me of Richelieu and Mazarin.[1] Like them his governance was artificial, arbitrary, vindictive, and absolute: exile and proscription appeared to me to march at his side; and although he had succoured me in my youth, I could not forgive his severity to the French magistracy. However, I could not keep my eyes off him. I had seen him benevolent and sensible in his diocese; as administrator, popular in Languedoc; full of humane feeling at the dearth of 1778, and during the ravages of zymotic disease; founding pensions for poor young ladies; establishing schools for the gratuitous education of a large section of society; and opening asylums for old priests and young clerics. All his benefits were present to my thoughts; and from that moment

---

[1] M. Loménie de Brienne passed for a man of much intelligence, having very wide views as to administration, but quite of the school of the philosophers and Encyclopædists. He was openly inimical to monks and all religious orders. Louis XVI. had refused him, in spite of the solicitations of Marie Antoinette, the archbishopric of Paris, at the end of December, 1781. He had nominated to that see a man of little merit, but of obstinate and fanatical character, M. de Juigné, formerly bishop of Châlons-sur-Marne. He was the opposite of M. de Brienne. The late Archbishop of Paris was the most intolerant of Catholics, but at least this archbishop, M. de Beaumont (whom J. J. Rousseau rendered so celebrated by the eloquent letter he addressed to him), was very benevolent, and each year distributed three hundred thousand francs among the poor.

my heart rejected all those accusations party spirit had made against him.

The procession of the blue ribbons amuses one for once. Formerly it took place in the city; now it is more a secular than a religious ceremony. The King was led from his chamber to the chapel. The Queen and the ladies of France were in the gallery. The King and his suite took their places in the chapel. The Archbishop of Narbonne officiated, and the Archbishop of Toulouse sat in the chancel.

I followed the procession to the chapel.[1] Everything around the King showed he was the central figure; the attitude of his brothers, the silence and obsequiousness that reigned everywhere denoted the presence of a master.

After mass the King dined in public. How I should have deplored being the centre of a ceremony so solemnly puerile! It is the same with the other princes and princesses, but with them it is only acting; they are served with a theatrical supper when they come to table, and the public only see, as it were, the ghost of a banquet. The princes afterwards really dine in their own apartments.

At four o'clock the King attended a sermon that a Parisian rector (a very vulgar preacher) delivered against philosophy. When he was not sleeping, the King was yawning. Marcus Aurelius would have better appreciated the merits of such a discourse. But the orator was lengthy and uninteresting; he quite justified the King's boredom.

---

[1] It then occurred to me to sketch the portraits of all the Royal Family and register them in my travelling note-book. They follow.

CHAPTER XXXIII

Some Portraits

Louis XVI.

THE King was about five feet five. His physical structure was large and common-looking, presenting an appearance of far stronger health than his pale face; he had pale blue eyes, without the slightest expression, and a loud laugh which savoured of imbecility. He was short-sighted, his carriage was most awkward, and his whole appearance was that of a badly brought-up rustic. His education had been much neglected under his governor, the Duke of Vauguyon, and this the King himself acknowledged. At the bottom of his heart he had, however, a keen sense of order and justice; but his extreme weakness of character prevented him taking his own way, and he blindly followed the advice he received from his ministers, and particularly from the Queen. This woman had immense credit for her tact, and did what she liked with him. He would have preferred the society of simple, modest people, whilst he was entirely given over to that of young and giddy persons, with whom the Queen had surrounded him. His one decided taste was hunting, and above all shooting, which he practised daily. His country tastes weaned him from intercourse with women; his temperament, besides, did not tend to give him any propensity for this sort of thing. It was nevertheless remarked that the Countess of Châlons pleased him better than anyone else; but his gallantry only took the form of gross jests that would have been insulting in anyone else, and in a few attentions of the most stupid order.

He ate like a pig, and drank like a fish; he scarcely ever left the table without being a little unsteady, and then his jokes with the one he wanted to entertain were somewhat gross. He disliked gambling,[1] and took pleasure only in backgammon and billiards; but as he was unskilful, particularly at the latter game, he often let drop the loudest and deepest oaths. He . was a gross feeder, and had, indeed, few intellectual gifts. However, his judgment was clear; he meant well, and would always have done well if his disposition had been supported by a true woman or a truly patriotic minister.

Queen Marie Antoinette.

The Queen was of middle height, but dignified. Her carriage was truly noble, and her sprightliness induced her to please everyone. During the first years of her stay in France, and when she was only Dauphiness, she showed a simplicity and an affability

---

[1] The Royal Family generally lost one hundred thousand crowns during the trip to Fontainebleau, to the profit of M. de Chalabre, who took the place of banker at faro. This gentleman croupier gained twenty-three thousand francs during one trip to Fontainebleau in 1779. Louis XVI., who never played at any game of chance, felt obliged this year to depart from his usual custom. The fact of the effect that a loss of five hundred louis d'or produced on him may be judged from the fact that he had not his brother's passion for heavy play. He told everybody of his bad luck, even to those he knew nothing of. He spoke of it as a folly which he had committed, and which he certainly would never commit again.

which made her generally liked. But her character quite changed when she became Queen; the sway she gained over the King rendered her despotic, and her influence on public affairs was fatal. She surrounded herself with a few partisans, a circle at last restricted to the Duchess of Polignac, her favourite, and to a few friends. Besides, she showed much attention to, and predilection for, interesting and handsome young folk. Those who had nothing more to recommend them than good conduct and established reputation gained but little regard or attention. She abolished all Court etiquette, knowing none but that of pleasure, for which she had a frantic taste. She was fond of high play, and delighted in theatricals, the gayer the better. She had no attachment or affection for the King, whose tendencies were foreign to her own; she liked the Count d'Artois, her brother-in-law, much better, and showed him marked attention. This made people think there was more between them than there should be. Those in contact with her declared her very kind; but she did not please the people generally; everyone thought her prodigious influence over the King was a national misfortune.

Monsieur, the King's Brother.

Monsieur was five feet three inches high. His stoutness, already great in 1779, rendered his walk heavy and ungraceful, and gave him a vulgar appearance. His bloated face spoilt the regularity of his features; he ate and drank to excess, and took no exercise. Naturally idle and indolent, he only betrayed one inclination —that of a love for gambling. He was characteristically politic, sly, and cunning. Though caring nothing

for the Queen, he influenced her greatly, and paid
her every attention, even when she was quite estranged
from Madame.   In spite of his pretensions to literary
knowledge, his ideas were most superficial on every
point; but he read attentively, and found means to
lead the conversation to the subject of his morning's
reading and to give quotations and criticisms, which
made him appear erudite; his great gift was a good
memory.

He was the only one of the princes who retained
a love of etiquette and the habit of being always followed by his guards and household appointed to accompany him.   Occasionally he showed a certain amount
of gallantry to the ladies; but it was taken for granted
that his constitution could not support such vagaries.
In spite of the King's shortcomings, the nation was
glad he was the eldest; he, at least, had in his character a kind of frankness and integrity, with which
Monsieur was by no means credited.

Marie-Josephe Louise of Savoy, Monsieur's wife.

Madame was short and undignified, ugly and sallow;
her eyes showed her duplicity, which formed the basis
of her character, of which, on many occasions, she
had given unequivocal proofs, especially in her refusal
to receive the Viscountess de Laval as a lady of
honour.   She hated the Queen and the Queen hated
her.   These two princesses lived in a political state
of mutual mistrust.   Madame possessed no kind of
influence, and bitterly regretted that she could only
exercise her love of intrigue at her own Court and
at that of Monsieur, where, however, she found many
opportunities of setting people by the ears.

The Count d'Artois.

The height of the Count d'Artois was five feet five; he had a handsome face, while an imposing and agreeable bearing distinguished his youth. He had a great love of pleasure, liked wine and women, and was very friendly with the Duke de Chartres and a number of young people, whose community of tastes and genial ways had much attracted him.

Solely occupied with his pleasures, and the desire of satisfying them in every way, he was most ignorant, and had no idea of study or work. He continually declared that if he were King he would try and find the best minister possible, and put all the burden on him, while he would give himself up entirely to pleasure. Otherwise, he was most agreeable in society. His politeness was easy and gracious, and he had such a desire to please as to make him most agreeable to women. The Queen, as I have said, made people think that her feelings towards him were warmer than those of friendship.

Marie-Thérèse of Savoy, Countess d'Artois.

The Countess d'Artois, the sister of Madame, was, like the latter, extremely small; but she had a good complexion, a very long nose, and eyes so small as scarcely to be seen, which, from her extreme timidity, were always kept lowered. She found great difficulty in speaking, and it was easy to see that she had to exercise great self-control to enter into conversation with the people who came to pay their respects to her.

The Count d'Artois was kind and attentive, although

it was clear he had not much love for her. Indeed, this lady showed that she characteristically possessed an indifference which she thought was necessary for her welfare. She continually said the Countess d'Artois should be happy, so she never interfered in anything. The passive condition in which she lived kept her clear of all the annoyances and perils of intrigue.

Adelaide, Victoire, and Sophie, aunts of Louis XVI.

The distinctive characteristics of these ladies were kindness and affability, so they were generally liked. They held a Court absolutely separate from their nephews and nieces, who, however, often saw them, and showed them all the consideration they had a right to expect.

The King had given them the estate of the castle of Bellevue, between Paris and Versailles, where they passed part of the year. Their manner of living was very different to that of the youthful Court. They only exercised their influence with the King to procure favours and posts for members of their household. Thus Madame Adelaide had heaped benefits on the Duchess of Narbonne, her maid of honour, her favourite. Madame Victoire did the same for the Duchess of Civrac, whom she particularly liked.

The ladies had a fourth sister, Madame Louise, but many years ago, under the reign of the late King, she became a Carmelite at Saint-Denis. Several reasons were given at the time for this proceeding, but the public never knew the true reason for this extraordinary step.

CHAPTER XXXVI

English Gardens.

OUR great landlords now seek nature unadorned, although they are not well-qualified judges of it; their fancy now is to have English gardens and lawns, as they wear English hats and English buckles. Perhaps we may rise from imitating gardens to imitating a constitution, and France may owe to the gardeners of a rival nation the regeneration of her rights and liberties. In this case it may be averred that the first English jockey was the cause of the present revolution. How often, indeed, have great events been referred to small causes!

CHAPTER XXXIX

Meeting of the Clergy at the Church of the Augustins, June, 1788.

IN Spain the higher clergy (by this is understood the bishops and archbishops) merit the respect and consideration of the people and aristocracy by their piety, their exemplary conduct, their residence within their dioceses, and their great benevolence. The inferior clergy, the priests of the second class as well as the monks, on the contrary, by their gross and unruly manner, by their fanaticism and inquisitorial spirit, are the scandal of religion. It is quite the contrary in

France.   Our higher clergy think nothing of the religion which panders to the luxury and what they call
its representation (I speak generally, for there are still
virtuous and religious prelates remaining) ; in their
feelings,   their   behaviour,   and   their   diocesan   administration there reigns a despotism heedful of all
that concerns their immunities, rights, and exemptions.   All the wealth of the Church is for them : the
most necessary section of the clergy, the most benevolent, and the most respected can barely gain a living.

In the bosom of the Church, which is the best endowed in Europe, the prelates have allowed a multitude
of priests to exist on a stipend of seven hundred francs,
and yet these priests are destined for a supernatural
governance, for civil and religious functions, for the
consolation of the unhappy peasants, where they are
respected as much by their virtues as by their labours.
The higher clergy have suffered a crowd of men, endowed with the same character, called to the same
sacred career as themselves, to hopelessly vegetate
under the degrading term of hangers-on.   It might be
said that for rectors and curates there was one religion, but for bishops and archbishops quite another.
Is not this the verdict the people should pronounce
after what they have seen ?

The higher clergy administer or rule the provincial
states, the provinces, and even the kingdom.   Their
Master has proclaimed, however, " My kingdom is not
of this world ! "   And still our modern apostles claim it
is for them to rule the world !

Alas ! how far this sort of work has led them from
the spirit of their calling, and destroyed the respect which
for so many centuries the people blindly awarded them !

How comes it that the rulers of the Church have developed into governors of provinces? During the early centuries of the monarchy it was easy to guide the ways of these ignorant kings, ferocious soldiers, and degraded serfs: their fluency, the authority of a new and venerated form of religion, the blind and superstitious piety of our ancestors, formed the privileges of the clergy. The public enlightenment of the eighteenth century will however put them back in their place.

What can one expect of these administrators who are not citizens, who cannot be fathers of families, and who give their country no pledge of their faith or loyalty? It little matters if a man be a celibate from inclination or interest. Being a celibate, having no stake in the country, he must be a bad statesman. Honour after all, as Montesquieu says, is but a weak motive in serving a mass of men socially united. The Romans only believed in a love of country; they treated bachelors with contempt, punished them with fines, and never let them interfere in the statecraft of the empire.

However, this class had seized the chief power in the national assemblies from the earliest times, and composed a separate caste. In the state, it took the first place: possessing an influence and power which acts fatally on the fate of a nation; for this sacred order too often imposed on the laity taxes and dues from which its own members were exempt. It is one of the greatest errors of government to allow a class to tax the people—a class which never pays any taxes, and which is always talking of its assumed right to make only voluntary and free-will gifts.

Why does not this order of the clergy, composed of nobles, amalgamate with the class from which it comes? Why should it vote separately, since by prejudice and interest it is always in favour of the nobility, thus leaving the feeble wishes and suffrages of the third estates in a hopeless minority? This latter class, like the donkey in the fable, has to bear the heaviest burden and to serve two masters.

For several years the English constitution has been lauded; and certainly it is both good and sensible, when compared with the present government of the other states of Europe, crushed by military forces and saddled by despotism.

But why servilely admire a legislation smirched with the blood of kings, and originating in English forests? Why try to seek such grand examples from the foggy shores of the Thames? In the south of France, in the midst of the magnificent scenery, which has given us our most popular king—in fact, in Béarn —a people exist who do not despise pleasure, and who love liberty. The highlanders, proud of their privileges, give us in their states and their ancient assemblies the model of an administration perhaps more perfect than that of England.

The states of Béarn are composed of two chambers. The clergy and landed nobility have but one vote. The third estate, after having, at will, heard the debates of this chamber, leaves to discuss matters in its own, where it possesses as much power as the two other classes united. It is only in cases where opinion differs that the King has the casting vote; but the two chambers generally come to an understanding, to avoid having to appeal to the sovereign.

Here is a sublime constitution, established at our doors, in one of our own provinces, carried out for centuries under the eye of successive French ministries; and when I spoke about it in Paris, everyone was astonished to find that the French had so perfect a constitution; for, since the publication of M. Delolme's work on the English constitution, Parisians talk of nothing save *constitutions*. It is the word of the day. Even the women want a constitution.

I return to the clergy. The Assembly of Notables has seen the birth of a great equitable idea—that the wealth of churchmen shall contribute to the land-tax.

The idea of the tithes is founded on principles no less just. The immunities of the clergy were reduced to the sole form of repartition, and the revenues of the ecclesiastical property had been already enrolled. In the states of Burgundy the nobility and the third estate added to their vote on the taxation of tithes the condition that the clergy should pay their quota. The same occurred in other provincial assemblies. Finally, there was the letter of M. Lambert, treasurer-general, to the intermediary committee of administration in the province of Poitou as to this subjection of ecclesiastical revenue to the same rule as that of the secular subscription to the tithes. The letter contained this clause: " . . . . . and to record the property recently taxable, such as real property, that of the clergy, the princes of the blood, of the Order of Malta, of the hospitals," &c.

Would it be believed that in the eighteenth century the clergy should have opposed this equitable scheme by the proclamation, in the most vigorous and solemn terms, of what they called their privileges, rights, and immunities ? Would it be believed that this wealthy body, enriched by the credulous piety of our ancestors, full of the benefits conferred by the third estate, composed of the nobility of the kingdom, fed by the peasants' sweat, should put to the front its privileges and rights, thus to crush the laity by taxation, while their rich dwellings and fertile land went free ?

If the maxims of the author of " L'Esprit des Lois " were followed, no interference would be made with the privileges of the clergy for fear of attacking the monarchical constitution. His intellect has constructed a very ingenious and very brilliant system. But as natural justice and reason are beyond all political and legislative systems, it is generally thought in France that the clergy ought to contribute to the land-tax in respect to their territorial possessions. One would not complain so much of absolutism if it led to popular principles. It is quite true that that most despotic prince, Louis XIV., by his edict of the 27th of October, 1711, exempted the clergy in perpetuity from the five per cent. tax imposed by his declaration of the 14th of October, 1710 ; but then there was no question of administration and political economy — notions which have cropped up in the present century. Religion had in its clergy very different supporters. Then religious opinions were not discussed and shaken by philosophers. Besides, nations are never of age, and kings are simply administrators having a mere life interest.

CHAPTER XL

The Manners and Religion of the Age.

MANNERS have now culminated into perfect politeness, always a sign of corruption. The heart has its
manners and vice possesses the heart. This demure-
ness of countenance, this amenity and mildness in
intercourse are the deceitful veneer of extreme licen-
tiousness and selfishness. The mind, debauched by
luxury, loses its spontaneity. The beggar in the
street is unrelieved, but as much is spent· in one
night at the opera as would keep him for a month.
A real misfortune demands no pity; tears are only
for Greek or Roman heroes.

The people live in the gutter, but are clothed above
their condition. Worn out by an unreasonable amount
of work, they drown their sorrows in wine every holiday.
They have diversions even more fatiguing than their
trade, and enjoyments more injurious than the foul air
of their workrooms.

All enjoyment is for the rich. But public opinion
revenges itself upon the pecuniary superiority of up-
starts by treating them with a sort of proscription when
they appear in what is called good society. This privileged class adopts a language, a style, and manners
which these upstarts copy with a farcical effect; the
nobility are no less proud of their manners than the
rich of their wealth. The latter go in for a senseless
luxury that sits ill on them, quantities of insolent

retainers, and gorgeous banquets eaten only by their parasites.

The aristocracy form a separate nation. The sun only shines for them. Like the mandarins, their language is not understanded of the people. The Court is their universe; the intrigues of the Œil de Bœuf their occupation; to rob the peasantry of their own, to pillage provinces under pompous and senseless titles, because their wealth does not suffice for their luxury and vice: these are the objects of their ambition. To act as courtiers is their only accomplishment; to gain a look from a purblind king, bow low as he passes, join in his hunting parties, assist at his toilet, form their heartfelt ambition. They often talk of the public welfare, to which they never contribute, but which, on the contrary, they generally obstruct. Everywhere and always separated from the populace, they are divided in the grave; and they fill the churches with their monuments and epitaphs. The ashes of the nobly born are alone worthy of preservation, and this says everything.

The populace has nothing but the religion of the senses; the rich wish there was none at all; the rich do not possess it. I never see but middle-class people at church, except a few society women, who go there as to a theatre, where they can loll at ease. And then they cannot go except with two footmen and a gold-embroidered mantle.

The religious processions are really imposing. I have witnessed one at St. Eustache; the number, the vestments, and the pious bearing of the processionists impressed me profoundly. The number of unfortunate children (those born blind) much touched me; they were consoling themselves by singing the praises of our Lord. But I was disgusted to see the troop of servants that two high and mighty lords, the Dukes of Penthièvre and Orleans, had sent. Would it not be better when uniting with the people in an act of noble and touching simplicity, to come themselves without these torches and servitors and prove to the crowd the power of the true religion?

CHAPTER XLI

The Parliaments.

SOON there will be no more parliaments. Their greatest enemy, sovereign authority, has taken advantage of the damaging light thrown upon these institutions by Chancellor Maupeou: the colossus of magistracy is overthrown; the nobility defend it strenuously; but the clergy, more diplomatic, only seek to retain their own privileges; the third estate has mixed up in the quarrel, for it owes to parliament the States-General. Moreover, this dangerous body must be stripped of that excess of power which, sooner or later, will inevitably destroy it. The mainspring of parliaments in the political machine is worn out. The present requirements need more intermediary bodies.

The provincial administrations, reformed and purged of their original imperfections, would form these intermediary bodies and create a truly national procedure. They would form a real basis of monarchical liberty, and destroy those aristocratic tyrannies which threaten France with anarchy.

It is, no doubt, the same with political.bodies as
with corporeal bodies : people require excitements and
shocks, disintegrations and creations. M. de Brienne
gave movement to that old immobile mass, the French
government. The movement will cause lots of ship-
wrecks, bring about minor evils ; but this expiring
nation, eaten up by egotism and luxury, will come
to life again ; its feeble springs, weakened by an
excess of power, will recover ; and patriotism, like
a new elixir of life, will circulate among all State
parties.

A glance at history shows the many phases
through which the institution of parliaments has
passed. Completely in the dust at the beginning of
the seventeenth century, obsequious under Richelieu,
unruly under Mazarin, a nullity under Louis XIV.,
rampant under the Duke of Orleans, the parliaments
arose when Louis XV. was seen to be unbusiness-like
and nerveless. Then they made war on the clergy,
became Jansenists and Molinists, and intervened in
the Breton troubles. They moved the whole kingdom
by a great league among themselves ; the provincial
parliaments were only, so to speak, colonies of the
metropolitan Parliament of Paris.

It would seem, however, that latterly, having undergone the drastic reforms of Maupeou, the Parliament
of Paris, strengthened by a signal triumph gained at
the end of some years, was able to put some pres-
sure upon the government. It might be supposed
to dominate ministerial tyranny, carried to its height
by the last ministers of Louis XV., and still more
by the Miroménils, the Dambrais, the Calonnes (who
destroyed the work of Turgot), Malesherbes, and

Necker. A lively fermentation was noticed in the provincial parliaments, which had been created by the ambitious restlessness of the Paris Parliament. Finally, it was widely felt that these bodies would form a sort of shield to protect France from excessive taxation. There was much room for doubt as to what concessions could be obtained or extorted from the Parliament of Paris, which was so much exposed to the cajolery and terrors of the Court. Nevertheless, public opinion was all on the side of the Paris Parliament, and encouraged it in its resistance. We awaited coming events which presaged the suspension of the two consecutive assemblies of the notables, which had now become the object of ridicule and contempt.

CHAPTER XLII

A Diplomatic Acquaintance.

IN the hotel in the Rue de Prouvaires, where I lodged, I made the acquaintance of a M. Mazzey, of Florence, the envoy extraordinary of Poniatowski, the new King of Poland, to Louis XVI. I had the opportunity of talking to this clever diplomatist as to the state of public opinion and this movement among thinkers, to which the events of the day gave unaccustomed vigour.

We often spoke of that civil liberty which was utterly unknown in France, but which he had seen so respected in the United States, where he had resided during the time of their enfranchisement. " While you

have a Bastille, you will never have personal liberty,"
he repeated. One day he proposed to introduce me
to the Duchess d'Anville, mother of the Duke de
Larochefoucauld. " You will meet persons there," he
said, " most distinguished for their philosophy and
enlightenment." I could scarcely refuse so advan-
tageous an offer.

The duchess received me with that kindness she
always showed to young people who were friends and
admirers of philosophers. In her drawing-room I saw
MM. Condorcet, Jefferson, Lafayette, an abbé, a celebrated chemist, the Duke de Larochefoucauld-Liancourt, the Duke de Larochefoucauld, son of the Duchess
d'Anville, and M. de Rohan-Chabot. America and
its recently-completed constitution were much talked
of. For my part, I ventured to express a few ideas
on the most pressing needs of France and on civil or
individual liberty. The duchess then said to me, " Sir,
you are doubtless not acquainted with a letter on civil
liberty, written by Turgot to Dr. Price, of London.
I will give you a copy of it. The great principles
of this clever statesman may one day be of use to
you."

I here place on record this valuable document just
as it was sent to the Prouvaires Hotel by the Duchess
d'Anville under cover to M. Mazzey.

CHAPTER XLIII

Turgot's Letter on Civil Liberty.

" To Mr. PRICE, London.

" *Paris, March 22nd, 1778.*

" SIR,

" Mr. Franklin has sent me, on your account, the new edition of your ' Observations on Civil Liberty, &c.' I owe you a double meed of thanks : (1) For your book, of which I have long known the value, and which I read with avidity, notwithstanding my multifarious avocations, when the first edition appeared. (2) For the frankness with which you have retracted the imputation of want of tact,[1] which qualifies the compliments you otherwise pay me in your additional Observations. I should have better merited this imputation had you only had in view the want of tact displayed in not being able to counteract those intrigues carried on by men much more skilful than I in work of this kind—work I never did or wished to undertake. But it seems to me that you charge my want of tact with having fundamentally shocked the public opinion of my country, and from that point

---

[1] What is here said refers to an account of M. Turgot's administration in the second tract on civil liberty and the war with America, page 150, &c. In the first edition of this tract I had mentioned improperly his want of address among the other causes of his dismissal from power. This occasioned a letter from him to inform me of the true reasons of this dismissal, and began that correspondence of which this letter is a part, and which continued till his death.—NOTE BY MR. PRICE.

of view you have not done me justice, either as regards my country or myself.   Here there is much more
enlightenment than Englishmen are wont to believe,
where it is perhaps easier than with you to inocu-
late the public with reasonable ideas.

"I reason thus from your nation having become
infatuated with the absurd plan of conquering America,
which lasted until the defeat of Burgoyne opened your
eyes.   I come to this conclusion also because of your
system of monopoly and exclusion which is explained
by all your political writers on commerce (I except Mr.
Adam Smith and Dean Tucker); a system which is
the real cause of your separation from your colonies.
I judge thus because of all your polemical dissertations
on questions which have been crucial for twenty years,
and before your treatise appeared, I scarcely had read
one, if I remember aright, that seized the real point
at issue.   I cannot conceive how a nation, which
has cultivated all branches of natural science with so
much success, has remained so far below itself in that
science which of all others is of most interest to public
welfare; a science in which liberty of the press—a boon
you alone possess—should have given you a prodigious advantage above all other nations of Europe.   Is
it national pride that has hindered you from profiting
by this advantage?   Is it because, you being a little
less diseased than others, all your speculations are
directed by the theory that you are quite well?   Is it
party spirit, and a desire to be backed up by those
popular opinions which retard your progress, that
makes your politicians treat in an ideal, metaphysical[1]

---

[1] See Mr. Burke's letter to the sheriff of Bristol.

manner all those theories which tend to establish fixed
principles as to the rights and true interests of people
and of nations?   How comes it that you are almost
the first among your writers to have true notions of
liberty and to demonstrate the falsity of that idea combatted by the most republican authors, that liberty
consists in obeying laws only?   For how could a
man oppressed by an unjust law be free?   That
would not even be true supposing all the laws ema-
nated from the assembled nation, for the individual
has the same rights as the nation, and cannot be deprived of them except by violence, or by an illegal
exercise of general policy.   Although you may acknowledge this fact and fully explain it to your own
satisfaction, it perhaps merits greater development,
inasmuch as it has had so little attention from even
the most zealous partisans of liberty.

"There is another strange thing, which, if it
did not concern England, would be a mere truism.
One nation never has the right of controlling another; such a government could only be founded on
force, which is the basis of brigandage and tyranny.
Tyranny of a people is of all known oppressions
the most cruel and intolerable, one which gives the
least chance to the oppressed; for at least the despot
is restrained by his own interest; he suffers from remorse, or from the disapprobation of public opinion.
But a multitude heeds nothing, has no remorse, and
awards itself fame when it has earned nothing but
shame.

"For the English passing events are a terrible
commentary on your book; for several months they
have accumulated with increasing rapidity.   America

has proved the sum, for here she is—independent for ever. Will she be free and happy?

"This new people is most advantageously situated to give the example of a constitution where a man may enjoy all his rights, freely exercise all his faculties, and be governed only by nature, reason, and justice, if he but know how to found such a constitution. Is it possible to act on eternal principles, and to foresee all those causes of division and of corruption which little by little are sure to undermine and destroy the structure?

"I admit I am not satisfied with the institutions so far established by the different American states. You justly criticise that of Pennsylvania, in which a religious oath alone qualifies a man for entrance into the representative body;[1] and it is much worse in some others.

"I see, in the greater number, a useless imitation of English usages. Instead of subjecting all authority to one, that is, the nation, different bodies have been established—a representative body, a council, and a governor, simply because England has a House of Commons, a House of Peers, and a king. They are busy in balancing these different powers, as if this equilibrium of authority were necessary to counterpoise the enormous preponderance of royalty; but of what use is this in republics founded on the equality of all the citizens, as if all establishment of different bodies did

---

[1] It is the constitution of Delaware that imposes the test here referred to; that of New Jersey, with a noble liberality, orders that there never shall be in that province any establishment of any one religious sect in preference to another, and that Protestants of all persuasions shall enjoy equal rights and privileges.

not lead to contention. In desiring to avoid all chimerical dangers, real ones have been created. It was assumed that nothing was to be feared from the clergy, and yet all were enlisted under one banner of proscription. In ignoring the right of eligibility, a foreign element has been introduced into the State. Why should a citizen who has an interest as great as his fellows in the common defence of goods and liberty be denied the exercise of his intellect and virtues because he belongs to a profession especially requiring the possession of such qualities? The clergy are only dangerous as an incorporated body of the State; when they think they have, as a body, common rights and interests; and when they imagine they have a religion as by law established. As if men could have any law or any authority to regulate the consciences of others! As if an individual would sacrifice the opinions on which he believes his salvation to depend to the supposed advantage of society! And as if peoples were saved or damned wholesale. Real tolerance is to admit the total incapacity of government to deal with individual conscience, and to admit the cleric into the national assembly as a mere citizen; he is only a cleric when outside.

" I do not think enough pains have been taken to reduce to the smallest limits the number of business men to whom the government of each state will be entrusted, nor to separate the work of legislation from that of administration, whether general or local; to establish standing local assemblies, which, while fulfilling all the functions of the petty details of government, relieve the general assemblies of this work, and take away from the latter all the means, or perhaps the wish, of abusing authority which should be exercised in a larger field, and thus, too, stifle those meaner passions which so often excite mankind.

"I do not see that enough attention has been paid to the great distinction, the only one based on nature, between two classes of men, the proprietors and the non-proprietors of land; to their different interests, and consequently to their different rights relative to legislation, to the administration of law and police, to the contribution to the public expenses, and to their employment.

"There exists no general principle as regards taxation. It is assumed that each province can tax itself at will, collect personal taxes, taxes upon food and imports, thus creating rival interests in each province.

"The right to regulate trade is supposed to be free everywhere; the executive bodies and the governors alike may prohibit the exportation of certain staples under certain circumstances; so little has it been seen that absolute free-trade is the corollary to the rights of property; so deep are they plunged in the fog of European illusions.

"In the general union of the provinces between themselves, I see no coalition, no fusion of the elements which should make one united and homogeneous whole. At present there is nothing but an aggregation of parties only too separated, which always preserve a tendency to differ by the diversity of their laws, customs, and opinions, by the inequality of their actual strength, and still more by the inequality of their future progress. This is nothing but an imitation of the Dutch Republic; and this even had nothing to fear, as has the American Republic, from the undue influence of some of its states. Up to now this new edifice has its foundation on the very old and false political ideas, upon the prejudice that nations and provinces can have interests, as provinces and nations, other than those of a free people, in defending their property from brigands and invaders; a false advantage in doing more business than others, in not buying foreign merchandise, forcing foreigners to consume their own products and use their own manufactures; an imagined interest in acquiring a bigger territory, annexing such and such a province, such and such an island, such and such a village; a desire to be a terror to other nations; a craving for military glory, and for distinction in arts and science.

"Many of these prejudices are rife in Europe, on account of the ancient rivalry of nations and the ambitiou of kings, which compels all the states to have large armies to defend themselves against their armed neighbours, and to look on military power as the principal object of government. America has the benefit of not having had for a long period to fear any foreign enemies, if she escape internal dissensions. Thus she can and ought to appreciate to the utmost these injurious interests, the sole drawbacks to her liberty. With the sacred principle of free trade, looked upon as the natural sequence to the rights of property, all the false principles of commerce will disappear; the false idea of possessing more or less land will vanish from the conviction that land does not belong to a nation, but to the individual proprietors of estates; that the question as to whether such or such hamlet or village should belong to a certain province or state should not be decided by the fact of the interest of any province or state, but by that of the inhabitants of the hamlet and village in question possessing the most convenient spot where to assemble for the transaction of public business ; that this interest should be regulated by the distance from his home a man has to go in order to transact his daily work, which is a natural and physical reason for the extent of jurisdiction and states, and establishes an equilibrium among all[1] as to extent and strength, which avoids all danger of inequality and all pretensions to superiority.

"The benefit of being feared is *nil* when nothing is asked for, and when one is in a position in which one cannot be attacked by overwhelming force with any hope of success.

"Martial glory is not to be compared with the boon of living in peace.   Renown in arts and sciences is free to all who care to grasp it.   Here is a harvest for all the world.   The field of discovery is inexhaustible, and all profit by the discoveries of others.

"I do not imagine the Americans have yet a full sense of these truths, as they should feel them in order to secure the welfare of their posterity.   I do not blame their leaders, who had to provide for the immediate wants of a union, such as it was, to confront a powerful enemy at their doors.   There was no time even to dream of correcting the faults of the constitu-

---

[1] This seems to be a particular of much consequence. The great inequality now existing, and which is likely to increase, between the different states, is a very unfavourable circumstance; and the embarrassment and danger to which it exposes the union should be guarded against, as far as possible, in laying out future states.

tion and the suggestions of the different states; but they should avoid perpetuating them, and busy themselves in uniting diversity of opinion and interest, and leading up to a uniform procedure in all their states.

"On this point they have important obstacles to overcome :

" In Canada, the corporation of the Roman Catholic clergy and the existence of a body of nobles.

" In New England, the rigid puritanism still existing—always, it is said, a little intolerant.[1]

" In Pennsylvania, the fact that a large number of its inhabitants hold as a religious principle that the profession of arms is wrong, and consequently refuse to fall in with the arrangements necessary for the foundation of a national military force, that is, the union of the functions of the citizen and of the soldier or militiaman. This idea would involve a mercenary army.

" In the southern states there is too much inequality of wealth and too large a number of negroes. To enslave the latter would be incompatible with a sound political constitution ; to free them would be even worse, for then there would be two nations in the same state.

" In all colonies there exist prejudices, a clinging to established customs, the fear of a new and untried taxation replacing that to which its inhabitants are accustomed, the colonial vanity in the possession of power, and a sinister commencement of national pride. I believe the Americans must become a great people— not by war, but by agriculture. If they leave behind

---

[1] This had been once true of the inhabitants of New England, but it is not so now.

them the immense prairies which extend to the western ocean, a horde of outlaws and evildoers, escaped from the severity of the laws, will consort with the savages ; bodies of robbers will ravage America, as the barbarians of the north ravaged the Roman Empire. Thence will the danger arise of the necessity of a frontier force and a continual state of war. The frontier states will consequently be more warlike than the others, and that military inequality will be a terrible temptation to ambition. The remedy for this inequality would be to raise a standing army to which, according to population, all the states should contribute. But Americans are dominated by the distaste of the English for standing armies, and dread them above all things. There they are wrong. Nothing is easier than to connect regular troops with the militia, by which the latter become more disciplined, and by which combination liberty is strengthened. But on this point dread is not easily allayed.

" Here are difficulties indeed ; and it is possible the hidden interests of certain powerful persons will cause them to inflame popular prejudice to obstruct the designs of really wise and patriotic citizens.

" It is impossible not to hope that this people will gain all the prosperity of which they are capable. They are the hope of the human race, and ought to become its exemplar; they ought, indeed, to prove to the world that men can be at once free and peaceable, and throw off the fetters with which tyrants and humbugs of all kinds have chained them in defiance of public welfare. The asylum thus opened to the oppressed of all nations should be a boon to the whole world; the facility of profiting by it to evade the effects of misgovernment will force the powers to act justly and in an enlightened manner. The rest of the world will, little by little, awake to the utter stupidity of the old system of politics. To accomplish this, America must guarantee that she will never become, as has been so often predicted by your ministerial writers, a copy of our Europe, a mass of divided powers, fighting for territory or commercial profits, and continually cementing the slavery of the people by their blood.

" All enlightened men, all lovers of humanity, should now unite their efforts and join their experience to that of learned Americans to aid them in their great work of legislation. Such a task will, sir, be worthy of you! I fain would excite your zeal; and if in this letter I have given way more than I should to my own ideas, that end has been my only motive. This, I trust, will be my excuse for the trouble I have given you. I hope that the blood which has flowed, and will flow, in this contest will not be shed in vain for the welfare of the human race.

" Our two nations are probably about to do each other much harm, out of which will come no real profit. The only result will undoubtedly be a huge increase of the national debt and the ruin of many citizens.

" England seems more inclined for this even than France. If instead of this war she had gracefully given in at first; if it were given to statecraft to do at the beginning what must be infallibly done at last; if public opinion had impressed on the government the importance of the coming events which it foresaw ; if the independence of America had been conceded without war, I firmly believe your nation would have lost nothing by the change. Now she will lose what has been expended and what she must still spend; she will experience for some time a serious loss of trade, even if the nation be not forced into bankruptcy; moreover, whatever happens, there must be a serious loss of political influence abroad. But this last is of very little importance for the real welfare of a nation, and I do not at all agree with the Abbé Raynal in his epigraph upon you. I really do not think this will render you a contemptible nation or throw you into a state of slavery.

"Your misfortunes will take the form, perhaps, of a necessary amputation—perhaps the only method of saving you from the gangrene of luxury and corruption. If, by your agitations, you can repair your constitution by annual elections, in rendering your representation more equitable and better proportioned to the interest of those represented, you will perhaps gain something as good as America by this revolution, for your liberty is intact, and with and by it your other losses can easily be repaired.

"You may judge, sir, from the frankness with which I touch on these delicate points, of the esteem with which you inspire me, and of the satisfaction I feel in thinking we are actuated by the same principles. This letter is entirely between ourselves.[1] I even ask

---

[1] In compliance with M. Turgot's desire, this letter was kept private during his life. Since his death, I have thought the publication of it a duty I owe to his memory, as well as to the United States and the world. I can add, with much satisfaction, that my venerable friend whose name introduces this letter, and also, that some of M. Turgot's intimate friends who have been consulted on this subject, concur with me in this sentiment.

you not to reply to me in detail by post, for your answer will surely be opened in course of transit, and I shall be found too true a friend of liberty for a minister, even a disgraced one!

"I have the honour to be, sir, with all possible consideration,

"Your most obedient humble servant,

"TURGOT."

————

CHAPTER XLIV

Reputations (July).

PARIS is a changing scene where reputations are made and lost with equal rapidity : cool imaginations, fired by the chaos and tumultuous excitement of this capital, carry everything to extremes. To-day that which was applauded to the echo is furiously denounced; mud is thrown at what was adored a little time ago. The golden calf is the only deity now.

Necker.

The Parisians have gone mad over M. Necker, who had the cleverness to prosecute a ruinous war without cash. To see the popular enthusiasm one would have thought he had turned on Pactolus through Paris. *O quantum mutatus ab illo!* Now they call him a rascal, a buffoon, an errand boy, and a banker. Let us add him up without prejudice, following public opinion in a *résumé* of various private judgments ; or, rather, let us record what all the world thinks of him, since he can no longer exercise power, but has only the weight of his intellect.

A stranger in France, he found himself at The-
lusson's bank.   He was only a man of figures, accounts,
and arithmetic, aided, however, by much sense and
great ambition.

Under Turgot's administration M. Necker, still a
banker, attracted public attention by a work on free
trade in corn.

The French Academy proposed Colbert as the subject for an essay.   M. Necker immediately wrote a
pamphlet on his administration, which was so full of
errors and of praiseworthy success.   His ambition
was to pose as a wit, under the mask of gravity and
solidity.   He obtained the prize.

When money and Court intrigue had made him a
minister, blind confidence reigned everywhere.   War
was carried on without extra taxes ; the navy flourished
efficiently without crushing the people.

For M. Necker universal enthusiasm reigned, for
had he not discovered the philosopher's stone of
governing ?

The report soon came in.   They said no minister
had ever possessed so much public and private integrity ; and yet he put obstacles in the way of free
trade in corn.   His early writings on this subject
were forgotten in his later operations, so different to
the principles he loudly proclaimed before.

To-day the people who judged him are no longer
the same.

This foreigner of republican birth is but an agent
of despotism, all the more dangerous for having concealed his designs beneath a most plausible style.

This republican gained the confidence of the nation
by his report, and attacked the constitution by his

secret memoranda. He fettered us by his provincial administration. These creatures of despotism may one day lose the vices of their origin, but we shall unceasingly denounce their originator, who was vicious, and is now doing all he can to ruin us.

The report is accused of bad faith by a statesman of acknowledged bad principles. M. de Calonne has published pamphlets in London which challenge Necker to justify his procedure. Until now Necker has not replied. This report is looked at askance as a new departure. But had not that scoundrel Terray already published one?

He praised Colbert, but did nothing to imitate that eminent minister. Manufactures, languishing in France under Necker, can no longer rival in demand those of England.

He carries on the war without fresh taxes, but he crushes the nation under a mass of new loans. To the lenders he mortgages two or three generations of Frenchmen; for governments are like private individuals: if one generation lives by loans, the next is sure to be ruined.

M. Necker has failed as a minister, but by no means as a writer. The latter no doubt consoled him for his exile during the time of the Assembly of Notables, and the persecutions he experienced in Paris. Was not Colbert persecuted to the tomb? And he had made the kingdom both wealthy and glorious. M. Necker should make this comparison, and think himself happy in being allowed to write his work on religious opinion in peace. This book, full of truth, interest, and philosophy, planned on a grandiose scale and full of political facts, has been drastically criticised, as is usual with standard works. The ex-minister has been accused of humbug, both in his religious tales and his reports. But epigrams die while the book lives on. It is written for sound thinkers.

Maurepas.

M. de Maurepas, who was so much praised when he ruled, passed for a featherhead, whom time happily moderated. A statesman more by instinct and natural finesse than by far-sightedness and principle, he was rather a clever courtier than an enlightened adminis-trator. Nature had endowed him with a subtle and cheerful temperament. Trained by his reverses to read men, he had that tact lacking to so many govern-ments, and which is as good as royal beneficence.

The partisans of the royal prerogative now (1788) reproach him with revolutionising the parliaments. With the sole end of creating creatures, they say, he re-established these dangerous magistrates, shook the crown, and woke up his inveterate enemies. It was he who brought about the present crisis, and did harm to the whole of France. But this is not my opinion. Maurepas saw it was necessary for a monarchy to have honourable and honoured judges, and for Frenchmen just judges who deserved their trust. He re-established the magistracy, he restored the monarchy, he got rid of the cleverest despot France had had since Duprat—the Chancellor Maupeou. He opposed those great tribunals of despotism towards which monarchy always tends; unknowingly he paved the way for disastrous revolutions, it is true, but they are as innate in government as they are in the elements.

Storms and thunder purify the air and clear the atmosphere.

Turgot.

This is the name that rises to our lips when we wish to indicate an honest minister, one that was a friend of the human race. Turgot would have been the happier had he never been a minister; but no one would have known the good an administrator could do. The only reproach he seems to merit is that he was too energetic in the pursuit of what he thought good; and excess in anything is a great evil. He was too eager in the enunciation of his well-thought-out and well-weighed schemes for human benefit. The people for whom he laboured, in spite of all their enlightenment, were not intelligent enough then to profit by his great projects. Some years after his retirement his decree on forced labour was carried into effect, and one of these days his excellent plan for buying up feudal rights will be carried out. By this time, the new decrees of 1788 have weakened seigneurial power, and shaken the sway of landed proprietors. In several provinces the nobility were dead against this, and it was to weaken and subdue them that the commonalty were allowed positions in the high courts and the army.

This was a great step towards the utter destruction of the feudal system. Why should not an enlightened age sweep away all traces of those abuses which barbarous times have left us? Do vested interests stand in the way? But were not the serfs, those attached to the soil, all the property of the feudal lords? Why have not the wretched remains of feudal barbarism been cleared off amid the universal cheers of the people? The adoption of Turgot's plan is in the wind; it would indeed be a happy event were feudalism knocked on the head, provided the expense were not too great.

The Archbishop of Toulouse.

In his youth Loménie de Brienne gained renown by that celebrated thesis which was so fatal to the Abbé de Prades. From the moment he entered the Church he was ambitious; and from the time that he obtained a mitre at Condom, his morals were dubious. When he became archbishop of Toulouse he displayed much talent in the administration of his province. In Languedoc they spoke of his intelligence, of his talents in guiding men and things. Love of notoriety, and still more the passion for destruction, caused him to conceive the plan of regenerating Toulouse, of building harbours, cutting canals, of founding educational establishments for young ladies of quality, and retreats for old clergymen. Through being intimately connected with M. de Choiseul, he acquired his despotic manner, his destructive tastes, and ruinous schemes. The King's dislike to the duke kept De Brienne from the cabinet for a long time. Ever since the fall of M. de Choiseul he thought of it. M. Elie de Vermont, who was reader to the Queen and had known her at Vienna prior to her marriage, was his intimate friend. The moment was seized when Calonne imprudently assembled the notables, in 1787, to put the archbishop in his place.

The first idea of the nation was to congratulate itself on having such a statesman. Paid by the Church, he was not burdensome to the people. Connected with the parliament of Toulouse, and having taken the part of the parliaments during the revolution of 1771, he was bound to support these institutions. Rich, both from his see and his family, it was thought he would be actuated in his plans by the love of honour and glory.

This anticipation was not verified. The new minister acquired fresh wealth from the Church, and he gave numerous posts in the ministry to incapable relatives and friends. He declared war on the parliaments, which he longed to destroy; the seigneurial justices were superseded; the provincial treaties were violated. Finally, he involved all parties in the State in trouble and confusion, and sowed dissension among all classes. De Brienne had all the despotic tendencies of Louis XI. and Richelieu without their great talents. Cruel and false as they, in eighteen months he brought the monarchy to the brink of ruin, and it was not his fault that civil war did not again break out.

They did not give him credit for having head enough to weld into a whole a proper governmental scheme. He showed too great a tendency to reform one department only of the administration, and too much haste, violence, and pigheadedness ever to gain political success. He went his way, always pulling down, never building up—only acting on one idea, that of ruling general disorder; toying with each party in the State, and everywhere governing by means of artifice and deception.

This iconoclastic priest was at last dethroned by general opinion (which was shown by the lowest classes, and even by the soldiery and the workmen, people who as a rule never reason). Fireworks illumined his fall. He was considered absolutely incapable of governing. He knew no more of finance than he did of legislation; weak and cowardly in politics, and only learned in intrigue, he was unable to resist those intriguers who beat him and drove him from office.

It was said he went to Italy. This is perhaps the only possible arena for his exploits. There he will see (chiefly at Rome) that kind of political and administrative spirit that he wished to display in France.

But in the midst of the disorder and political outrages which characterised his ministry, it will be one day said that he was the man who scattered the seeds of equality in taxation and equality of opinion amongst the masses. He was the man who raised the Third Estate by making it perceive its rights that had been usurped by the nobles, the magistrates, and the priests. Never was so much written in favour of the people and of liberty as during his ministry. It is true he had to oppose the other orders with the Third Estate. He only did from necessity what a good minister would have done from justice.

CHAPTER XLVI

An Evening at the Lycée of the Rue Saint-Honoré.

I subscribed to the Lycée to hear the scientific discourses of Fourcroy and the literary lectures of La Harpe. This assembly was composed of a crowd of brilliant men, of women who were lovers of learning, and of the most distinguished foreigners in Europe. La

Harpe was the oracle of the place. They committed his words to memory and received his maxims in favour of liberty with unanimous acclamation and with loud applause. At last the Lycée became a real moral and political opposition to the Court and the ministerial power, which, since the first Assembly of the Notables in 1787, were struggling with public opinion.

Besides the great hall for public instruction, there was a reading-room and a room for conversation, where the subscribers met every evening. There I heard most interesting literary and political discussions. Men like Champfort, Lebrun, La Harpe, Fourcroy, Condorcet took an active part in them.

At one of these soirées, animated by the news of the day about Parliament and the ministers, a great deal was said about a very warm altercation which had just taken place in Madame Necker's drawing-room between a priest named Morellet and Count de Guibert, both members of the French Academy, but diametrically opposed in politics. The priest, it was said, defended the monarchy of Versailles to excess, and the Count pleaded boldly for the new ideas; he commented on the recent example of the United States, and spoke of their beautiful federal constitution and of their Declaration of Rights. At these words the priest Morellet, restraining himself no longer, replied to the innovators that there had existed fundamental laws in France for many centuries; for example, the Capitularies of Charlemagne, the ordinances of Saint-Louis, the States-General and their ancient decrees; and that there was no need to overthrow the ancient institutions of the country under pretext of destroying some abuse. M. de Guibert refuted the Gothic pretensions of his adversary by dwelling forcibly on the excesses of ministerial despotism, on the perpetual conflicts with Parliament, and on the imminent necessity of a reform in the government. He succeeded in silencing the priest only by saying to him, "I can show you two letters addressed by the Duke de Choiseul, minister of Louis XV., to one of his intimate friends, then French ambassador at Vienna. They will show you that, according to Choiseul himself, this ancient and so-called constitution of France is no great thing. The first of these letters treats exhaustively of the limited power of Parliament; the second of the system of taxation and of the financial *régime*. I will give them to you to read and to reflect upon, and you will be convinced that France has never had another constitution than feudalism—rather, the absolute wish of the kings and that of their ministers."

Thus finished this great political controversy, the report of which spread immediately throughout Paris. Everyone desired to read these letters, so precious under the present circumstances. I will endeavour to procure a copy from some Academician or some man of letters who knows M. de Guibert. If I can obtain it, I will religiously insert it in this part of my journal.[1]

---

[1] I succeeded in obtaining copies of these two letters, just as they had come from M. de Choiseul's private study. I think I am doing France a service by publishing the personal opinions of so weighty and clever a statesman, who was foolishly sacrificed to a court intrigue of one of the royal mistresses.

CHAPTER LI

Two Letters from the Duke de Choiseul to M. N——
on the Parliaments and on the Financial Régime
(written in 1763).

First Letter.

"Fontainebleau, October 10th, 1763.

"SIR,—I have just received the letter with which you honoured me on the 8th inst., as well as the accompanying memoir, and I hasten to reply to it.

"You are aware of the change which has come over the Department of Justice, and although I had no trust in M. de Lamoignon, I was sure of my position in his consideration, whereas, not knowing M. de Maupeou, nor his ideas on the actual circumstances, I am sure of nothing ; thus we are both in the same position, and what we write in private is only to enlighten our own ideas, to make them valuable, when they will seem good to us mutually, without either of us being able to take any action.

"The preamble of your memoir, which is relative to the basis of justice, is speciously just. It is certain that force and liberty of opinion do not go together. It is certain that, chiefly for the financial edicts, it were to be wished that people saw no contradiction between the promulgators of the law and the legislator. I will not enter into the very extensive discussion of this thesis, whether the legislator in France requires the consent of Parliament to establish a law, or whether in the true

constitution of the State, the same legislator only
sends his law to Parliament to promulgate it. It is
certain that if it were true that the King, the sole
legislator in France, required the consent of the parliaments (which are not political bodies, but distinct
courts of justice) for making a law, it would be
shown that the parliaments, and not the King, were
the legislators.

"We must grant that the parliaments have the
means of remonstrance, that they can repeat it, the
forms in use teach us that the imperative legislator
in France, if he persists, must send letters of command,
and finally that the last degree of authority of our
kings is the *lit de justice*. Very often the letters have
produced their due effect, but for some time past
they have lost their force, and the parliaments attack
the *lit de justice*.

"If this act of the authority and of the majesty
of our kings is abolished, I pray you to tell me what
will remain to the legislator for the support of his
law? In truth, if this foundation of our French constitution were destroyed, I should regard the kingdom
as very unfortunate in changing its legislator. I
assure you that in a few years it would be the prey
of its neighbours, and an object of contempt to the
universe; I think this as true as that parliaments
and forms are a first necessity. It is then necessary
to moderate the authority with the form, to observe
due distance in things and in persons; the different
powers must tend to the good of the kingdom, to its
splendour in Europe, to the glory of the legislator
and the good of the people; for, let us not be deceived, the people are a pretext in the remonstrances

of the present parliaments, and the people would be very miserable if their industry, the defence and management of the provinces, and the fortunes of the citizens were overturned by the trouble which the resistance of the parliaments might produce.

"I regard the collection of taxes by means of troops as civil war. Now, a civil war neither contributes to lessen the debt of the State, nor to improve the fortunes of the people. We are, however, at the point of civil war or general bankruptcy. This last course would be dishonourable; but the resistance of the parliaments may bring it about if the King, moved by the misfortune which his people may experience, dared to sacrifice his honour to the diminution of the taxes.

"I believe you do not know the state of the King's affairs when you say the expenses of his Majesty amount to 160 millions. The army and navy cost 80 millions (this sum seems excessive—it is not sufficient); the pay of the soldiers, the hospitals, food, fodder, the generals, officers, employés—this fixed expenditure amounts to 58 millions. All our magazines are empty, and our forts in bad repair; 12 millions are wanted for the artillery, and 4 millions for the engineers—there remains, for the navy and the colonies, 6 millions. The colonies alone cost more, and the Royal Navy cannot be maintained with less than 16 millions.

"You will say perhaps that it will be possible to reform the troops. Never has a greater reform than the last been effected. Consider that we must guard three hundred leagues of coast, and places which extend from sea to sea. Reflect that we are inferior to our enemies on sea, and that we have some superiority

on land; but if we weaken the army we shall lose
this superiority, and cannot again regain it.

"In spite of this picture I have prepared two
bills for 80 millions, and I hope by much attention,
by deferring some bills and by advancing others, to
maintain the honour of the army. Foreign affairs
cost 12 to 15 millions—they cost 52 when I took
them over; the royal household costs from 17 to 18
millions—it has not varied since the time of Louis
XIV. The finance amounts to 25 millions. I do
not know the bill—it is very extensive; the superior
courts and intendants belong to this department.

"There is besides the military school; so that
with 140 or 143, all the expenses of the King ought
to be paid, and, with attention and economy, I believe
they will be sufficient.

"Besides, there are 147 millions of interest for
the debts and 20 millions of reimbursements, a total
of 167 millions, in addition to the 143 above mentioned.

"Finally, there are what are called the small
debts, those made during the war, and the salaries,
wages, pensions which have been suspended in the
bill for the army and navy, these amount to 100
millions. I do not know the other bills, but I believe
they are not less. Such is the true state of the situation, by joining to it the East India Company, which
we must take into consideration.

"I am certain that the Controller-general, even
with these decrees, will not be able to go to the end
of the year. I will add that it would be possible to
form a fixed plan if we were down to the present
month, but, in spite of the situation which I have
just revealed to you, we are at least eight months in

advance; thus the second twentieth is spent for the year 1764, a fact that completely prevents your plan of carrying its product direct to the royal treasury. This change in the collection of taxes would discredit the rescriptions, and the rescriptions are the only means of making the machine move.

"From this picture I think there is only one means of quieting the disturbances and of re-establishing order and tranquillity amongst all parties—by waiting till a system of finance shall be worked out, understood and agreed upon by the parliaments. I think the King ought to publish an edict interpreting those of the month of April, in which, in ordering the collection of the two-twentieths, his Majesty will fix a time for the duration of these imposts. While there is life there is hope. Besides, this term will persuade the ministry of finance to find a method for its simplification. I believe that the levy of the sous per pound ought to be at stated times, like the twentieths; this tax falls on the food supply of the cities, and is the most just.

"The gratuitous gift of the cities ought to be explained and the hundredth denier abolished; an explanation must also be given of the assessment in the introduction of the edict, which may say that this assessment will be worked at by the deputies and all the parliaments. Such an edict is necessary, though burdensome. I would vote, if I were at the Parliament, for the registry.

"As to the sinking fund, I would wish that you would confer with M. de Laborde, and in the registry of the edict of the Parliament of Paris, there may be a mention of the security of the sinking fund. I give you, sir, my ideas in confidence, as I would give them at the council. I inform you, moreover, that the King cannot fail to manifest a burning resentment to the parliaments, which have dared to oppose him. This act can only be endured in anarchy, and we are not in this position.

"I have the honour to be, with sincere attach-ment, sir,

"Your very humble and very obedient servant,

(Signed) "THE DUKE DE CHOISEUL."

Second Letter.

"Fontainebleau, October 18th, 1763.

"SIR,—All that you have said on the management which is necessary to render an acknowledged and respectable authority valuable is true. I think also that a wise, deliberate, and energetic administration is the surest means of maintaining this authority in all its purity. I am more convinced than anyone that the combination of the government is infinitely more necessary than force, and that this should be known, but should never appear in the State, but for the support of the laws.

"We are then agreed upon the principles, but these principles ought to have been understood twenty years ago. All parties have gone beyond their limits, and the question is to make each return to its proper sphere. This is, I believe, the principal and difficult part of the situation, for it is absolutely necessary that all should return equally.   .

"It will be easy to moderate force. Will. it be equally easy to bring back by gentle methods men excited by imperfect opinions, who think that their

state participates in the sovereignty, whilst it is
only a simple agent of the sovereignty? I see such
complete folly exhibited amongst some of the magistrates daily that I do not know any means to correct
the balance. In other respects this matter does not
concern me.

"I am sorry that in my department a chamber of
vacations takes the liberty of convoking parliament,
and, without it being assembled, decrees the arrest
of the lieutenant-general of the province, president of
the parliament, and representative of the King. It is
an act they could not have been done to a councillor
who had robbed on the highway. He ought to have
been judged by the assembled chambers. I do not
honour myself on being a member of a chamber of
vacations that can order my arrest. Extravagance is
carried to the highest pitch; the means of suppressing
it ought to be similar. If the wisdom of the law does
not replace these excesses, is it M. de Viarne, and
such people, that will be the legislators of this empire?
Will the King permit the constitution to be changed
by folly and ridiculous resistance? That is what the
magistrates must consider, and this is not at all within
my province. I will even say, like the prince, that I
am not at all clever in a war of chamber-pots, and that
the King ought not to sacrifice more than a hundred
of his troops; they will be sufficient to annihilate with
one four-pounder the great parliamentary fire. But the
taxes will not be collected, they say. All becomes a
crisis in such circumstances. I believe this will neces-
sarily lead to general bankruptcy. The King at the
first resistance must suspend all payment of interest;
the farms, estates, State properties, and about sixty-

four millions in taxes will be his. These will be suffi-cient for the expenses; they will even exceed it, and the excess will serve to fulfil the anticipations, and to bring the accounts up to the present; moreover, the troops will be paid by the provinces that will require them, and the royal treasury will be out of straits in a few months.

"It will be evident that not only will it be the resistance, but the form of the resistance of the parlia-ments that will produce this bankruptcy.

"The King will have no more credit, it is true, but he will be rich and will have no more debts; the people will have less taxation, and can thus bear an increase of taxation for a new war, if the Parliament insists on such a situation. I believe a great part of the Parliament of Paris will not be very content, and will regret not having appeased the fire that destroyed its fortune.

"Believe me, sir, this is the unfortunate operation of finance which will be carried before the month of January, if tranquillity be not restored. As I myself shall lose 90,000 livres a year, which I have from the city and from my wife's property, I shall be just as sorry as anyone else to support this enormous loss through the resistance of the parliaments.

"As to your calculations, permit me to tell you they are not correct. Be assured that the charges, if all are to be paid, amount to 332 millions. M. de Laborde can give you the details: 147 millions of annuities, 37 millions of reimbursements, 143 millions of expenses, 8 millions for the discount on the revenue. Amongst the debts and reimbursements are those of the army and navy, as well as those of the finance and the royal household, which amount to a great sum.   Now it is certain that the Controller-general only procures 316 millions by his edicts.   Then if it be shown that the account is correct, you will agree that his fault is that he has not asked enough, for it is vain to say the 143 millions of expenses are absolutely necessary, and for the debt we must either raise the money or go bankrupt.

"Your account of the revenue is as incorrect as that of the expenditure.   The general taxes only yield the King 118 millions net, the tax-gatherers retain 6 millions for the reimbursement of their funds, whether right or wrong, but it is done all the same.   The hides are not worth more than 3 millions.   The general receipts, which you raise to 95 millions, do not amount to that except with the twentieths; without the twentieths, and considering the annual reductions which must be made in the taxes to the countries which have suffered during the year, the general receipts are 70 millions. The estates are only worth 3 millions ; the post-office, I assure you, is not worth 6 millions, and the stewards will not take a seven years' lease.   The clergy pay nothing in times of peace ; 4 or 5 millions every five years are demanded of them.   This time 6 millions may be demanded, which they cannot give in the year 1765 without difficulty.   The countries of the States produce little, on account of their debts, from which I conclude that with the two twentieths and the six sous per pound, as well as the two sous per pound of the twentieths, the Controller-general will have much difficulty to get out of his embarrassments.   Very far from wishing to diminish the moiety of a twentieth, I believe we ought to finish the parliamentary fermentation on the present footing, and during the year to introduce a real system of finance, which, whilst sustaining national credit, may appease the people and assure their property to the citizens.

"I am of your opinion on liquidation. I think it is just, even necessary, that all the first twentieth should be carried directly to the sinking fund. I would add to it half at least of the second twentieth—perhaps the whole twentieth—and registering it with this clause, as in the first twentieth. I do not depart from the form of liquidation you propose, nor am I opposed to this—that an account of the operation of each year be made in the presence of the chief president and general procurators of the Parliament and Treasury. Here is an essential modification which I would advise the King to grant in his edicts; I would add the gratuitous gift of the cities according to justice; I would explain the idea of the register; and I would abolish the hundredth denier. That is how the arrangements could be carried out. The rents could be raised one tenth by reducing the gratuitous gift of the cities; but, considering all, that would be worth nothing, for it would be necessary to break faith, and at least that must be done to some extent.

"I do not think you ought to return before the time you have fixed. There is nothing here but clouds, and they must be dissipated, that you may occupy yourself with your affairs, and make your journey of use.

"I beg of you to regard all I have said as the musings of a private individual. Relying on your honour, I am persuaded that you will at no time use these to compromise me. I deserve this discretion on

your part from the sentiments of affection with which
I have the honour to be

"Your very humble and obedient servant,

(Signed) "THE DUKE DE CHOISEUL."

CHAPTER LVI

November 6th, 1789—Second Meeting of the Notables.

WHEN Philip the Fair wished to convoke the
States-General, in 1301, Marigni, his superintendent
of finance, being in want of money, tried to gain
the favour of the people. The Royal Council was
assembled, and the people were admitted in the
assembly of the States as the third body or order.
That is the origin of this strange and dangerous
distinction.

Now, it is proposed to assemble the States-General
because the King wants money, and the nation a constitution. But how are the rights of representation
to be regulated in a just and legal manner? It is
proposed to limit the pretensions of the permanent
bodies, the influence of the supreme courts, the ambition of the clergy, the privileges of the nobles. What
can one expect from an assembly of aristocrats? What
can eighteen mayors do against one hundred and fifty
priests, nobles, or magistrates? Public opinion alone
can compel them to be less aristocratic than they are.
We must consider what America has done in a short
time. If liberty, equality, and fraternity were now
established, too much would be done in one moment.
Prudence recommends us to use this assembly to obtain

at first a slight amelioration in the condition of the people, for experience teaches us to do, not what ought to be done, but what can be done. Besides, America, whose liberty is our model and our phantom, was in a different position. It boldly attacked the greatest of all abuses—national slavery. It used moderation and firmness in its fight, and succeeded.

But it had not a rich, ambitious, and hypocritical clergy, styling themselves the first order in the State; nor a nobility also calling themselves an order; nor persons exempt from taxation by privilege. It had not an absurd system of criminal law, nor contradictory civil laws carried out arbitrarily by perpetual tribunals which pretend to have a negative right in the legislation. It had not ruined agriculture, commerce and industry by numerous prohibitions. It was not paying huge taxes, more onerous from the manner of collection than from their amount. America demanded the inalienable rights of man, the abolition of inequality among citizens, and the termination of perpetual tribunals. We shall be very content if we slightly diminish this inequality and these powers. We shall be happy if we do not give them fresh sanction, and render the abolition of these abuses impossible. Now, that is what the aristocratic spirit will not fail to do at present, as it dominates and makes the greatest efforts after the recent successes it has obtained.

In the Assembly of Notables the debate will arise whether the nobles and the clergy are willing to grant the nation half the votes in the assembly. A revolution will ensue if a National Assembly should be formed of which one-half was composed of deputies of the nation and the other half of deputies of privileged bodies, and, as such, enemies of the nation. In other words, they will try to show themselves as enlightened as the Dauphin, who has already established this system in his states.

We are also promised liberty of the press and individual liberty, which have been hitherto chimeras for Frenchmen.

But will it deprive Parliament of the power to pass whatever it thinks fit, and to prosecute the writers? Let us recall what it has done against the " Annales " and their author. The arbitrary power which the government had, and which in its hands was much less dangerous, will simply be transferred to a hundred provincial magistrates in each province.

Thus we shall have an aristocratic assembly in act and constitution, an arbitrary power in the hands of a perpetual body; that is what awaits us in this Assembly of Notables, the principles of which ought to influence the National Assembly itself. Will it be the spirit of liberty or will it be the spirit of aristocracy? We ought to have a constitution based on equality and having in itself the power of reformation.

But are we as powerful as the Americans, and are we in their position? A Bill of Rights, acknowledged in some states and tacitly accepted in others, defended them against a legislature which wished to abuse its power; their laws were tolerable and superior to those of nearly every nation. Thus the inactivity of the American legislature for the reform of abuses was not very inconvenient; besides, England had left the Americans without public authority.

Here all circumstances are absolutely different and prescribe an opposite course. Besides, how can America in her revolution be compared with France? The former had for leaders Jefferson, Franklin, Washington. We have only D'Esprémesnil, Bergasse, and a Duke de Praslin. Do the latter inspire the same confidence?

The Assembly of Notables held its first meeting on Thursday, the 6th of November. The King arrived at noon, accompanied by the princes his brothers, the Duke of Orleans, and all the concomitants of royalty.

The spectacle was noble and imposing. The King seemed satisfied; he appeared well and did his best. But what were the wishes of the ministers, the privileged classes, and the princes?

The King announced that he only sought the most agreeable means of rendering the nation happy.

The Keeper of the Seals expanded this idea in a public speech. It was not L'Hospital speaking like Lycurgus to the assembly of the States of Blois, in a more barbarous time, with sterner manners, and a Court very differently composed.

M. Necker presented the different plans of convocation which national history and reason seem to suggest. His speech, full of views and love of beneficence, made the greatest sensation.

M. d'Ormesson, first president of the Parliament of Paris, spoke in a commonplace magistrate-like manner. He also spoke of the form of convocation of 1614. How blind *esprit de corps* is! All the privileged classes are alike. Decidedly it is for them to receive the light of the century, and not to transmit it.

The 24th of November.

The officials are at work. Those of Monsieur have declared for the people or Third Estate—that is to say, he has consented to grant them an equal number of deputies as to the clergy and nobility. In truth, this view obtained only the barest majority.

The five other offices are in favour of the form of representation of 1614. And yet, if they consult the history of the Assembly, they will see that the Third Estate almost always sent a greater number of deputies than the other two orders.

In general it is asserted that the nobility were nearly all in favour of the Third Estate except M. de Bouillé. The Church, with the exception of the Bishops of Aix, Bordeaux, and Narbonne, declared against it. The magistracy is totally opposed to the Third Estate. The mayors, the natural defenders of the people, have become their enemies, except the Mayor of Rouen and the Provost of the merchants of Lyons.

It is believed, in spite of these unassuring preliminaries, that the decision of Monsieur's officials will carry the day in a general meeting of all the offices, so strong and irresistible is the rule of reason and necessity.

The provinces are in a ferment. The corporation and the municipality of Rennes have sent twelve deputies to the King to claim for the Third Estate a representation equal to the other two privileged classes. M. Cotin, an Anglo-American living at Nantes, and the owner of a beautiful property in Brittany, is at the head of the deputation. It was well received by the King as he was going hunting. He smiled upon them on his return. The Queen also received their report, which has been already agreed to by the King. Monsieur received them in his cold, reserved, but honest way. The Count d'Artois received them more favourably, and had the report read in his room, the deputies having retired to the ante-chamber, but being able to hear it, as the door was open on purpose.

M. Necker treated them well, whilst M. de la Luzerne invited them to dinner. This they did not accept, as they had not the character of representatives of a body which had the right to send a deputation to the prince.

On the 8th of November Archbishop de Brienne wrote a letter to the King in the name of the three orders of the Dauphiné, to demand the equality of the Third Estate with the other two orders.

This letter is full of strength, respect, sense, and liberty. Nîmes has made the same demand as Nantes. The Parliament of Toulouse wrote to the King asking that the Third Estate might be made equal to the other two. Everywhere the same cry arises. It must reach the ears of the sovereign, if the nobles are not willing to listen to it.

The latter protest, saying too great a change is sought at once. They reproach M. Turgot in the same way; they will say the same to whoever attacks abuses. Everybody declares that they must be destroyed; but no one wishes to begin by that by which he profits. People are excited against one another, and the abuses remain.

What cannot be expected from a government which has destroyed statute labour, established provincial assemblies, liberated the serfs of Jura and Saint-Cloud, given civil rights to Protestants? from a government which in all its operations had used bad principles only through fear of offending the defenders of aristocracy? We must expect that it will render to the nation, and above all to the citizens, the greater part of their rights if it gets any assistance from the nation itself. Good citizens who cannot endure despotic or aristocratic servitude ought to exert themselves at least to deserve liberty.

Let us fear nothing more than aristocracy: it has real strength, whilst the despotism of one man has but imaginary strength. Ministers of a prince are compelled to end abuses, to make sacrifices, they are even driven from office; this is proved by the cases of the Archbishop of Sens and of M. de Lamoignon. Aristocrats can only be compelled by force, and this the people cannot do in a single town when they are not united.

It cannot be denied that as to the abuses of justice, the judicial power entrusted to permanent — almost hereditary—bodies is an obstacle to every reform so long as it wishes to unite itself with the head of the government or the army. Now, this is what will happen as soon as the judicial bodies think they are threatened by a National Assembly. If the nation will not take advantage of the moment in which the Parliament of Paris, led by a disciple of Mesmer, has had the imprudence to break this union with the government—if the Parliament is allowed to take sufficient authority without any fear of the Court, and thinks itself sure of self-management, then we shall see very long intervals between the different convocations of the National Assembly. What is being done is but a scarecrow adroitly set up by the Parliament to show the Court how much it has to fear for itself.

It is the same with the nobility and clergy: their leaders know that it is to the esteem they have at the Court of Versailles they owe their influence in the provinces; it is because ministers give appointments at their solicitation that they receive the support of the nobility and even of the clergy. Thus by uniting with the parliaments in giving an aristocratic form to the National Assembly, they will be assured of power to make the ministers afraid; they will continue to throw the burden of taxation on the people, and to have themselves and their followers supported by the nation.

What then is the pretended difficulty in destroying abuses? Who imagines that there is in the kingdom a province so blind as not to wish to be judged by jurors rather than by a parliament of nobles? Who thinks that soldiers should be sent to compel the people to elect deputies without distinction of order? All would be done easily if they wished; there are but those two points, with which the liberty of the press and the absolute destruction of arbitrary orders would suffice to reform all abuses.

If that were impossible, better remain as we are than risk leaving to our descendants an aristocracy to combat. It is of all the governments against nature the only one in which the progress of knowledge and reason do not refine manners and weaken tyranny. There occur in the aristocratic government of Switzerland horrors such as no aristocratic government of the century has offered examples. Why give us this odious form of government in the sweet hope of one day changing it? Is it not, on the contrary, giving it a new sanction?

The improved provincial assemblies will lead us to

a rational constitution; but they have been sacrificed to the parliaments. Why not join the National Assembly to them? Why commence by destroying them in introducing the distinction of orders? The party which styles itself patriotic makes no step that is not in favour of inequality, has passed no measure that is not in favour of an abuse fatal to the people. That is not advancing slowly and prudently; it is going backwards.

Doubtless it is to the people's interest to live under a monarchy till it is fit for democratic government. When a nation agitates in slavery, it is treason to lead it away from that goal which alone is reasonable and accords with justice and humanity. Let us remember that we have not an aristocracy concentrated in one town, as in Berne. This aristocracy is timid; it has neither strength nor numbers. A popular insurrection would suffice to destroy it. Ours, on the contrary, are everywhere—in the temples, in the castles, in the courts, and round the throne—and would have nothing to fear. Was anything ever more dangerous, unless attacked openly with force or with the best combined skill?

Good politicians fear lest this Assembly of Notables become pupils of M. Necker. He ought to consider that the opponents of territorial taxation ought not be the partisans of a form of government which ought to abolish the privilege of not paying taxes. Can one expect anything from virtue? Montesquieu tells us that virtue is not the spring of corrupt monarchies or depraved constitutions. Ought the principles of honour to direct all minds? The meaning of this word is changed. Nothing is left but honour; interest has conquered the ancient chimera of the French. Honour has perished with chivalry; virtue is fled with our ancient manners. Gallantry has succeeded honour since the time of Francis I., and virtue has been replaced by pride and magnificence since the days of Louis XIV. The honours of despotism date from the reign of Louis XI.; the abuse of ministerial power reached its zenith under Cardinal Richelieu. Abuses of all kinds belong to this reign.

Honours are affected for riches. Honour is a word of luxury and good dress. Reason, supported by the interest of the majority, is the only word which can be employed to-day.

Louis XVI. is, as his ancestors were, contesting with the great vassals, liberating the serfs, establishing communes, and rallying the nation to the commune from policy. But this epoch in our history is reproduced with more strength in the aristocratic bodies, with more light amongst the people, with more freedom of thought. There is need but of a firm, intelligent prince who would love the people. What can be expected from a good minister surrounded with traps, liable to be dismissed by caprice, moving in a dangerous place, and at the side of a Court where writings are in sand, where they think only for the moment, where nobility acquires strength by union, more by servitude?

The 28th of November.

The Prince of Conti, excited by the aristocratic spirit of the nobles, brought forward a motion at the committee, where the deputies of all the offices were assembled. He addressed Monsieur, who presided, and begged him to inform the King of the writings and dangerous systems published in the kingdom, which would terminate in the destruction of the monarchy. That is the monument of the feudal theory sanctioned by a prince who one would have believed to be more profound in administration, more politic, and, above all, more popular.

Next day, the King replied to Monsieur in a simple note, forbidding the nobles to enter on that subject, which was quite different from the purpose for which they were convoked.

Then they confined themselves to the publication of the motives which induced them to decide against the people in favour of the form of 1614. But whilst they were making this odious publication, the Parliament of Paris, dismayed at seeing the popular favour desert them, retraced its steps, but not without using the obscure language of pagan oracles. Lost labour; the modern false gods were already unmasked.

The 5th of December.

The Parliament has just passed a resolution in which it wishes to be excused for having demanded the form of 1614, and in which it showed its pretensions to participate in the authority with the States-General. It claimed the liberty of the press after having ruined it by its sentence on Linguet; it reserved to itself the judgment on the writings, and constituted itself judge of this liberty.

The 9th of December.

On the 9th, this resolution was presented to the King in the form of a petition. The King's reply delighted good citizens and just politicians. Never did words so beautiful, so full of sense and justice, emanate from the French throne. Here are his words: "I have no answer to make to Parliament on this petition. It is with the assembled nation that I will concert the proper means of consolidating public order and national prosperity for ever."

The parliaments are at last put in their places. The kings alone could not subdue them, but when the kings *will* understand the people, there will be no more resistance to be feared from those respectable but too eager bodies. The parliaments have always had the fatal art of joining their cause to that of the people when the government wished to act against them. They have been kings during regencies and minorities, usurpers under weak princes, popular and beneficent under foolish and cruel ministers. The time has arrived to determine their functions; they are appointed to render justice to the nation in the name of the King; the nation can and ought to restrict them to serve public order instead of destroying it.

The 12th of December.

The King, tired of the laborious inutility of the Notables, dismissed them without assembling them in a general committee. Public opinion has accused them of injustice, aristocracy, and personal interest; the sovereign has treated them accordingly.

CHAPTER LVII

Since the State has once more the happiness of being directed by M. Necker, the French will probably be pleased to cast a glance on the financial principles of this great man. Here are examples drawn from the beautiful and consoling moral ideas which form the greater part of his work and which paint his character so nobly. Unfortunately these examples are not all equally beautiful, as can be seen from the following:

" The sovereign of a great empire like France can always, when he wishes, maintain the balance between his expenses and his revenue. The diminution of the former, always seconded by the popular wish, is in his hands; and, when circumstances demand, the augmentation of the taxes is in his power."

" It is the power to impose which essentially constitutes sovereign greatness."

" But because in a monarchical State the sovereign is the bond of political interests, and because in such a constitution he alone determines the sacrifices of the citizens, because he alone is the interpreter of the wants of the State, because he alone orders, because he alone has the power to enforce obedience, the principles of justice are not changed, and the duties of the representatives of the State no less exist in all their force."

" A threatening truth for the conscience of kings is seen to emanate from these reflections; it is that in confiding to the tribunals the decision of the differences which arise between their subjects, they are left sole arbitrators in the greatest cause which exists in the social order, of that which ought to fix the measure of the rights and pretensions of the public treasury on the property of all the members of society, and to decide and know this on all occasions, not only is a just heart requisite, but study and knowledge still more."

"The simple power (in the provincial assemblies) of making observations in the case of new demands, so that the will of the King may be always enlightened and never obstructed; finally, the term *gratuitous gift* absolutely forbidden, and that of *country of administration* surrogated to that of States, that the resemblance of the names may never involve similar pretensions: one feels that it is easy to fulfil these conditions, especially when there is no obstruction from an anterior convention, and when from the part of the sovereign there is nothing but concession and beneficence."

"I will add, moreover, as an essential condition, that the duration of the perfection which is believed to have been given to this new constitution ought to be only for a time, and should be confirmed afterwards for a new term, and thus again as long as your Majesty would demand it; so that, after having taken all the necessary precaution to perform a good work, your Majesty would always have the means of suppressing it. With such prudence, what inconvenience could arise?"

"In a monarchical country, where the will of the sovereign is law, the sovereign's anxiety ought to be limited to ascertaining that his just and beneficent intentions are fulfilled."

" But there is no part of his revenue which a king of France has not the power to expend as he pleases."

" The ancient connections of France and Switzerland, the natural rampart which their alliance assures to a part of their frontier, the long and loyal services of that patient and courageous nation, and finally the utility it is to a sovereign, in times of trouble or effervescence, to possess a certain number of foreign troops, all these reasons show us the wisdom of always maintaining a good number of Swiss troops."

" In the care one takes of one's reputation there is a feeling apart from the judgment of others. It is a glass in which one looks at oneself, and we wish that it be as pure as our hearts."

" One must attach oneself to the form of account most susceptible of contradiction. It is the only guarantee that can be offered to a nation whilst it is deprived of representatives and has not the right of questioning."

CHAPTER LIX

January 1st, 1789—The People's Christmas-box.

A GREAT question is agitating the kingdom. Philip the Fair, in 1303, called the Third Estate to the National Assembly. The barons and bishops consented to deliberate in the same chamber with them. But in the century of light and philosophy the barons and prelates have different ideas, and do not wish the nation to have representatives equal in number to the two privileged orders. The nobles thought that custom and personal interest should prevail over reason and justice. At last the council—or, rather, M. Necker—decided otherwise, and on the 1st of January this virtuous minister published the result of the Privy Council of the 27th of December.

Immediately feudal fury broke out, the prelates intrigued, the magistrates threatened. But politicians and wise men have carefully examined the result; and here are the sentiments I have gathered.

In this report there are such excellent things and such principles of justice that we can pardon the minister for his display of pride in offering himself as a sacrifice to the intriguing powers, even where he would do so uselessly. One would think that he wished to put his seal to the end of this admirable work to shield himself from the suspicion of not being the author of it.

The only essential defect which I find in the report is to allow the States-General to determine whether the vote will be by number or by order. The manner of voting ought to have been provisionally prescribed by the King. If the two privileged orders persist in adhering to the old custom, the Third Estate will be sacrificed. Now, as the Third Estate cannot be blind on this point, one ought to expect that it will protest, and that all will remain in total inaction.

M. Necker can only be excused by saying that in his anticipations, if the parties of the assembled nation did not agree on this point, the King as arbitrator would prescribe the counting of the votes by number. Unhappily this hypothesis, which would suppose much foresight on the part of authority, seems contradicted by several features in M. Necker's report.

However, the enthusiasm which reigns here at present regards as a great advantage the abandonment which the monarch makes to the States-General of the right of determining whether they ought to vote by number or by rank, and prevents reflection on the numberless difficulties which the two privileged orders will cause before arriving at this conclusion. Yet it seems that public opinion, the example of Dauphiné in its mandate to the deputies, and the force of things, ought to make the vote by number prevail.

I only demand moderation in the means which the nation will employ; the strongest ought not to impose his opinions by force; the man who has a good cause should not degrade it by excesses. Oh! how well things would be done in this beautiful assembly if pride, self-interest, and prejudice did not prevent reason, justice, and nature from being consulted.

END OF VOL. I

H. S. NICHOLS, PRINTER, 3 SOHO SQUARE, LONDON, W.